CW00690679

# The Autobiography of
# James Gregson

## Edited by Barry D Smith

Published by E R Smith Publications, Brighouse, 2011

First Published 2011
By E R Smith Publications
4 Thornhills Lane
Clifton
Brighouse
HD6 4JG


Printed and Bound in Great Britain by
The Amadeus Press
Ezra House
West 26 Business Park
Cleckheaton
BD19 4TQ


ISBN: 978-0-9570001-0-0


A Catalogue record of this book is available from the British Library

All rights reserved. No part of this publication may be reproduced, stored in a retrieval system, or transmitted in any form or by any means, electronic, mechanical, photocopying, recording or otherwise, without the prior permission of E R Smith Publications.

The Publishers and Author have made every effort to ensure the accuracy and currency of the information in The Autobiography of James Gregson. Similarly every effort has been made to contact copyright owners who have kindly permitted them to reproduce photographs and illustrations in this publication and also extend their thanks to those copyright holders of material which is reproduced but whom the Publishers have been unable to trace.

# Acknowledgements

To obtain the Gregson family permission to publish James R Gregson's Autobiography, I managed to track down, after some effort, his son-in-law Patrick Dowling who was living in Sydney, Australia. Gregson's daughter, Jane (her acting name, although she was christened Florence) had died in 1993. I contacted Patrick by e-mail and received the following reply on October 19th 2008.

> Your request has been forwarded to me by Pete Woronkowicz and I am happy to allow you to go ahead and publish as you ask. I would request only that you send me a copy of your work when it is ready. Indeed it's very good to hear that Dick is still remembered and valued. I have copies of several of his plays if you have any difficulty in finding any of them. I am in fact Dick's son-in-law as I married his daughter, Jane, now sadly also dead.
>
> With very best wishes
>
> Patrick Dowling
>
> Patrick died on June 17th 2009, aged 89. He was a TV writer, producer and director.

My thanks to Alan Petford for his help, advice and constant encouragement.

Also, the staff in the following archive departments who have assisted me on my travels: *Calderdale, Huddersfield, Leeds, Manchester, Stockport and the Victoria & Albert Museum of Childhood.*

Richard Macfarlane, Curator of the Bankfield Museum, Halifax for introducing me to Miles Sharp's paintings.

Images & Illustrations were supplied by the following :

> *Steve Gee*
> *Chris Helme*
> *Molly Brook – for permission to use a Peter Brook painting*
> *Ross Parry Agency (Yorkshire Post)*
> *Mander & Mitchenson Collection (MM)*
> *BBC Photo Library (BBC)*
> *Manchester Archive & Local Studies (MALS)*
> *V & A Enterprises, London (VA)*
> *Bankfield Museum, Halifax (BM)*
> *Lancashire & Yorkshire Railway Society*
> *Calderdale Archives : Gregson Collection HAS : GRE 1-3 (CA)*

In addition, the *Yorkshire Dalesman* for kindly allowing me to reproduce the article written by James R Gregson, *Yorkshire Speyks*, in their February, 1971 publication.

Also, the Society for Theatre Research, London, for permission to reproduce from their book *Everymania*, by Norman Macdermott, the Calendar of Plays for the years 1923 & 1924.

And finally to all the kind and patient people who read and re-read the manuscript – many thanks

# Foreword

James Gregson's *Autobiography* is an undiscovered gem. It is the story of a boy born into a poor family in Brighouse in the heart of the industrial West Riding who became briefly a household name by virtue of his writing, acting and broadcasting.

Gregson achieved his eminence by writing and the *Autobiography* ranks with the best of his literary work. There are many autobiographical accounts of the journey from rags to riches; few are told so well. Gregson's vignette of his childhood is masterly and frequently moving. His experiences as a young man working in the textile trades and in a foundry are told with panache. Who could forget his depiction of the maniac steel smelter swinging a crucible of molten metal, intent on humiliating his young assistant. Nor does Gregson neglect the inner life; in the early pages he weaves something of a spiritual Autobiography into his narrative of popular religion and nonconformity. Ultimately Gregson's religion drew him into politics, the I.L.P. in the years just before the First World War and conscientious objection and the No-Conscription Fellowship from 1914 onwards. Fascinated from an early age by the theatre, Gregson began to write and his first play was performed in 1917. Like all his subsequent dramatic work it belonged to the school of northern drama that he helped to shape between the wars.

*James Gregson (1946)*
*Publicity Photo (BBC)*

In the years following the First World War Gregson was an important figure in the development of amateur theatre, not only as a playwright but also as a performer and manager and his *Autobiography* has much to interest the student of drama. When drama failed as a livelihood, Gregson became a journalist and a very prolific one. No doubt it was his experience as an actor combined with his reputation as a journalist that moved the B.B.C. to call upon his services during the Second World War and so launch Gregson on another career. His *Autobiography* not only provides interesting insights into war time broadcasting but also into the heady years of post war expansion. Moving often in the centre of events and meeting frequently with the stars of the day Gregson might easily have become vain and pompous. His *Autobiography* shows that he kept his feet firmly on the ground. He tells his story with considerable skill and great modesty. We reluctantly close the book regretting that our genial companion has come to the end of his story.

Gregson never intended his *Autobiography* for publication. Aware that he had had an extraordinary life he seems to have written it for his own amusement and for his immediate family. It was probably written in the 1950s when many of the people he worked with were well known to his family and indeed a wider world. They are forgotten now and, if we are to have a proper appreciation of Gregson's world, we need to know who they were. Happily the *Autobiography* has found the ideal editor in Barry Smith who has spared no pains to track down details of those with whom Gregson worked. This edition is the richer for the extensive footnotes which help to illuminate the personalities who people Gregson's pages.

The name of James Gregson has slipped from public view. Once a familiar figure on the wireless and a playwright well known in amateur dramatic circles, his name is little remembered even in his native town. It is a paradox that those who work in the media and are well known in their generation are amongst those most securely consigned to oblivion by posterity. The publication of Gregson's *Autobiography* will revive the memory of a writer of considerable merit. It throws light on what it was like to grow up in the industrial West Riding in the last decade of the nineteenth century and will make available an important source for the history of repertory theatre and broadcasting in the first half of the twentieth century.

AJ Petford MA

# Introduction

James Gregson was born in 1889, the eldest child of working class parents, in the West Riding of Yorkshire mill town of Brighouse. This account of his early life, growing up in a very poor part of that town, gives a fascinating and intimate glimpse of the joys and tragedies of family life in late Victorian England, and of his early working life in the Edwardian era. Gregson was someone who lived the life he wrote about, he was no social commentator looking back many years later. His *Autobiography* shows with stark realism and emotion what it was like to survive, with very little money and no work. The welfare state had not come into existence, people were dependent on the family, charity or the workhouse. Like many others of his class, his education was rudimentary. However he persevered and educated himself to a high standard of literacy and through his theatre work strove to enable others to expand their horizons. It is not often that people on the lowest economic rungs can tell their story as eloquently as James Richard Gregson.

Unlike many luminaries in the arts world James Gregson had to earn his living in ordinary jobs well into middle age. And yet his artistic output was prodigious. He became well known as a journalist, playwright, actor, producer and broadcaster. He had a formative influence on the emergence of modern repertory theatre and was an early broadcaster and radio personality.

James Gregson's long and varied life was well summed up by Professor M W Beresford when the University of Leeds conferred an honorary degree on Gregson in 1969.

"Even a social historian reviewing Mr. Gregson's 80 years of super-activity, might hesitate in case he seemed to be deserting fact for fiction", said Professor Beresford, presenting Mr. Gregson. "Some of these varieties of Mr. Gregson's experience were simply to keep himself alive while the boy who had left school at 12 turned himself into an actor and dialect dramatist. Others, like a year's labouring in a chemical factory were enforced when the stage darkened in the mid-1930s and the cause of provincial theatre took its all too familiar air of loves labours lost. His contribution to a Northern culture in the inter-war years extended from the stage to journalism, the cinema and the new art of broadcasting. A pioneer, he made his debut 45 years ago (1924) and both as a free-lance and as staff member served the BBC as actor, producer, raconteur and playwright.

In the war, like his friend Wilfred Pickles, his voice and pen were enlisted when a provincial accent was thought to give more authenticity to a news programme – particularly if it included bad news – than the tones of Oxford. He became principal scriptwriter and announcer for Radio Newsreel. Later he was the first BBC reporter to be accredited to the Parliamentary Lobby and sitting in the Press Gallery of the House, perhaps remembering the theatre galleries of Stockport and Manchester where his tastes and talents had been shaped nearly half a century before, and the many galleries – the Leeds Civic and the Bradford Civic among them – that had applauded him as actor, playwright and producer and which as a theatre's manager he had desperately tried to keep filled."

*Quoted in the Brighouse Echo*: May 23rd 1969

This publication of James Gregson's previously unpublished *Autobiography* has come about through my involvement with an extra-mural class in Local History run by the University of Leeds. One of the projects involved comparing the early years of certain Yorkshire writers and to see what influences, if any, made them into regional writers. J B Priestley immediately came to mind, and for a comparison I suddenly remembered James Gregson, a native of Brighouse like myself. I had come across him once, back in 1954 at the fiftieth anniversary of the Birds Royd Wesleyan Methodist Mission. As a twelve year old boy I was suitably impressed when I was told that the guest of honour was an 'old boy' of the Mission, and a famous man. In the following years I only occasionally came across him in the local press, and for the last twenty years his name and his work seemed to have disappeared completely.

It was, therefore, with no great expectation that I went into Calderdale Archives to see whether or not they had any information concerning James Gregson. They did and the quantity of material far surpassed my most optimistic expectations. Along with his unpublished *Autobiography* there were three folders of press cuttings, photos and programmes, together with typescripts of several of his plays. In addition, there was a treatise, dated 1933, entitled *J R Gregson's Yorkshire Dramas*, by Karl Heinrich Thomas.

So there was a virtual treasure trove concerning James Gregson. The material had been deposited in the Archives in 1984, by Ernest Sands (a former editor of the Brighouse Echo) on behalf of Gregson's daughter, Jane Dowling and was far more than I needed for my essay. To start with I attempted to write a biography of Gregson, using his unpublished *Autobiography* and bringing in all the other relevant information that I had come across in the archives. However, having discussed this approach with Alan Petford, one of my tutors from the local history class, we decided the best approach would be to publish the *Autobiography* in its entirety, together with explanatory notes. Gregson's story is a fascinating one and we felt that other people would be interested.

There were other surprises whilst delving into archives, such as finding documents lodged in the Calderdale Archives relating to the foundry he worked at in Foundry Street, Brighouse, in 1906-07. These gave information as to why a Swiss national had started a foundry in Brighouse to manufacture steel by a new process. Whilst researching in the Manchester Archives, for information on James Lansdale Hodson, his partner in their touring repertory company, I was confronted with over eighty boxes in the J L Hodson private collection, which apparently no one had asked to see for over twenty years, until I and another researcher turned up in the same week. In addition Stockport Archives were very helpful in providing information on the early days of the Stockport Garrick Theatre, together with references to Fred Pennington, one of its founders and a very good friend to James Gregson.

Trying to find information on Fawcett Simpson Ltd., the pram manufacturers where

Gregson worked for several years in the 1920s, was a very difficult and frustrating task. I spent many hours in the Leeds archives with no success. Contacting other archives likewise proved fruitless. It was as though all trace of one of the largest pram manufacturers in the country had disappeared completely, along with archive evidence of the Leeds Industrial Theatre, which the factory had established. I had just about given up hope when a trawl through the internet brought up a reference to Simpson Fawcett on the Victoria and Albert Museum site. On contacting the archivist responsible, I was told they had just begun cataloguing some Simpson Fawcett material that had been passed on to them. The story was that Simpson Fawcett had been taken over by Lines Brothers (makers of Triang toys) in the1950s. At the time Lines Brothers. had requested that some archive material be sent down from Leeds for publicity purposes. When Lines Brothers. themselves stopped trading, all their archives, including the Simpson Fawcett material were donated to the Victoria and Albert Museum – Museum of Childhood. There must still be some archive material for Simpson Fawcett and the Leeds Industrial Theatre somewhere in the Leeds area, which would, I am sure, produce some fascinating stories.

The text is faithful to Gregson, except for one factual error which has been corrected and noted. The only other change is to the layout, in that films, plays, poems and newspapers have been highlighted in italics to enhance the text. When I came to try to find suitable illustrations for the book, I had a lot of help from a number of local people whom I have thanked in the Acknowledgement section. The illustrations have been placed for the most part where they are relevant to the text. However, especially in the chapters relating to Brighouse, a number of illustrations have been included to give a feel for Brighouse at the turn of the twentieth century. One suggestion I received was from Richard Macfarlane, curator of Bankfield Museum, Halifax, which concerned a Brighouse artist I regret to say I had never heard of, Miles Sharp. Bankfield Museum has a collection of Miles Sharp paintings and engravings of Brighouse scenes from the early twentieth century, some of which I have included in the book. The one small problem is that there are two Miles Sharps, father and son.

Robert Goulding, head attendant at the Smith Art Gallery, Brighouse, has been most helpful in pointing out that the paintings and engravings of early twentieth century Brighouse that are in the book are all by Miles Sharp Snr. Robert mentions that in some of the paintings you will see a tall, white bearded figure, with a hat and a walking stick. This is Miles Sharp making an appearance.

Miles Sharp died in 1948, aged 84, leaving two sons. Gilbert, the eldest, was an architect like his father, unfortunately dying the following year, aged 54. The youngest son, Miles Jnr, was a landscape artist, working with oil, watercolours and making line engravings. Much of his work has been exhibited at the Royal Academy.

An appreciation of Miles Sharp Snr, given by an old friend, commented "Who didn't know Miles, and to whom wouldn't he exchange a kindly greeting in our dialect? Upright as a Guardsman, well groomed, immaculate in dress, and always on the look-out for someone to give a cheery word. Miles was our drawing master at Larkhill Academy in my time there from 1885-1889."

Whilst researching Gregson's career I came across a number of interesting stories that are not mentioned in the *Autobiography*. They enhance his story and add other dimensions to his varied career. These have been included in the Appendix.

Gregson was a man of many talents. He was a significant name in Yorkshire in the 1920s and very highly thought of in the theatrical world nationally. At the peak of his popularity, he was claimed as "Brighouse's own". He was also claimed as "Huddersfield's own", "Leeds's own" and even Manchester put in a bid! He was in at the beginning, when amateur theatrical's popularity took off after the First World War, and throughout his long life always encouraged amateur productions. Professional theatre seemed to leave him uneasy, with theatre managers concentrating on popular, commercial plays at the expense of the more experimental. He did, however, act and produce professionally when times were hard and he had to earn money to look after his family. However he never took the final step of committing himself wholeheartedly to the professional theatre, whether by acting, producing or playwriting. We shall never know what he might have achieved had he done so. His background, as a poor working-class boy, at times out of work, at times hungry, stopped this final step. He did not wish to return to those days, so he played safe.

BRIGGATE . BRIGHOUSE .
AS IT APPEARED IN THE YEAR 1858.
This view shews the old Mansion House with the garden in front, on which a shop was built in 1859.
The house occupied by the late Mr John Bottomley maltster, was pulled down in 1875; and the Malt Kiln demolished in 1885.

*The engraving is signed MS 91, which indicates Miles Sharp 1891*  (BM)

*Miles Sharp - Yorkshire Waterway (early twentieth century) : canal looking towards bridge, Huddersfield Road, Brighouse* (BM)

This was in contrast to J B Priestley, who had a much more comfortable and secure upbringing, which gave him the confidence to move South, go into writing full-time and appeal to a much wider audience than James Gregson ever did. Not that James Gregson ever had any resentment of Priestley; they appeared to get on well when they met and respected each other's abilities. And yet, perhaps there was a tinge of regret later in his career when Gregson thought back on what he had achieved and what he could have achieved, and he said to himself "if only".

I must, at this point mention his daughter, who was called Florence like her mother. She flits in and out of her father's story. Calling her Florence obviously caused problems when she herself took up acting. Mother and daughter couldn't both appear on the bill as Florence Gregson! Initially young Florence was known as Von Gregson. This then changed to Jane Tann, Gregson's stepmother's maiden name being Tann, under which name she appeared in plays and on BBC TV. When not acting she was known as Jane Gregson, and when she married as Jane Dowling.

James Gregson's portrait is hanging in Smith Art Gallery, Brighouse. Unfortunately, little or nothing is heard of him now. I hope this book, in some small way, makes amends.

# Brighouse 1893

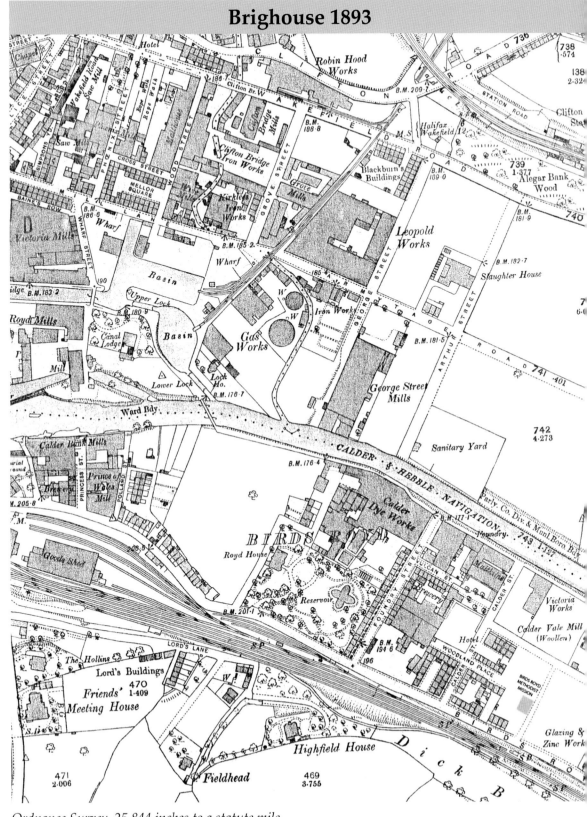

Ordnance Survey  25.844 inches to a statute mile.

Yorkshire (West Riding)  Sheet  CCXXI . 15.

Surveyed between 1888 and 1892, Published in 1893.

Please note : Birds Royd Methodist Mission (built in 1904) has been added.

# Chapter One

"What about going off to Scarborough these holidays lass?" asked my father, happily ignorant of his condition."Holidays!" retorted my mother, quite as happy (I hope) if not quite so ignorant about hers. "I've got another use for that brass".

"Eh!"
"Aye! For a wedding!"
"Oh!"
"Aye"
"So that's how things is?"
"That's how they are lad!"
"Then we'd better get spurrins in sharp!"[1]

And so, as my stepmother (the best of all stepmothers) used to tell the story, the banns of marriage between Charles Gregson, batchelor, and Ann Ramsden, spinster, both of this parish were published forthwith. A tiny one-up and one down house was rented and furnished and in due course the two careless spendthrifts shook themselves down into something resembling domesticity, to wait and prepare for my disconcerting arrival.

I've never bothered to trace my ancestry any further than my memory takes me. I've never needed a pedigree for moral support. If a man can't find justification, or apology, for his existence in himself, then it's useless and cowardly looking for either anywhere else - least of all in his forbears who probably wish they weren't![2]

The Gregsons were cotton operatives in, I believe, the Lancashire mill town of Blackburn. They migrated to Brighouse, in the West Riding of Yorkshire, during the hard years of the Cotton Famine.[3] James Gregson, my father's father, appears to have been a man of some reading and culture - enough, at any rate, to mark him off from the usual run of working men in his day. Soon after he settled in Brighouse he became a publican, but a publican with unusual ways, for he never touched a drop of liquor himself, and discouraged his customers from taking too much. He took a keen interest in politics, was a staunch Radical, and lent his premises for public debates.[4] He didn't transmit this puritan strain to his children, and either their upbringing in the beer house, or some weakness derived from my grandmother, about whose antecedents I know nothing whatever (I don't even know her Christian or her maiden surname) played the very devil with all of them.

Where the Ramsdens came from I don't know, but they were bargees until a growing family reaching the working age made it necessary to have a fixed abode. My mother,

---

[1] Yorkshire dialect for wedding banns.

[2] Appendix 1 : Census details of the Ramsden, Gregson and Hine (Florence Gregson's maiden name) families.

[3] The years 1861-1865 saw a depression in the textile industry in north west England brought about by the American Civil War, and the resulting shortage of raw cotton which at this time came principally from the southern states of America.

[4] *The West Riding Directory of 1877*, published by Kelly Post Office Directory of West Riding, shows a Mrs. Mary Ann Gregson as a beer retailer in Mill Lane, presumably after the death of her husband.

along with her numerous brothers and sisters, was brought up in the cramped quarters of a canal barge, and whilst she was still a babe-in-arms, had a narrow escape from drowning.

My maternal grandfather, Richard Ramsden, was a hearty, bluff, black-bearded fellow, very fond of his glass. He returned to the barge one evening when they were "hove to" in the "basin", to find my grandmother almost at her wit's end with the fractious child. Nothing would satisfy his drunken humour but that he should try to quieten her, and after some argument, he grabbed the crying child and started to walk the deck with her, roaring a lullaby to the startled night. It wasn't long before the discordant duet between the singing father and the protesting daughter was ended by a splash as he toppled over into the dirty water. Up from the cabin rushed my grandmother, seized a boathook, and, after missing him once, got a firm hold of him as he "came up for the third time". She dragged him to the side and, with no little difficulty, finally hauled him aboard. He was still clutching the baby - a baby as quiet and sober as himself. And, after making sure they were both alive, she proceeded to give him the "best leathering" he'd ever had.

I heard this story many times before it dawned on me by what a narrow margin I'd escaped being drowned before I was born, and, being young enough to believe it really mattered I got quite a kick out of it.

Anyway born I was, the first grandchild of the two families, the first nephew of a large circle of uncles and aunts, the first child of a young and graceless couple who, in their own rough way, were always more lovers than parents.

I never boast of my working-class origins. It's a matter for sincere and grateful

*No's 14 to 20 Park Street, Brighouse, photographed in the 1930s, prior to demolotion. In the 1871 census it was at No.15 that Ann Ramsden was recorded as living, aged three (Appendix 1). Halifax Reference Library.*

humility. But I was, indeed, born into the very purple, for my parents were of the aristocracy of their class, both as regards skill and earnings.

My father was a wire-galvaniser, never earning less than fifty shillings a week, a truly princely wage in the eighties. It was skilled and responsible work, but hard and unpleasant; the hours were long, averaging sixty-six a week; conditions were far from ideal; partly open to the weather, the shed was never clear of evil smelling fumes, and clothes were quickly rotted by acids. Careless and easy-going, he refused offers of the more responsible position of foreman, both by his own employers and others who tried to tempt him away. He lived to regret his lack of ambition, working in that same shed on the plant to within a few months of his death. [5]

My mother was a "gasser" in a silk mill, holding down a highly-coveted job worth anything from twenty-eight to over thirty shillings a week. [6] A "gasser" could always be recognised by her superior working attire. In those days, if you were sufficiently prosperous, you had a new suit or dress for "better days and Sundays", your second-best was reserved for Saturday afternoon and evening, and the rest of the week you wore your working clothes - serviceable, but rough; not infrequently patched and usually stained with grease from the machines; or sand or coal dust from the quarries or the moulding shops. Even in the week evening courting was pursued in clogs and shawls, mufflers and caps. Collars and ties were strictly reserved for Saturdays and Sundays.

But the "gassers" broke through this rigid convention. As befitted their superior status, they were a law unto themselves. Not only did they lead the fashion in Sunday finery, but they went to work dressed as for a Saturday. They wore shoes instead of clogs, and instead of swathing their heads in their large woollen shawls, they sported them rakishly on their shoulders, and topped the ensemble with a "straw benjy"[7] perched at a saucy angle on their high buns and frizzy front fringes or "toppins".

There's no doubt that I had a couple of sparks for parents. Careless and improvident and pleasure-loving, they spent their money and their energy with a royal disregard of the future. Straightened times were to come upon them about the same time that I was, but their courtship was unclouded by any shadow of prospective poverty. Working hours were long, but not too long for them to spend their evening dancing when they got the chance. Very often the dances were held miles away from home, and except on rare occasions those miles were covered on foot.

Weekends saw them roaming even farther afield - to Leeds for a play or a pantomime; and, if the cheaper parts of the theatre were full, then more expensive seats would do just as well. There was one occasion, reported by my stepmother with fitting awe, when the only seats left were one or two expensive boxes. My father, without hesitation, plonked down a terrific slice of his week's wages and topped off the evening with a typical flourish. There was no train to bring them any nearer home than Halifax,

---

[5] Charles Gregson died in 1926, aged 63.

[6] A "gasser" was a person who worked in the "gas room" of a cotton or silk mill. The job was to remove, by burning against a hot plate or in a flame, unwanted hairs on the thread thus making it smoother. The operation was usually performed before bleaching and finishing.

[7] A straw hat, usually worn by men with a low flat topped crown and broad brim.
A.Kellett, *The Yorkshire Dictionary of Dialect, Tradition and Folklore*, Otley, Smith Settle, 1994.

and it had been their intention to walk the last four miles, but my father bundled his sweetheart into a cab and startled the sleeping town by rattling over its cobbles in the early hours of the morning. The sensation he caused can readily be understood when you remember in those days cabs were only used by the working class for funerals and weddings - and not always then.

*Halifax Railway Station (1900)*                                        *(Steve Gee)*

My stepmother doesn't really come into the story yet, but I can't resist pointing the pathetic irony of the contrast she presents at this stage. She was working in Brighouse, alongside my mother, and lodging with a couple of father's aunts. She was quiet, gentle and retiring; and whilst my parents roistered and squandered their money, she sent every penny she could spare to support a large family of fatherless brothers and sisters. She even eked out her factory earnings by needlework in her leisure hours. But there was never the slightest touch of envy in her recalling of these memories - on the contrary, she always seemed to revel by proxy, as it were, in a rakish extravagance of which she herself was totally incapable, and the memory of which still took her breath away.

Although no thought of the future shadowed the light-hearted full-blooded, yet almost callous courtship of my parents, something caused a break in it. What exactly, I don't know. The nearest my stepmother ever got to explaining it was, "I fancy your father was a bit too keen, like - and yer mother didn't want to be tied too soon. And then, you know, like all the Ramsdens she'd a temper, and were a bit willy-nilly like! "

Whatever the reason, the break nearly drove my father frantic. And when the tiff, or quarrel, was made up and the courtship was resumed, the affair left with him a rankling wound - a bitterness of which we were to catch glimpses as we grew up and the drink was in him.

But the reconciliation was apparently complete enough and warm enough, for it was during the first weeks of their re-union that I was conceived.

*Miles Sharp: Back Bonegate 1913*

(BM)

*Miles Sharp: Bow Market 1923*

(BM)

*Miles Sharp: Bridge End 1915*

(BM)

*Miles Sharp: Briggate 1911*

(BM)

*Miles Sharp: Daisy Croft 1914*

(BM)

*Miles Sharp: Holroyd Buildings 1914*

(BM)

*Miles Sharp: Rastrick Bridge and Bridge End 1917*

(BM)

*Miles Sharp: Yorkshire Mills, c1930*

(BM)

# Chapter Two

I was born on the second of April, 1889, and, being the first grandchild of both families, was given the Christian names of both my grandfathers. It was the age of double-barrelled, often grandiose names, and although I was always referred to as James Richard in public, in the intimacy of the family circles my name was mercifully shortened to Dick.

I'm told I cried so much as a baby that I ruptured myself. I remember seeing, years later, the truss I had to wear - a tiny, ridiculous affair that today would hardly serve as a garter.

My earliest memory is vague and incomplete. I am being carried down stone stairs by someone wearing clogs. I am almost smothered in a blanket. I am put into a tin bath waiting for me on the hearth before an unbearably hot fire. The bath is filled with a yellowish liquid which is more slippery than soapy water. The steam from it tickles my nose and makes my eyes water. I'm terribly hot, the blanket in which I'm rolled again is hotter still, and I'm struggling to push it away to reach cool air as I'm carried back upstairs.

There's a break of, as near as I can guess, two years before my next definite memory. By then I must have been between four and five years old. I'm perched on the square kitchen table, swinging my legs, and reading aloud with steady fluency to an admiring circle of relatives, the leading article of the *Yorkshire Evening Post*. But of how and when I learned to read I remember nothing. I had yet to make acquaintance with school.

There's another early memory of about this period. I'm in bed, wakened from sleep by a tremendous hullaballoo from downstairs. Men are shouting and laughing, women are shrieking. I tumble out of bed, go downstairs - into bedlam. My mother is rolling and crying with laughter in the rocking chair. Three or four neighbours are there, all helpless with excited amusement. My father is sitting collapsed on the hearth-rug helpless in a paroxysm of mirth. And in the centre of the room, our solid foursquare table is prancing and cavorting about, first on one pair of legs, then the other; and following it about, his hands spread flat on the scrubbed top, is a little man with a bald head, whom I get to know years later as a local spiritualist. But the terrifying sight of that table so far forgetting itself is too much for me. I let out a yell and bring the seance to an abrupt conclusion.

Until I started my schooling, my world comprised three houses - three little pulsing worlds, like the two houses in *Wuthering Heights*, apparently existing in a geographical void. The streets one traversed between one and the other meant as little to me in those very early days as the string in the bracelet of brightly coloured beads of which my sister was so proud. I knew those three houses so well, even to their smells, which varied according to the day of the week, that even now I can recall each piece of furniture as vividly as the folk who owned and used them. Some of these household goods, in fact, are, now more real and individual than the grown - ups who petted and fussed me.

Judged by the standards of my class and time, my home was a "fine" one. For one thing, the stone-flagged floor wasn't bare and sanded, but boasted a square of coconut matting; and, instead of a home-made rag rug, the hearth was distinguished by a rich red affair of fine twisted threads known as "yelds". The uncovered surround was scoured an immaculate bluey-white with "donkey stone ".

Then again the furniture was surprisingly homogenous, considering the different sources it had come from. We had a complete suite - sofa, four upright chairs and rocking chair, of mahogany and horsehair. It was "grand" but far from comfortable. We weren't allowed to use this furniture, but, as it scratched our limbs, we much preferred the bare wooden stool which got a weekly scrub just as we did. And there was always the floor. This suite was new - a typical piece of parental extravagance which roused the ire of Grandmother Ramsden.

She was a great haunter of sales - a female Autolycus - and it was at a sale that she had found the handsome dresser which helped the suite to give our house such tone. [8] This also was of mahogany, but it had been stored in some stable or hen-house before it had come into the market. The drawers were fouled with poultry droppings and the lovely veneer, so smooth and grateful to a child's sensitive, enquiring fingers, was hidden by the dust and filth of years. It was a disreputable affair at which my mother turned up her nose in disgust. Her story of the cleaning and polishing it had to undergo was a household saga. I found its history of neglect hard to believe as I studied its imposing proportions and its near florid carved ornamentation of fruit and flowers. With the thought of it comes a chilling little memory of the first time I saw its plain unvarnished, almost poverty-stricken back. Majesty died. I felt cheated. I don't think I ever took anything at its face value again after that earth-shaking exposure.

But even after I had surprised its guilty secret the dresser still dominated the house and set the characteristic note of spick-and-span, cheerful cleanliness. Everything glistened and shone. Everything was either scrubbed or polished to a scrupulous spotlessness that made the fire seem twice as large and twice as cheerful as it really was. The shine and glisten was on everything from the lustres on the dresser, the dresser itself, the heavily-framed pictures, the brass fire-irons and fender and the black-leaded grate down to the pots and pans.

And as they shone, so did my mother's face. I have never seen anyone wash herself so thoroughly and vigorously as she did. Standing stripped to the waist at the cupboard sink, her full breasts as firm as her splendid back and shoulders, she not only made a lengthy and exacting ceremonial of soap and water but the towel in her hand became a scouring instrument of high purpose. It gave her face a high-lighted veneer which seemed as hard and smooth and lasting as that of the dresser. In the firelight I could catch tiny flickerings on her finely-drawn nose, cheekbones and chin. They were only less bright then those in her eyes; tiny echoes of those which danced so warmly and gaily on the glass and mahogany around us.

It was a comfortable, comforting house, as I remember it during that early happy

---

[8] A Greek mythological figure, a renowned thief and "a snapper up of unconsidered trifles" amongst other things.

period of my life, with my mother as its centre and soul. My father at that time comes back to me as little more than a quiet, friendly, entertaining comrade, giving scarcely a hint of his importance as the breadwinner, but behaving more like an older child and setting us a charming example of deference to the mistress of the house. He seldom, if ever, gave a direct command. He was the leader in a conspiracy to keep the reigning power in a mood of serenity; the leader in a pretence which deceived no one, at once comical and serious and always wholly delightful.

And yet, in spite of his homely charm, his fascinating stories and his unpatronising stooping to our level, he remained something of an interloper whose presence disturbed the "nesty" atmosphere. I was conscious of having to share my mother with him, in a way I never felt in the case of my brothers and sisters or as easy when he was there.

Warm and settled, cleanly routine. That's my first impression of life. Every day bringing its own special colour and flavour, its own established course of comfortable seclusion. Sunday, shining-white and starchy - the house dressed for the day with the best, most elaborately crocheted anti-macassars on sofa and chairs, the square centre-table gorgeous in its red plush cloth with intricately laced and tasselled fringe, the hearth a glory of brass and blacklead - except for the copper kettle which, one felt, would have hated not to be different from everything else. Sunday, which, just before dinnertime, almost forgot itself and, warmed by the use of the oven and scented with roasting meat, pretended it was going to be a dressed-up Thursday. Monday, beginning like a half-Sunday and ending like a half-Tuesday, a greyish day when the lordly fire-irons, carefully wrapped in an old shawl, were put away on the sofa; when all the weekend finery of mats and doylies (reminders of carefree spinster days when nimble fingers were busy getting ready one's "bottom-drawer") went back into seclusion away from the bustle and turmoil of the workaday week. Even the food on Mondays felt the chill of the approaching washday - the meat apologetically aware it was merely a cold leftover from Sunday's largesse, missing the companionship of the Yorkshire pudding, and only too painfully conscious it would not be followed by a warm sweet but beggarly jam or treacle and bread. Tuesday, dripping wet, yet palely shimmering with soapsuds flecking the naked floor, with the wan smell of washing and the tepid taste of cold rice pudding cut out of the solid and eaten like cake - a penitential, meagre cake, but lacking the sharp edge, the salty tang of tears. Tuesday, when one's mother was farthest away, driven by demons from tub to wringing-machine, her fringe as limp and damp as the clothes she pummelled and rubbed through many waters.

Wednesday was the colour of newly planed pitchpine, grained and streaky, but warm with the smell of ironing - warmer still with the promise of Thursday. Thursday, royal with banners - banners of yellow, orange and red - redolent with the odour of new baked bread and currant loaves and seed cake; a day that was a regal progress of goodly smells, when the fire became a glorious benison. Friday came marching in chain mail, with a backward eye on Tuesday soap and water and the other forward to Saturday's dry polish. It was a day of harsh and pungent smells, beginning as a grimy mess of blacklead on a cold fireless grate, then the biting tang of metal polish on the fire irons, and the soft hiss of bath-brick on the cutlery. But it was all bringing Saturday nearer - Saturday, which didn't really begin until just before the dinner was ready, when the fire-irons resumed their rightful position and put the fire in its place, that of a distant relative instead of a close friend.  Saturday brought fried steak and sausage as a fore-runner of Sunday's joint, a penny to spend on sweets and after a quiet tea, melted into a starchless Sabbath mood.

And suddenly, as I remember it, this seemingly eternal and unchanging cycle is shattered. One Thursday morning, hurrying downstairs from the nothingness that all days were beyond the stairs door, hurrying towards the most royal of all days now reigning, as I thought, in his glory below, I stepped into cold, dull emptiness, with no Thursday in the world at all.  With nothing but a very black man with very pink gums and very white teeth, busy with brushes in the hearth.  I ate my breakfast that morning, sitting on the doorstep, watching without really seeing the busy traffic of lorries and coal wagons.  When the stranger had gone with a last flash of his pink gums and white teeth and when the sour odour of soot had faded somewhat and the fire had been lit, Thursday crept back into the house.  But it was a frightening Thursday and I had another disturbing memory to keep company with that of the grand "maggony" dresser.  Even Time had a poverty stricken backside.

Grandmother Ramsden's house (I always thought of it as hers although Grandfather lived there!) ranked next in importance to ours.  Not only did we visit there oftener than Grandmother Gregson, but it was near enough to home, and its ruling genius so awe-inspiring as to make it difficult to forget even when one was far away from it.

It was a larger, darker, stuffier house than ours; overcrowded both with furniture and people.  There was a long-case (we never called it a "grandfather") clock in the darkest corner. It had a stern, heavy tick and a watchful air.  You felt it was in league with Grandmother to see you behaved yourself.  All the furniture was older and heavier than ours.  There was a long settle instead of a sofa, cushioned with horse blankets.  The rocking chair had a roomy drawer beneath the seat.  The fender and fire irons were of steel and the floor was smothered in a crazy conglomeration of dingy, stuffy-smelling rag rugs.  But the most notable feature was the large shut-up bed, which in the daytime masqueraded as an overgrown tallboy and at night sprawled and spread itself to within a yard of the hearth.

It was a noisy, busy house. In the daytime there were usually two or three old women discussing with appalling frankness and considerable din, the affairs of the neighbourhood. In the evening it was crowded with Uncles and Aunts who argued, laughed, squabbled and sometimes fought with disturbing vigour and vehemence.  I remember one terrifying occasion when my youngest uncle and aunt, both near their twenties, rolled about the floor in a fierce and bloody battle quelled in the end by my grandmother's intervention with a horsewhip.

The whip was always close to her hand, and she never hesitated to use it, whether on her recalcitrant family or the fearsome looking goat which haunted the stable yard next door. She was a stern, callous old matriarch.  She needed to be with such a roistering husband and such a lively brood (all of them twice her size) to manage. But manage them she did, driving them with a cold, implacable harshness which always made me tremble.

She dominates the scene to the utter exclusion of my maternal grandfather.  She outlived him by years. She seemed as permanent as the smell of the corn sacks she was forever darning. In all my memories of her except one, she sits on a hard chair between the sink cupboard and the window, her curved bodkin flashing in and out of the sickly-sweet smelling sack; her cold sharp eyes flashing, missing no sign of guilt or shortcoming in anyone or anything. Always at her elbow, on the long table beneath the window, stood a jar of brimstone-and-treacle, and always there was one dreadful, unchanging ritual to be undergone on one's arrival.

"Open thi gob!" she would bark. Then she would dip a large spoon into the jar twirl the sticky, sickening mess, with the expertness of long practice, towards one's mouth.

"Wider nor that!" she would bark again as she jabbed it in.

"Lick it clean!" And her eye never left you, not even for one second of the dreadful struggle with incipient nausea; and her regard never softened, no matter how much of a show you made of licking the last lingering ghost of flavour from the instrument of torture.

As I grew older, I learned many things about her which increased my awe of her. She was a moneylender in a small, ruthless way. She backed horses diligently, making quite a profitable business of it. But she never made a song-and-dance about anything. Curt and secretive, she spoke little, but always to the point. If you didn't obey at the first bidding, there was no second word, but such sudden action as shocked you into compliance. And she had no use for you if you wouldn't stand up to her tactics. She taught me to take my medicine in more senses than one.

Two memories of that household so impressed me that they forced themselves into plays - early plays which I quickly scrapped before completion knowing, without knowing why, that they were no good. The reason I discovered later. I was, at the time of writing, still too emotionally involved in the theme and with the characters, to get either in the right perspective.

Both memories are connected with the death of the indomitable old woman.[9] For some reason or other, I was sleeping at my Grandmother's that night. Sleeping as best I could between two of my uncles. My sister Cora was sleeping between two aunts in another bed in the same room. The room was curtained and closed, and before the faintest glimmer of dawn I was fully awake. Everything was close and dark and silent except for the regular, heavy breathing of the grown-ups. As stealthily as I could, I wriggled out of my stifling prison until I was sitting on the pillow, panting for air. I daren't try to get completely out of bed for fear of disturbing the others - especially my oldest uncle, a morose, taciturn man of whom I stood in childish awe. He had been in the Army, and I used to wonder fearfully what dreadful thing he had done in his younger days and what consequences he had escaped by taking such a disreputable way out. In those days soldiering was the last refuge of the ne'er-do-weels, and to have a son in the Army was almost as shameful as having a jailbird in the family.

Suddenly, the intense quiet was broken by a different sound. There was the scuffle of a chair downstairs where Mother was watching by the bedside of the sick but

---

[9] Jane Ramsden died in 1898, aged 61.

uncomplaining tyrant. I began to climb out of bed, still cautiously, but was halted by her voice, low and urgent, from the foot of the stairs.

"Jack! Jack!" Something in the call made me shiver into prickly gooseflesh.

"Jack! Get up! All on yer! She's gooin! "

Overlooked in the hurried, scrambled awakening, I followed them downstairs to the sprawling bed. Amongst the tumbled sheets lay the hunched-up, incredibly tiny figure of dread. Fascinated, I watched one aunt rip the pillow, take from it a small feather, and place it on the silent lips. It stayed there motionless.

*Dale Street, Brighouse (c1890s-1900s): A typical working class street in Central Brighouse, similar to the ones off Mill Lane and Wakefield Road. I remember it looking like that in the 1950s, apart from the posed inhabitants!* *(Steve Gee)*

"Better get her straight!" said the ex-soldier uncle after a silent exchange of glances. Kneeling on the bed, astride the corpse, he started to pull it into some semblance of order, then I was observed, hurriedly dressed and sent home through the dark streets to call my father. Full of the scene I had left, I forgot to be frightened of the darkened, empty world.

My last memory of that house is of the funeral and what followed.

The ceremony itself was nothing new to me. We were rather given to funerals in those days – grandiose affairs, to which the remotest and youngest members of the clan were bidden as a matter of course, but this was the biggest and grandest I'd known so far. It was a new experience for my sister Cora, and her curiosity, combined with her natural waywardness, gave me some humiliating moments. She howled because she wasn't allowed to gorge herself on the funeral biscuits; stamped and created because she wasn't allowed to hold the glass of funeral wine for herself; she coughed herself blue in the face at her first and only sip; she laughed and waved at outsiders who were "showing respect"; in short, she behaved with such a disregard of the decencies as to fill me with shame and dismay. She was getting on for five and should have known better. Besides, I was afraid that I might be bidden to take her home and so miss the rest of the day. I felt nothing but satisfaction when she was sick after stuffing herself with the funeral baked meats. For once, I felt, justice had been done!

It was a splendid affair, that funeral tea! It cost a shilling a head! At least sixty persons sat down to the long table in the hall of the Sunday school, and set to work with a will. Beef, ham and pork, a various assortment of pickles, white bread, brown bread, plain tea-cake, currant tea-cake, hard cakes, spice cake, seed loaf, queen buns and all kinds of tarts and pastries were swilled down with copious draughts of strong, hot, over-sweet tea. The gravity fitting the occasion had begun to melt from the moment we got into the coaches for the return journey from the graveside. By the time the feast had begun the talk was jovial. Before it was over the talk and the laughter were loud and, at times, ribald. In the general jollity I forgot all the flaws of that great day – even that dreadful moment at the graveside when I'd tried to cry, found I couldn't squeeze a single tear, and caught the eye of the gravedigger on me in what I fancied was stern disapproval.

The grand affair came to an end at last. We were taken home and divested of our mourning finery. Then just as I thought it was all over, we were taken by Mother for, although we didn't realise it at the time, our last glimpse of that old house.

It had already lost its character as a home, for the pictures were down from the walls, some of the furniture out of the way as though ready for removal. All the aunts and uncles were there, and no time was lost in disposing of the effects. The larger pieces of furniture offered no difficulty, for nobody wanted such old fashioned things. Not even the long-case clock which had been stopped whilst the dead was in the house. It was agreed promptly to sell everything for what it would fetch and share the proceeds.

The china and crockery evoked more competition, and so the eldest uncle turned auctioneer, trying to control the bidding which at times grew acrimonious, and keeping an account of the prices each lot fetched. I was a little puzzled that Mother bid for nothing.

This over, all the womenfolk, daughters, daughters-in-law and daughters-in-law to be, knelt or squatted in a circle on the floor, and the household linen, of which there was to me a surprising quantity ( the old lady had been something of a magpie ) was shared with noisy but scrupulous impartiality.

It was a queerly disturbing scene. I suppose it was the first time I'd seen the end, the break-up, of anything – the first time I realised that things just didn't go on for ever. Then again, during this "one for me, one for thee" process, things were said which sometimes meant something else, and although I shouldn't have put it like that to myself then, there were cross-currents of feeling which I sensed in a dim fashion but didn't understand. I'd heard the phrase "Breaking up the home", but in a vague fashion I began to see something else was breaking too, and these people whom I'd thought of, or rather taken for granted, as the "family" were, in fact, all separate, vitally differing individuals. They were persons as well as relations.

And there was another queer thing. Under all the keen chaffering of the womenfolk and the depreciating, peace-making efforts of the men, there was something in the attitude of them all towards Mother which I uneasily and vaguely resented. The unease was sharpened when the sharing proper was finished and there began a lengthy process of swapping and discarding.

I noticed that all sorts of almost valueless things would be tossed on to Mother's pile with some remark such as, "Here Ann ! Tha'll do moor wi' this nor me!" And I noticed, too, that Mother would readily exchange some elaborate trifle of a table-mat or antimacassars for a couple of patched sheets. And whilst the oddment was a gift made kindly, or an exchange effected after some bargaining, I felt that all of them, in their different ways, were somehow "looking down" on Mother. I didn't know then that things weren't going too well with us at home, and therefore couldn't understand their rough patronage. But I felt it, and I knew that Mother, in her quiet, proud fashion, also felt it – and resented it. She laughed and argued with the best of them, giving as good as she got, but there was a touch of white about her nostrils and a hard, but suspicious brightness in her eyes. And I had already learned to recognize these as suppressed temper or emotion.

I helped to carry the booty home with a vague, sick feeling which not even the possession of a quaint mug with a frog in the bottom could dispel.

Mother's share from the sale of the furniture and insurance was promptly spent on a week's holiday at Scarborough. It was the only holiday we ever had as a family. I remember only one tiny item about it – that Mother carried the slender store of sovereigns in a little canvas bag tucked safely away in her corsage.

My very last memory of that dark, fusty house was later to provide the play-off in a short story. Just as everyone was packing up his or her bundle of household goods, my youngest uncle gave a shout of surprise.

"Eh! Look what we've forgotten. Anybody want a whip?" he laughed as he made the ownerless sceptre crack viciously. He sensed the shocked disapproval of the others and his grin faded. Then he broke the handle across his knee and said "That's the end o' that! "

Grandmother Gregson's house I never visited willingly, and always with distaste. It was not only poor and bare – after all most houses I knew were – but almost always untidy and unclean. The few odd chairs had always to be cleared of clothing or pots and pans before you could use them. The dresser was scratched and chipped instead of being polished and the door of its centre cupboard was broken off its hinges. Its badly scarred top was always "cluttered up" with dirty crockery or cooking utensils, or dirty clogs. There were no ornaments on the mantelpiece – nothing but an old wooden clock that never went, and a jam jar to hold spills. There were no fire-irons – not even a tidy betty to hide the ashes which were allowed to pile up to the bars before being cleared. The deal top of the large square table was as innocent of covering as the stone floor – and little cleaner.

Upstairs there was nothing but untidy beds which apparently were never "made" – their quilts of dilapidated patchwork trailing on the fluffy floor. Under one bed an earthenware jar, holding at least two gallons, served as a chamber-pot, and I remember one shocking occasion when it was it full to the brim.

This house had two ruling smells, both equally pungent. Downstairs an ever-present odour of vinegar (or alegar as my father's people always called it) and upstairs, equally constant, the stench of stale urine. It was a slovenly, "offald" house.

But I once saw it in the throes of a cleansing which even Mother could not have bettered in thoroughness and ferocity. I arrived to find every stick of furniture on the flags outside, and Grandmother Gregson inside the naked living place, flooding it with buckets of water and raising hell's delight with an old broom. As her face was flushed and her speech thick, I made short work of my errand and fled. But such bouts of cleanliness must have been most rare for, when the family finally left the house it had to be disinfected by the sanitary inspector, to the shame and distress of my parents I need hardly add.

The reason for this shiftless slovenliness I was to learn and appreciate only too fully later as I gradually became aware of the Gregson weakness for drink, and also began to feel its effects at home. But even then, child as I was I sensed something was wrong about a grown man such as one particular uncle who had a good trade in his hands yet spent whole days and nights in bed, doing nothing at all, not even reading, not even sleeping all the time. That particular uncle was to end his days as a broken down tramp in a workhouse; his mother in an asylum for the insane.

But it wasn't only their needless poverty and improvidence which made our visits embarrassing and distasteful, though like most children, we had a strong streak of snobbishness in our make-up. It wasn't that we weren't welcome. They were kind and generous, all of them, to the point of lavishness, and their affection for us was little short of idolatry. We could do no wrong in their eyes. Nothing was too good for us. And I suppose it was this almost slavish adoration, their humble gratitude for the honour of our presence, almost as though we were young royalty, which went against all my childish instincts of what was fitting. Such humility in older folk didn't fit in with the world as I knew it. There was something wrong behind it I felt, long before I knew what.

The only time I saw Grandmother Gregson in our home was the last I ever saw of her. I'm anticipating my story again by a few years, but I set it down here to round off this account of my stock.

I should be between nine and ten years old, I think, when she made her last appearance in my life. It was an appalling day. I got down to breakfast to find a stranger at the table. An old bedraggled creature with untidy hair, her face and rusty black clothes smeared with mud, her eyes red and swollen with tears, was sucking tea from a saucer. Her voice recalled an almost forgotten three years old past.

"Doesn't tha know me, doy?" she whimpered. That "doy" flooded me with hot prickly memories. I slipped uneasily on to my stool, pretending I hadn't noticed her half-stretched arms. She began to weep noisily – uncouth chokings as she drank her tea, blubbering.

"Now don't fret yersen! Finish yer breakfast now "said Mother, quietly chiding. But the old dame made more noise than ever, and the bread was dry in my mouth.

Not a word of explanation was given to us as we were bundled off to school, but I learned afterwards that she had escaped from the asylum a day or two before, had slept no one knew where, but had managed to find her way to us during the previous night. She had made a mistake as to the house and had stumbled into the house of a bedridden old woman, thrown herself across the foot of the bed, and nearly scared the invalid out of her wits.

She was still there when we went home for dinner. So was my father. He was raging drunk – the first time I remember seeing him so, though I was to learn later it was his invariable refuge when things went wrong, he was alternately storming at his mother for the misery she was causing him and then blubbering as noisily as she in self pity. Once he snatched up the carving knife, but Mother held him off. We youngsters added our frightened voices to the din.

Then came the Relieving Officer - in a cab, round which unwanted sight all the children of the street clustered and chattered – to take the old woman back to the institution. He was a bluff, bearded, heavily built man, with a rough, unprepossessing voice. I suppose custom had bred in him a property of surface hardness, and that in reality he was quite a decent kindly man, but his dry matter of factness seemed to my boyish mind both callous and cruel. I drew on this memory of him for the character of "Frowse" in my one act play *Liddy*, and though it is perhaps unjust to him, it is in the light of later experience of Public Assistance work, true enough of certain of his breed.

In spite of her struggles and cries, he soon had the pitiful scarecrow out of the house, and I never saw her again. But she left a legacy of fear which was strengthened as the years went by, by the example of my father and that lie-abed uncle. A joint fear of what I learned to call the "Demon Drink"and of an inbred laziness and apathy. The fear of self-indulgence kept me a rabid teetotaller until I was well past thirty. The laziness I have fought all my life, far from successfully, for it still comes over me at times, a malaise that numbs my faculties. The dread of it makes even the normal fallow period between spells of creative work a time of sickening self torture.

Looking back, it seems that all my life I've been a battleground between the two warring strains; the Gregson diffidence against the Ramsden self conceit, the Gregson humour against the Ramsden wit, the Gregson lack of energy and self-assertion against the Ramsden [10] ambition to get on; in short, the Gregson putty against the Ramsden steel. The one positive virtue I inherited with the Gregson strain came from my unknown grandfather – a sense of obligation to my day and generation, which stepped in to act as a spur when disillusion broke the spring of ambition, and prevented me from sinking into utter indifference and indolence. What ever the reasons, inherited tendencies, acquired moral principles, or sheer economic necessity, I've never been able to relax or play with an unclouded conscience.

---

[10]  The text reads Marsden, but in fact Gregson must have meant Ramsden.

# Chapter Three

I was followed at mathematical intervals of two years by three sisters and two brothers, and very soon the halcyon days of enclosed, comfortable seclusion were over, and I was engaged in the more serious business of life. I took my place as nursemaid to my successors and general assistant to Mother. But although I was often teased by the grown-ups about having "my nose pushed out", I knew with absolute certainty that I held a very special place in the affection of my parents, especially my mother's.

There's no doubt I was a "mother's boy", and I ran true to type. I was timid and sensitive, abnormally observant, and alive to the most delicate nuances of voice, mood and changing relationships between my elders. I was finicky except, thank goodness, as regards food. I shrank from physical violence whether in fun or earnest, except when goaded to the utter extreme, when I would flare up into insensate, almost hysterical ferocity. I was law-abiding to a morbid degree; neat and precise – "as good as a lass, any day", said my mother.

My eldest sister, Cora, on the contrary, was a born rebel – a "besom", a "nowt", and on particularly outrageous occasions, a "little bitch, God forgive me!" in mother's phrase. She was the most intransigent child I've ever known, and never a day went by without a stubborn battle between them, usually ended by an explosion from Mother who would seize her as she screamed and danced, up-end her unceremoniously, give her a good "tanning" and then plank her down on the pavement or the doorstep to cool her knickerless bottom.

Next in age came a boy, christened "Ramsden".[11] He gave promise of being a male edition of Cora, but died suddenly, soon after his second birthday. I remember he lay in his small coffin on the long table under the window, whilst my mother lay in the big bed suckling the fourth of the family, another boy, John George.

The tiny living room was overcrowded, and when the street door was closed for the evening, unbearably close and stuffy. Unthinkable as it may be today that a woman should lie in childbed able to see and be seen by passing pedestrians, with the heavy traffic of a busy thoroughfare rumbling by a few yards away, the lack of privacy and the intrusion of neighbours, helpful or otherwise, was quite a matter of course to us.

I remember being puzzled at the seeming poverty of the dead child's funeral, wondering why there was no hearse and only one coach for the mourners. It also puzzled me as to how the coffin was to be borne to the cemetery, until I noticed the box like compartment under the driver's seat being opened, and the logic of it all dawned on me. Little lives got little funerals as was only fair. I made up my mind to live long enough to merit at least six coaches and a proper tea in the schoolroom, not just a "family do" as this was going to be.

But even the modest tea we did have was quite an occasion, for it took two "sittings-down" to accommodate the dozen or so guests. I remember two unmarried Ramsden

---

[11] Ramsden Gregson, born June 1893, died June 1895.

*Funeral carriage, Atlas Mill Road, Brighouse (date not known): definitely not used for Ramsden Gregson, more likely for his grandmother, Jane Ramsden.* (BM)

aunts dropped in on their way home from the mill, and I remember my mother trying to eat, and turning away her head on the pillow to hide the two slow tears that stole down towards her pinched, deadened nostrils.

She seldom wept, but always in that hard, quiet fashion; the deeper and keener the pain or sorrow, the less she showed it, and it's one of the curious, heart warming things of life to notice that same trick in my daughter, linking past and present, and heightening the remembered tragic-comedy of those funeral baked meats which also served as a christening feast.

Some time before this our financial fortunes had worsened considerably. My father's earnings, in spite of a strike, had been cut to about half, although his working hours remained unaltered. My mother made a better shot at the necessary economies than did my father, but she was a drastic rather than a competent manager.

Possibly because we were better stocked as regards clothes and household linen etc, than most of our class, it was some months before the real effects of the cut made themselves felt, and I do not remember any signs of our growing poverty in the first home, nor any signs of strain between my parents, nor any signs of deterioration in my father. It remains in retrospect a happy, unclouded period, and in it he remains a kindly, humourful creature with a great fund of entrancing stories based mainly on the plays he had seen. I never saw him reading anything but the evening paper, though he must at some period have pored over the *Leopold Edition of Shakespeare* – the only book we had in the house until we began to collect Sunday School prizes.

It was a rare treasure, this Shakespeare, with its pictures of terrifying apparitions, muscular men and Junoesque women. I still have it, tattered and rebound several times over, still heavily scored with the marks left by his acid-stained thumbs. We pored over its dark, heavy illustrations to such effect that even today I find myself comparing the players in modern productions with that gallery of dynamic, if sometimes beefy creations.

Another line of father's stories was drawn from his reading of various criminal histories, playing down the horrific side, and stressing some queer accident by which the criminal was discovered, or some eerie happening which drove him to confession. Detection in these crude, homely "whodunits" seemed a very hazardous affair, but the telling of them left us in no doubt that crime never paid, but always had to be paid for in the long run – a conclusion which satisfied our childish sense of right and justice until we were old enough to know the truth.

For the rest, our imaginations were fed by the "witch tales" we overheard the ancients retail round the fire on winter nights. You could always be sure of hearing some of these superstitious yarns in the little dark house occupied by two maiden aunts of my father. One of them was "a bit touched", and when disappointed of some small treat, would kneel up in her rocking-chair, her arms over the back, and rock herself furiously, crying the while like a baby. The elder sister supported both of them by taking in mangling. The mangle was a huge monstrous contraption, taking up more than a third of the house space, consisting of a long box-like affair in a stout wooden frame. The box part contained three blocks of stone each about a yard square and a foot thick. It ran on rollers round which, wrapped in a long, long sheet, the newly washed clothes were wound. Everyone in the neighbourhood brought their clothes to be mangled. Whilst my great aunt was engaged placing the articles on the winding sheet – a process calling for no small degree of skill to avoid uneven packing for one customer, an earlier one would be turning the mangle backwards and forwards over her own consignment. As there were always, or so it seemed to us, three or four clients in the house at once, you can understand why it was known as the "Gossip Shop". There was one occasion when a client, so interested in the talk around her that she forgot to keep her mind on the job, turned the mangle too far. The strap broke under the strain and the "coffin" of stone blocks slid to the floor, blocking the doorway, and it was some hours before order was restored and the customers able to get out of the house.

It was a queer, crabbed, dark little place, squeezed between frowning factories, and here on dingy winter evenings I have cowered by the fire, wedged into the coal bucket, and listened to the chatter about ghosts, omens and warlocks until I was benumbed at both extremities, scared to death of the dark journey home.

By this time being nearly seven, I was old enough to have several daily and weekly chores, principally "baby-minding" and running errands, the most regular of which was taking Father's dinner or supper, according to which shift he was on, to the work's gate. Other boys were there on similar errands, and we usually compared notes on what we'd brought for our respective parents. There was one boy whose mother was known to be "slack set up" – that's to say, lazy and shiftless. The meals she sent were always makeshift affairs of bread and potted meat, or some such sandwich filling – never warm suppers of newly cooked fry and potatoes, meat and potato pie, such as most of the men got. And we gathered from the boy that his father felt this very much, especially as his workmates chaffed him about it, and advised him to put his foot down. He must have taken the advice, for one evening the boy arrived in something of a dither. "There's going to be another row!" he said. "We had one before mi father set off to come here. He said he'd leather mi mother if she didn't send him a hot supper. So she has, an' I've to tell him to eat it while it's hot! An' it's only a mustard sandwich!"

I've often wondered how that affair ended.

Shortly after the death of my first brother we left our first cosy home in Mill Lane for one in Foundry Street which was to all intents and purposes a cul-de-sac running from the railway to the river and boasting about thirty houses, a dyeworks, a foundry and a brewery, not to mention the inevitable pub.[12]

*Brighouse Borough Market: preparing for an important visitor (General William Booth), c1900s. Halifax Reference Library*

---

[12] The name Mill Lane itself is interesting. An act of 1847 gave local authorities the right to name streets. Nothing was done in Brighouse until 1868 when the Local Board surveyed the streets and named them. Local people resented the loss of such old nicknames as Zingo Nick (a snicket off Commercial Street) and Ganny Bar, and the new street signs were repeatedly torn down until finally the Board ordered prosecution.
One road was named Cabbage Street! A Board member admitted that it was done as a joke, though protesting that the cabbage was a noble vegetable. It became Dale Street. Brighouse Lane became Police Street (now Lawson Road) and Larkhill Terrace was renamed Haigh Street.
Mill Lane, notorious for its pitted and dirty state, was named Parliament Street. This was too much for the locals, who refused to use the name, until in 1869 the *The Brighouse News* was able to report "it is with pleasure we record that the objectionable name Parliament Street has been changed back to Mill Lane by Order of the Board."
*What was happening in Brighouse 100 years ago*, Brighouse & District Historical Society 1992

It housed a cross-section of the working class of the day, from comparatively opulent foremen to out-at-elbows, very casual labourers; from children who wore boots on weekday to children who hadn't always clogs even for Sundays; from a handful of families who went to church or chapel and were teetotalers with "a bit put by" to those who drank everything they could earn, and often had recourse to the pawnbroker first thing on a Monday morning. Ultra clean and respectable next door to the sluttish and disreputable. Some at the top of the artisan tree, most of them trying not to slip down, a hopeless minority who'd given up the struggle – given up caring about being down and abandoned all idea of trying to keep up appearances – objects of disgust to the majority of the adults, not because they were poor and insecure, (who wasn't?), but because they flaunted their poverty and were so lost to all notions of independence and self-respect as to sponge and beg wherever they could. They welcomed charity, and no one could sink lower than that.

These social differences meant nothing whatever to us youngsters. Like children everywhere before their world loses its innocent wisdom, we were a true democracy in one respect at least. We knew little liberty, it is true, and fraternity was a most inconstant factor, but equality was so absolute that we were no more conscious of it than of the air we breathed.

The new house in Foundry Street was a slightly bigger version of the back to back dwelling we had left, but it boasted an extra bedroom. It stood back from the pavement and above it, and, in the sunk area in front, we had our own special privy. This, bringing emancipation from the bondage of a key and bobbin and a walk through a dark passage to a communal convenience, was a great delight which had to be sampled as soon as discovered.

Life became more public. Not only did the house seem more exposed because of its elevation, but we used the front steps and flags as an extra apartment, and the roadway, free of passing traffic, became a playroom. We were no longer in a nest but out on a branch.

It was a noisy, brawling street. Even after darkness, when the last squalling, yelling youngster was indoors, the women would sit on their doorsteps, shouting their gossip, banter and disputes. We knew everyone's business almost as well as they knew ours, and would take sides in the rows which would break out with sudden ferocity and be made up with equal din and heartiness. It was almost impossible to "keep yourself to yourself", and in the end we gave up trying.

The street was rich in characters, as indeed seem all the scenes I knew as a lad. There was the hard callous old woman with only one hand and a deadly tongue of vitriol, the bitchiest creature I believe I've ever met. She never seemed to miss the hand she'd lost in the factory – indeed the scarred stump was better than any hand as a weapon of offence, and she could use it with deadly effect, whether in a brawl with someone her own size, or in knocking the breath out of a youngster by a vicious jab under the ribs.

There was a big, strident Amazon, to whom life seemed one long, rare joke. She would laugh even whilst fighting. She was always the one to collect for wreaths when Death paid one of his frequent visits to the street. She was something of a heroine in my eyes because during the Anti-Irish Riots in Brighouse which followed the Phoenix Park murders she had felled a policeman with a three-legged stool she'd looted from some house or other. [13] And I regarded her with awe until, one hot Saturday afternoon, as I sat sucking the sweets I'd bought with my Saturday penny. I saw her come flying out of her house in a screeching panic and bang the door to behind her. I think she meant to try and hold the door shut, but a heavy dull thud from inside sent her scurrying across to Mother. And sticking through one of the lower panels, thrown with such force as to split it, was one foot of an iron last – the sort most families had for putting irons on clogs. When I heard that it had been thrown by her meek little husband who never spoke to a soul, but slipped out of the house to his work as though he was going to commit a felony and returned in the same fashion as though he had, I couldn't – simply couldn't believe it. But the iron last, which couldn't be shifted, stuck there all weekend, and the new raw panel, which replaced the damaged one on the following Monday, provided glaring evidence of the incomprehensible ways of grown-ups.

There were plenty such puzzles to occupy the mind of a growing, perhaps precocious child. Life had become wider, fuller, yet leaner and grimmer, and if this were romance instead of prosaic fact, I should work in some graceful symbolism about my discovering an affinity between existence and that unvarnished dresser back. But the fact is that I didn't think of my new life as seamy or sordid. It was too exciting to be thought about. It had to be lived.

By the time I was eight my weekly round of household chores was full and varied. It included the scrubbing of the bare wooden stairs, the polishing of the family's boots, the cleaning of the cutlery, the black leading of the grate and the scouring of the front steps and flags. There were also errands to run and the other children to "mind". The cradle never seemed empty, and I spent ages rocking it. A long piece of cord made it possible for me to sit on the doorstep and watch the life and play of the street, but this was confiscated when I absentmindedly upset the current baby.

Don't think I imagined myself as an ill-used drudge, or that I resented the taunt of "lad-lass" from more fortunate youngsters. It was the accepted thing that the eldest of the family, boy or girl, should "help out" with the domestic work until the younger ones could take their share too. If I thought about it at all, it was to wish that I hadn't been born first. But it was good training for which I've many times in domestic crises been grateful.

During the earlier years in the new house Father began to spend less and less time in the rather crowded restless home, and I began to dread the weekends when he had time for solid drinking. He was never unkind to us, but his unusual talkativeness, and sentimental – sometimes maudlin – displays of affection reminded me uncomfortably

---

[13] The anti-Irish riots in Brighouse seem to have been especially serious. On 6th May 1882, the most senior Irish civil servant, the Permanent Undersecretary, Thomas Henry Burke and the newly appointed Chief Secretary for Ireland, Lord Frederick Cavendish, were stabbed as they walked through Phoenix Park in Dublin. Cavendish (M P for Yorkshire West Riding, Northern Division – his constituency including Brighouse) had only arrived in Ireland on the day he was murdered. Anti–Irish riots followed in Brighouse.
The riots, taking place over four days, were probably the worst disturbances in the town's history. Brighouse's reputation was badly damaged. I remember in the early 1950s my grandmother talking about the riots and she was not born until 1884. See Appendix Two for further information.

of his family's weakness. He was quarrelsome only when he had "mixed his liquor", but at these times he proved himself an amateur bruiser of no mean ability, and I basked in reflected glory. But the envy of my schoolmates was a poor exchange for the growing discomfort at home and the struggle Mother was having to make ends meet. A wage of twenty-five shillings a week, even in those days when beer was two pence a pint and three pence would buy enough stewing meat for a family meal, was a tight fit when it came to clothing and feeding two adults and four children.

And so, about this time, I am initiated into the mysteries of low finance. "Dick!" says Mother. "Just slip an' meet thi Aunt Sar'Alice leaving t'mill, an' ask her to lend me six pence till Friday!" And by and by I am sent for a shilling and then there comes a week when it isn't repaid. The next time I'm sent I meet with a blunt refusal.

"What!" says Mother when I report failure. "Here! Hand me mi shawl! I'll just tell yond skinny bitch what I think about her!" And off she dashes to have a royal, flaming row which relieves her feelings, no doubt, but not the family finances.

For the next week or two I am sent to tackle another Aunt – always at the factory gate – until another default provokes another row, and I'm switched to another target. I don't like these embarrassing errands, but they are no more than a bit of a nuisance, until I am brought face to face with something near tragedy.

It is just before my eighth or ninth Christmas. It occurs to me that I have seen no "spice cake" as yet, and I blurt out a question that makes Mother suddenly quiet and hard.

"We're having none this year!" she says with some difficulty, and the bottom drops out of the world. No spice cake!

Spice cake meant much more to us than turkeys or plum puddings have ever meant to anybody. And its preparation and baking were almost as much a domestic festival as Christmas itself. A whole day was devoted to the all important job, and the cleaning and drying of the fruit, the mincing of the candied peel, the special washing of the loaf tins, and the mixing and baking of a score or so of generous sized, gorgeously smelling loaves made the October day as happy and glorious as a month of ordinary Thursdays. Put away carefully to mature through the weeks, they appeared at the festival one by one in the place of honour on the dresser, flanked by a huge hunk of cheese. It was a point of honour that everyone entering the house during the festivities should partake of both. Each piece meant you'd have a "happy month" during the coming year. Not to offer it to a visitor was unforgiveable. Not to have it on show would be nothing less than disgrace – a confession of poverty almost as shameful as begging.

I was not surprised, after that quiet, cold reply, to see Mother's usual slow tears glistening in the firelight. I knew what she was feeling – felt sick for her.

How long she sat without speaking I don't know, but she stirred at last and said quietly, "Go to thi Aunt Sar'Alice. She'll be just leaving t'mill. Tell her she can have mi seal skin coat for half-a-crown!"

Another staggering blow. I knew how she prized that magnificent relic of her carefree, pre-marriage days. She must have seen something of my dismay, for she said quickly, "It's alright – it's no moor use to me!" and bundled me out of the house.

"What! That old-fashioned thing!" said my aunt. "She can keep it! But here's a tanner for thisen!"

Mother heard my report without a word, left me in charge of the children, and went out muffled in her shawl. How she managed to get the things I never knew, but about an hour later she was back with various small packages, and set to, there and then, to bake two pitifully small spice loaves.

"An' remember!" she commanded us sternly. "This is for folk coming in! Don't any o' you dare to ask for it!"

The family face and the sealskin coat were both saved for the time being.

That must have been the Christmas when my stocking held only an orange and an apple – not counting two sugar mice, costing a halfpenny each, which I'd bought and put in myself. I've another tragi-comic memory of that seal skin coat. It provided the only overcoat I ever had until I was old enough and able to afford to buy my own. My heart sank when one day I saw it being pulled to pieces and learned it was to be remade for me. Apart from the pangs I knew it cost Mother to part with it, I knew only too well the torments I should go through when my schoolmates saw it.

The result proved Mother to be but an indifferent tailor and me to be an only too accurate prophet. I wasn't ungrateful, but I couldn't stand the ridicule that "bum-starver" let me in for. I wore it as little as possible, and "lost" it as soon as I decently could.

# Chapter Four

I cannot recall a single outstanding incident of my schooldays. Not a fight, not a scholastic success, not a sensational thrashing, not a schoolmate who later was to make a great name for himself. The one abiding impression is the smell of slate pencils and corduroy clothes. I was neither the poorest boy there nor the "best-off". I was never at the top of the class nor the bottom.

Looking back, it seems to me that the only things I learned at the various Board Schools I attended proved a handicap rather than a help in later life. I could read, write and count before I began to attend school. I could do little more or better when I left. It's true that I was initiated into various branches of arithmetic, or rather had cumbersome, long-winded methods of calculation drummed into me. As I remember, all the emphasis in the so-called teaching we got was on the "how" of things, never the "why". For example, the teacher's explanation of long division was something I could never grasp. In the end I copied a sum from the slate of my neighbour – he'd been fortunate to get the answer right – took it home, and ferreted out the principle for myself by working out the sum backwards.

This was whilst I was attending Rastrick Common Board School, but it was neither better nor worse than any of the others I knew, either as regards the curriculum, the standards of accommodation and equipment, or the methods and quality of the teachers.

Even by the standards of those days, Rastrick Common was poorly equipped – a place of four classroooms, not too well lighted, its walls painted with drab colours and broken by a few dingy maps and tonic-sol-fa sheets. Paper was a scarce commodity reserved for the use of the upper classes. I came to the conclusion that slate pencils were made "squeaky" on purpose to give the teachers an excuse to cane us for "noisy writing".

It still surprises me how many reasons were found or invented for punishment. The fact was that like most similar schools, it was manned by teachers to whom teaching was a job, not a vocation. They taught from economic necessity with little or no sense of calling. Few of them, it appears to me now, had either the real aptitude or the right temperament for teaching. The result was that we were driven, not tempted, to learning. We feared and hated, rather than respected, much less loved our so-called teachers.

The last word on this subject was said by one of the teachers himself. Years later, when I began to attend evening classes at the Brighouse Mechanics' Institute, this bright spark, I found, was our tutor in Commercial Arithmetic. On the first night of the session he rose and said, "I see among you four – no, five – of my old pupils at Rastrick Common. And I want to say to you straight away – forget all we tried to teach you there! Forget all the silly, roundabout ways we tried to drub into you. I'm here to show you the simple, easy commonsense ways of calculating and reckoning!"

But the worst feature of the school was not its failure to make the best of its youthful material, but its success in confirming, if not arousing, some of the worst in us. Clumsy and wrongheaded as the methods employed were, the fact does remain that most of us emerged with a fairly sound knowledge of the three Rs, that it did achieve a decent, modicum of its limited aims. But if any of those teachers, except the headmaster, had any glimmerings of the notion that their job was to inculcate in us some idea of our place as citizens of the world we were to occupy, it was far from apparent to us. Quite the opposite, in fact. Let one illustration suffice.

In spite of the honourable example of the headmaster, favouritism, on the part of the teachers, was open and rank. And this favouritism was not governed by a boy's merit so much as by his clothing and his parent's standing. Nor was it merely a passive preference revealing itself in various small privileges. It was often active and vocal; and ill-clad boys, or those from the poorer, rougher families, were often held up to ridicule merely for those reasons.

It was the most pitiful kind of snobbery, and its implication that mere possessions was a virtue and poverty a crime was not the strongest incentive towards decent citizenship. Compared to this, the occasional injustice and the too frequent recourse to physical punishment were mere fleabites. It bred all kinds of unhealthy resentments, discontents and rivalries, and cut at the roots of a child's innate sense of equality and fair play.

The deficiencies of my official schooling were, fortunately, in some way made good by the Sunday School and the theatre. Both came into my life about the same time - before I was ten – with sensational abruptness.

Religion was brought into our godless neighbourhood by a band of home made, self educated "missionaries" from a large chapel in the centre of town.[14] They came with a skirl of concertina for a fanfare. Besides announcing in colourful though not always grammatical phrases that they brought us "the good news of the gospel", they invited us to the opening of their new mission hall. They had taken an old workshop, cleaned it, erecting a platform at one end and an inner porch at the other.

All the activities of the mission – Sunday School, Sunday Evening Services, Band of Hope, Sales of Work, Concerts – were housed in this one room.[15] In Sunday School the various "classes " were huddled so closely together that it was easy, almost impossible not to hear at least three teachers giving three separate lessons.

---

[14] St. Pauls Wesleyan Chapel, which stood on the corner of King Street and Police Street, Brighouse.

[15] It was agreed to rent a room on Woodland St. (adjoining Calder St.) from a Mr. Lord at 2/6 a week for 18 months. It was also agreed to spend up to £30 on refurbishment. At a later meeting it was agreed, in view of the large amount of money being spent, to extend the rental period to seven years. The mission was duly opened on Sunday, January 9th 1898.
Birds Royd Wesleyan Methodist Mission, Brighouse. Minutes of meeting, October 4th 1897. West Yorkshire Archive Service (Calderdale) PA76.
After a few years, land was purchased on Woodland St. and a new church built, at a cost of £1041.18.0, including £100 capitalised value of ground rent. It was opened on Saturday, December. 3rd 1904.
At the Jubilee celebrations on December 4th, 1954, the *Brighouse Echo* reported : "Mr. Gregson, who was introduced by Mr. Saunders, told those present that he had associations with Birds Royd even before the present mission was built. The pioneers who built the present building, did as much according to their abilities and capabilities, as did any statesman for his country. Describing life in the Birds Royd area at the turn of the century, Mr. Gregson said that it was not a well-liked district morally before the mission opened. He mentioned that he first learned to sketch and speak, as a lay preacher, at Birds Royd. He said it was their duty to do their utmost for those who would come after them, as did those pioneers fifty years ago".
The mission closed in 1969 and was converted to industrial use.

The "mission" were all working men and women, frequently confessing in their prayers and "experiences" that they were "unlearned and ignorant" men, but this humility did not deter them making the most fiery and dogmatic assertions as to heaven, hell and Holy Writ. Straightlaced and narrow-minded and bigoted at times, they were nevertheless devoted and sincere, and they brought to the neighbourhood a dash of energetic, dramatic endeavour, providing it with a sadly needed example of unselfishness and sober living.

Charlie Brook, my first Sunday School teacher, was typical. He spoke badly, stumblingly and found his scholars rather a handful. I remember little of what he told us except that, no matter where or how he started the lesson, it seemed always to end on what was obviously his "King Charles Head" – a theme which had" Ask and ye shall receive " as its text. [16] He was a foundry labourer, and his wages couldn't have been more than a pound a week, but he managed, somehow or other, to buy a pair of boots for one boy in the class. Rather ironically, that particular boy was the least deserving case among the lot of us, and the boots soon found their way to the pawn shop, but that didn't lessen the impression of gentle goodness which the incident left on me.

Sunday School was to play a much more important part in my life later on, as I shall tell, but very soon after the opening of the mission, I made my debut as a reciter. Stage fright made me funk the ordeal twice, but when I eventually got *The Charge Of The Light Brigade* off my chest, I was promptly roped in to play the part of a naughty boy in a sketch item to be given in the Choir Concert – a great occasion when people actually paid to come in! Having tasted blood, there was no holding me back.

I had, by the way, already written my first play. It was in five sets and twenty scenes. It began with Robin Hood and ended on Spion Kop.[17] The whole script didn't run to more than four pages of a copybook, and the dialogue couldn't have averaged more than two lines per scene – but it was decidedly rich in action. I've thought many times since that the coming cinema must have cast its prophetic shadow on me, inspiring me to draft one of the earliest scenarios ever written!

This fledgling flutter was prompted by my first visit to the theatre and it convinced my father, who was always boasting "Our Dick'll never have to take his collar off to work!", that we'd a genius in the family, and if that genius was to be trained and fostered, a weekly visit to the theatre was called for.

Accordingly, for some months, I was given threepence weekly for a seat in the pit, with the proviso that I gave him a full and detailed report after each show.

The Albert Theatre was a new affair.[18] I'd watched it being built. As theatres went

---

[16] This is a persistent idea or thought, an allusion to a character's irrational obsession; Mr. Dick in Charles Dickens' *David Copperfield*, with the head of Charles 1, ( beheaded 1649 ). Apparently, a well known expression in late Victorian times.

[17] The battle of Spion Kop, was fought in the Second Boer War, January 1900, 21 miles West South West of Ladysmith, on the hilltop of Spioenkop. It resulted in a well-known Boer victory.

[18] Opened in 1899 in Huddersfield Road, Brighouse, closed as a cinema in 1972.

*Huddersfield Road, Brighouse (c1890s)*                                    *(Steve Gee)*

in those days it was quite well fit up, though small. It was lit by gas throughout. The decoration was gaudy and most of the plays were crude both in content and presentation. I know we have reformed all that, indifferently – I have, indeed, had a hand in the process – and that in acting, production, staging and writing, our standards are on the whole immeasurably higher now than they were then. But I often wonder whether, in raising our standards, we haven't lowered the emotional response and weakened the magic. Audiences today are spectators and critics rather than participants in a communal experience – a state of affairs to be noted in our churches and chapels too. I'm not sure where the fault lies, but I'm certain the result is to be deplored.

Enchantment was the essence of my first theatre. From the hurried scamper to join the noisy mob milling round the pit entrance to the breathless recapitulation of the evening's traffic, punctuated by gulps of bedtime milk.

The place itself was so right! It even smelt right. And the staring advertisement curtain, the painted set-drop with a scene from a Venice that never was on sea or land flanked by painted heavy red hangings pulled aside and held up by painted gold cords, the grinning, scowling masks of Comedy and Tragedy, all fitted and contributed to the whole. So did the one circle above us where the nobs sat in state on plush, its curved front ornate with plaster wreaths and cupids whose round bellies sported navels and burst into extravagant foliage just at the point where they promised to become really interesting.

The stock fare of the blood-tub was, of course, melodrama, ringing every possible and

*Albert Hall, Brighouse (c1900)*

*(Steve Gee)*

35

impossible variation on the themes of battle, murder and sudden death. Not always so sudden though. And not always death in the outcome, either. For if there was one trick which those old journeymen-playwrights had mastered thoroughly, it was the use of suspense. By the time I was twelve there was neither a stratagem nor a means of torture and death, nor a comedy sub-plot which I didn't know.

Long before I met Shaw's semi-termagant huntress I watched their melodramatic ancestresses at work.[19] One I vividly remember because she was involved in a superb bit of theatre. She was a female spy pursued (for political reasons only!) by the detective hero. This abandoned creature in one scene had the unconscious hero absolutely at her mercy. She worked up my agonized feelings to the pitch of frenzy as she slowly approached him, half hiding a wicked-looking knife, held it poised for the deadly thrust then dropped it harmlessly and flung herself upon him, kissing him in her hysterical revulsion of feeling. The sudden change of mood, the snapping of the tension, had on me something of the stunning, numbing effect of a thunderbolt. I knew then, and for all time, the meaning and power of great theatre.

And long before I saw Rinehart's masterly use of the revolving stage in Berlin, I saw a change of scene which called for the use of three such table-stages.[20] The setting was the ground floor of a double fronted house. There was a bow-windowed room on either side of the hall, looking out on a snowy night at the back of the scene. The action passed freely between all three compartments until the hero thrashed the villain towards the hall door. Just as they reached it, there was a momentary dimming of the light and the next instant the exterior of that house was facing us, snow was falling between it and us, and the struggling pair were emerging through the doorway towards us and the climax of the scene. Bearing in mind the small stage, the split-second timing of that change to coincide with the switching over of a two-fold lighting plot and the snow effect was little short of miraculous.

Out of all the welter of blood and thunder puddings (with very occasional excursions into classical drama) which proved my elementary schooling in the theatre, two shows stand out pre-eminent.

One was a melodrama called *The Klondyke Nugget*, presented by Bill Cody and his Wild West actors, both red and white. It was an orgy of sensations! Real horses climbed a mountain pass. One of them was flung headlong into the gorge when the foot-bridge (tampered with by the villain!) gave way. One Red Indian had an attack of delirium tremens in a bar-room, and the stage swarmed with pink, green, blue and yellow snakes! A shack was blown sky high. Halfway though the show, the play was suspended and the houselights brought up for an exhibition of truly brilliant sharp-shooting from the auditorium at targets on the stage. Greatest thrill of all, perhaps, was the cutting of another Indian's throat, his head held towards us and stretched backwards, so that we could see the blood follow the knife.

That week Brighouse was the undoubted home of Romance, for these picturesque

---

[19] Termagant : a violent, overbearing person.

[20] Max Reinhardt (1873-1943) was an Austrian (later naturalised American) theatre and film director and actor. Reinhardt's productions were often lavish spectacles that integrated lighting, costume design, sets, stage form and acting styles into a seamless experience.

*Briggate from Anchor Bridge, Brighouse. Potential audience for cowboy and Indian show!*
*c1900* (BM)

fellows with their long curls and imperials, their sugar-loaf hats and their hearth rug trousers, walking and riding our streets, brought a fresh world to our doorsteps – a grand show, losing nothing because it cost nothing. [21]

And, though I didn't realize it at the time, I witnessed history in the making and aviation in its birth-pangs. On the vacant fairground during the day Cody and his men could be seen indulging in what seemed and was termed "babbywork" by some of the grown-ups. He and his company spent hours flying large box-kites making the first tentative experiments that were to result in man's conquest of the air. Progress from the profits of a penny-gaff! [22] There was real drama here if only I could have seen it!

The other outstanding production was that of a female Hamlet – a Mrs Bandman-Palmer, if my memory serves me right. [23] Whoever she was, she gave a weighty performance for she was heavy both in build and technique. Because of her bulk she

---

[21] An Imperial: a small tufted beard, which was originally worn by Emperor Napoleon III.

[22] A penny gaff: a popular entertainment for the lower classes in 19th century England. It consisted of short, theatrical entertainments which could be staged wherever space permitted, such as the back room of a public house or small hall. Clowning, dancing,singing and plays all featured, easy to perform, well-known to the audience, and with simple exciting stories.

[23] Mrs. Millie Bandmann-Palmer (? -1926), actress, was the wife of Daniel Edward Bandmann (1840 – 1905), a Shakespearean actor from Germany. For a time Mrs. Bandmann-Palmer directed her own company. She starred in Shakespearean roles such as Hamlet, which she took on tour for many years in Northern England.

very wisely stood and moved as little as possible and even then made all the use she could of properties and furniture to mask her nether limbs. For the most part she played sitting – even in the scene with the Ghost on the ramparts – but I must admit I was rather staggered to find she was sitting on a box which normally held two dozen bottles of mineral water made by a local manufacturer. I'd no idea the firm had been established so long or had such distinguished customers.

But the First Gravedigger was easily the best I have ever seen. He played the part as a caustic, dry old stick, never "working" for a laugh, apparently unconscious of having an audience. He was, compared with the rest of the company, under-acting or not acting at all, yet he was scoring every point as sweetly and neatly as anyone would wish. It was a first glimpse for me of the new school which I was to see in full flower years later in Manchester's Repertory Theatre.

But although this actor was using the new technique, he still stuck to the old "waistcoat gag"; that is, he took off in turn at least half a dozen waistcoats before getting down into the grave, getting a bigger laugh with each disrobing. I laughed, like the rest, at this "business", but a little uneasily. I knew from my father that Shakespeare didn't think highly of clowns and made Hamlet warn them about "saying more than is set down for them". I should have been more uneasy still if I'd suspected then what I've now suspected for many years – that the bulk of this scene, like so much of the Clowns' stuff in the plays generally, is improvised " gagging " by Will Kemp or some other droll. But I must keep off that particular hobby horse.

The curious thing is that in those days I never dreamed of being an actor, never wanted to go backstage to see the wheels go round. And though I was unconsciously absorbing a thousand valuable lessons, I never imagined that I should one day appear on that stage in my own plays and be hailed as the local boy who had made good.

# Chapter Five

Early in 1900 the big bed from my parent's room was brought downstairs again, an unwelcome sign to me, that another baby was soon due to make its appearance. I began to worry as to how we should "manage".

The house had become barer as it had become more crowded. It was still scrupulously clean, but it was shabby. There was no floor covering now; the horsehair upholstery gaped at the corners; the brass fire irons, which still monopolised the sofa except at weekends, were dinted and peeling in places, and the antimacassars were coming in holes. There was still enough food, plain and homely, with the emphasis on "fillers" such as bread and potatoes. Threepennyworth of liver one day, threepennyworth of "fry" another, a little sausage, an occasional herring, provided the mid-week trimmings to the midday meal. Breakfast, tea and supper were always of bread and jam, bread and treacle, bread and lard, and now and then, bread and nothing. Sunday was notable for the small joint we had for dinner and the butter on our bread for tea. Our clothes were not grand but they were well patched and whole. My one-time careless mother had learnt to square her budget – more or less.

But the bringing down of the big bed meant, I knew, an additional strain on the budget. A strain too, on our sleeping accommodation. We children were already sleeping four in one bed, not in the normal fashion, but across its width. The new-comer would also mean more cradle rocking for me.

There came an evening when the four of us had "to play out" until nearly nine in the dark and cold of a February night. It seemed ages before we were called in and hurried to bed – eating our bread and treacle upstairs, after a hasty glance at the little red and blue faced newcomer, and a curiously pale, drawn, large-eyed mother.

For the next fortnight I was kept away from school to act as housekeeper and nurse, and I never went out of the house except to run errands or to stand at the door whilst Mother used the chamber, or was examined by the doctor who, contrary to all previous usage, had had to be called in.

The first week of that fortnight was a truly happy time for me, unaware of any shadow or anything untoward. There was so much to do, and so many things to blunder over and laugh about. I was expert enough at all the rough work of the house, but when it came to washing the faces of the younger ones I was, I'm afraid, a trifle heavy-handed.

"Nay, Dick lad!" mother would chide gently. "Leave t'child a bit o' skin on, or she'll catch cold!" And if the child tried to take advantage of this correction and evade a thorough washing, she would declare, "nobody's going mucky because I'm in bed!"

Nobody went mucky that fortnight. I even "went through" the children's heads with a fine tooth comb. And nobody went hungry, though some of the meals I achieved, in spite of Mother's supervision, dulled the edge of even our appetites before we tackled them.

One thing I disliked intensely. Washing nappies. Mother sensed this, though I said nothing about it. "Don't curl thi nose up at it, lad!" she said gently. "Someone had it to do for thee, remember!"

I think it was this unwonted gentleness that first warned me that things weren't taking their normal course. But though she was both quieter and feebler, she was still her cheerful self. Her eyes were unusually bright, and her face, though it had lost its colour, still kept its shine.

And so the first week went by swiftly. Each day with its first noisy scramble to get the children off to school; its mornings of housework and amateur cookery; its midday of din and clamour as the children squabbled over the meal; its afternoons of easeful calm – short hours of quiet intimacy and lovely peace when I felt myself once again really "Mother's lad". In the evenings we returned to the world and the present, the house no longer ours alone, and I no longer its stay and prop, merely the eldest of a group of children.

At the end of that first week snow fell heavily. It lay at least four feet deep, blanketing the noisy street. The house, too, was hushed – filled with unspoken tenderness. I have a vague memory of neighbours coming and going quietly; of a bright fire lighting the dull, snow-grey afternoons; of a tired woman seen in its flickering light – a woman whose smile was touched with pain, and whose eyes were fathomless with love; a woman with the gentle, pitiful gratitude of the helpless. At times, in spite of herself, those slow hard tears would steal towards the fine nostrils. Once, when she caught me watching them, she said, trying to smile, "It's being poorly, Dick. It makes me soft."

Often, as I helped her to wash her face and tidy her long, dark plaits, the inarticulate love in her eyes made mine blink with tears; and, once or twice, there was a feebly fierce, yearning hug for me that filled me with wondering delight and a queer, faint dread.

On what was to prove our last afternoon together, after the children had gone back to school, I cleared away and washed the dinner things as usual. Then, as she seemed to be sleeping, I sat quietly where I could watch her. Outside, I could hear the voices of young children chattering in the snow house the bigger boys had built in the street. Inside, the fire was crackling and sputtering a little, and its flames were reflected in the copper kettle I'd polished that morning.

The faint squeak of the rocking chair must have disturbed her. Her eyes opened slowly and it was a moment or two before she saw me.

"Aren't ta reading, Dick?" Her smile was tired.
I shook my head.
"Tha's missed it lately, hasn't ta?"

I said something about having time enough for reading later on. She closed her eyes, and we were silent again until the baby began to whimper.

"She'll want changing," she said.

She turned her head on the pillow to watch me as I did my still inexpert best at the job.

"Good lad !" she smiled when I got through without disaster. Then, as I replaced my sister at her side, she pulled me down towards her, and her arms held me very closely as she murmured, "Allus a good lad, weren't ta? – Tha mun allus be a good lad, Dick!"

She let me go at last, whispering, "There's nowt to cry for – nowt to cry for"

That was our last moment alone together. A neighbour, coming to ask if she could help in any way, headed a procession of friends and relations that went on and on, apparently endless. All the children, including the baby, were taken to spend the night separately elsewhere. The visitors stood and sat about awkwardly, almost dumb, watching the tired woman dozing in fitful snatches. She seemed the least concerned of any of them. I crept to bed unnoticed, and cried myself to sleep.

It was towards morning, I suppose, but still dark, when I was wakened by a man's noisy, choking weeping. I stumbled downstairs in the dark to find my father huddled in the rocking-chair, and a still sheeted figure lying on the long table under the window. When he became aware of me, he rose awkwardly, went to what had been my mother, lifted the handkerchief, and kissed the waxen remote face. It was the only kiss I ever saw him give her. [24]

For the next few days I had my meals in various odd houses, but always returned home in the evening to keep my father company. Usually he was there to meet me, but there was one evening when he wasn't. The door was unlocked, but I sat on the doorstep until he turned up. It was obvious that he'd been drinking. Equally obvious, it had been to no purpose, if, as I supposed, he'd been seeking consolation.

Some nights after the funeral, the children all back at home and in bed, I was nursing the baby in my usual place near the oven, when two strange women came to the door. Father asked them in, and the older woman, acting as spokeswoman for the younger, shyer one, plunged at once into a low voiced, confidential explanation of their purpose. I caught odd phrases. "Tha sees, Charlie, they can't have one! " And later, "Nay, they've tried an' better tried, but they don't seem to manage to pull it off, like."And later again, "T'poor little thing will have a very good home."

Father spoke little. He got very little opportunity, for the older woman had all the relish and garrulity of Juliet's Nurse. But at last she faded into silence and waited for him to make up his mind. When it began to seem he would never speak, she said, with consideration, "Tha sees, Charlie, it isn't as if tha can manage with a child so young. I know tha doesn't like parting with it, but tha'll have to trust it to somebody! "

There was another silence which he finally broke with a sigh of assent.
"Yer'll call her Ann?"
There was an eager assent from the younger woman.

He took the baby from me, held it for a moment, touching its face with his calloused, acid-stained finger. The younger woman eagerly produced a lovely white shawl. I held my breath, fearful to the last that he might not let the baby go. But he finally

---

[24] Ann Gregson died March 1900, aged 32.

placed it in the older woman's arms, and at a quiet word from him, I quickly found and bundled together all the baby clothes – most of them had served us all in turn – and saw them to the door with heartfelt or, if you prefer it, heartless relief.

I hate to think what would have happened to that baby sister during the next ten or eleven months, during which a constantly shifting procession of relations, friends and various odd outsiders came to "do" for us. Some did, some didn't. With Father's people we "pigged it" in rough and ready, affectionate comfort. With Mother's people we were not so happy. Between them all we slumped to the underside of poverty and sometimes went hungry. All the outstanding memories of that period are of sudden, frightening quarrels when Father discovered some glaring piece of neglect and sent the offending "housekeeper" packing.

All the memories except one. There is one day that still glows in the memory like a jewel in a drab eternity. It was sometime in the latter half of 1900.

Father had begun to go off every Saturday and Sunday afternoon, always in his best black suit and never getting back until we were all in bed. But one Saturday, golden with Autumn sunshine, he told me I was to go with him. So I, too, was spruced up in my one whole suit – of black. A Norfolk suit, I remember, with buckles below the knees. It had been bought out of the insurance money for me to wear at Mother's funeral, and after it had been sponged thoroughly, it didn't look too bad. When I was sent to borrow a pair of black stockings from my youngest aunt, and made to polish my boots twice over, I felt something important was in the wind. I'd no inkling what, nor was I given any. Those were the days when children were taught "Theirs not to reason why"!

But there I was, dressed up on a Saturday as though for a very special Sunday with a new and very smelly celluloid collar at least four inches wide, walking solemnly by Father's side, with the eyes of the whole street, it seemed, upon us.

I made to turn down the main road into the town, but Father, breaking the silence which had lasted since we left the house, said, "Nay, we are going to t'station,lad." Then, as I said nothing, he asked, "Tha'd like a train ride, wouldn't ta?".

I nodded, wonderingly. I felt somehow he was nervous about something. He was so near and friendly, so different from the remote, withdrawn creature he had become since Mother's death. I knew there was something behind his attempt to make conversation. I tried to guess what. Perhaps he was taking me to be adopted by somebody, as my baby sister had been. I became aware he was speaking again.

"Tha's only been in a train once before, has ta"
"Twice"
"Nay, nobbut that time we all went to Scarborough!"
And the time we came back!" I explained. "That's twice"

He laughed at this and things became easier. "Well," he said, "this'll bring thi score up to four, becoss we're going as far as Huddersfield and back."

So we were coming back. This meant I wasn't going to be adopted. I wasn't sure whether I was relieved or sorry. But Father seemed to find it easier to talk from then on, and became more and more like the Father I had first known. We were bound ultimately, I learned, for a village called Crosland Hill.

Arrived at the moorland village, then a separate entity from the sprawling town which has now overrun it, we made our way to a little old-fashioned house with the long windows which told of its past as a handloom weaver's cottage. There were lots of plants in the window-sill, and long, red sausage affairs to keep out the draughts. It was a cheerful house, occupied by a cheerful family of grown up brothers and sisters. All six or seven of them were at home waiting for us. Of the two women, the younger had most to say and most to laugh at. The older one seemed shyer and much quieter, and said "sh sh sh" when the others made jokes which set everybody laughing but me.[25]

"Little sobersides, isn't he?" the younger one said after one sally whose point I couldn't fathom.

"Takes after me, Lily!" said Father, laughing. And whilst I was wondering at the change in him, Lily took me to see the hens and the pigs. Left to wander on my own and to take stock as it were, savouring the sunshine and the wide panorama of rolling hills around me, I wondered once again if, after all, these people were thinking of adopting me; that my father had brought me here to be "looked over". I decided that, on the whole, I should rather like living here. The wonderful tea we had made me quite certain. Apart from the variety and the quantity of the food, we drank out of cups, every one of them alike in pattern. I kept my ears sharpened for anything that might give me a hint. I also kept a tight watch on my manners, just in case.

But nothing happened to enlighten me, although everyone of the family made much of me. Tea over and the washing up finished, Father, the elder sister and I went for a walk. As we were leaving the house, Lily said something about a gooseberry. I joined in the laughter, though, for the life of me, I couldn't see what there was to laugh at.

There was nothing said on that walk to puzzle me – none of the "above my head" talk that grown-ups usually indulged in. It was a heart-warming companionable affair with plenty of sweets to eat without check and later, as a crowning touch, fish and chips which we ate out of the paper as we slowly climbed out of the grim industrial valley towards the cheerful old house. It wasn't quite dark. We seemed to keep just ahead of the actual night until we were at the top of the hill. We paused there a moment, and I had my first glimpse of a Yorkshire hill-scape, the land below us twinkling with fairy lamps, the sky sprinkled with starshine. I felt like crying because a lovely day was slipping from me.

"Hasta enjoyed thisen, Dick?" asked my father as we settled ourselves for my fourth train journey. And when I'd nodded, he asked awkwardly, "Did ta like "Vinnie"?" I nodded again. Even more awkwardly he said "I'm glad o' that!"

Nothing more was needed. Revelation came like a lightning flash. "Vinnie" – Lavinia

---

[25] Gregson was being taken to see his future step mother, Lavinia Tann.
   The 1891 census shows the Tann family living in Shepley, Huddersfield. The father, George, aged 48, was a maltster; the mother, Ann was aged 52. The children, Lavinia, woollen burler aged 26, Herbert 19, Jack 18, Joe 15, Harry 13 and Lily 11. There was an older brother, William, who, on the 1881 return was 2 years older than Lavinia. He had left the family home by 1891 and died in 1899, aged 36.

– was to be our new mother. I'd been with my father a-courting!

My father couldn't have made a better choice, and the life of Lavinia Tann, as our stepmother, was to prove a saga of patient, selfless devotion not to be matched anywhere and never to be adequately told. I've thought of it from to time as the theme of a novel, but always put it aside as a task beyond my powers.

As I've already mentioned, she knew both my parents well before they were married. I suspect she was half or more in love with him then. Country bred. She had known real privation in her childhood. She told me of having to scour the hedgerows for nettles which were stewed with oatmeal for dinner; of having one piece of bread and butter in place of cake as a special treat to Sunday; of running errands to the town some miles away and feeling generously rewarded by a lump of sugar. She began work in a factory before she was eight years old.

Her mother was left a widow with a large family of younger children, and Lavinia, as the eldest became the main bread-winner. Just when the family was getting on its feet and it looked as if Lavinia might begin to have an independent life of her own, her mother began to fail. Factory work was given up for that of nurse and housekeeper. It was a training that stood her in good stead during the hard days she had with us. It had bred in her a quality of meek tenacity and gentle heroism which kept her going through every crisis in a job that would have broken most women.

Under medium height and slight in build, there was a hint of frailness about her that belied the wiry vigour of which she was capable. She was a great contrast to my mother in ways as well as physique. Her voice was soft and husky, and she suggested and reasoned, rather than commanded as of right. The house was run with less fuss and noise and without those flashes of temper which at times made Mother terrible as an army with banners.

My father brought her home in time for tea on the day following the wedding – Sunday. It was quite a jolly meal. We all were specially spruced up for the occasion. But as soon as it was over, Uncle and Aunt left for their own home, and, incredible as it may seem, Father slipped away to the pub as soon as it was open, leaving his new wife to get acquainted with four young savages, three of whom she'd met for the first time an hour ago.

I never got her to talk freely about that evening. The most I ever got out of her was, "I didn't know where to start. All of you watching me all the time! I felt lost, like".

"I felt lost!" – No wonder! Pretty sick at heart, too, I imagine, as she began to take stock of the denuded, neglected house.

"I hardly knew where to start!" – Not until she'd spent a solitary two hours, between going to bed and Father's return from the pub, in facing up to what lay before her. Not all Gethsamenes are endured in a garden.

The very next morning she began a clearly mapped out campaign. Before I set off to school I was hurried to the chemist for a new fine-tooth comb and some ointment and the first attack had been made on my sister Cora's ratty, ill-kept locks. But a comb was of no use in the case of the younger sister, Jane, and when we came home to dinner, we found her close-cropped as an infant convict. It was pretty obvious the barber was an amateur.

By the time we got home for tea, the sewing machine had been put in order and was already being used to patch sheets. The Gregsons had taken the first steps on the long, seemingly endless climb back to decency and respectability. The start of an epic of infinitesimal gains and minute disasters in which a new pair of clogs or curtains, the cleansing of a child's head, the provision of a new pie-dish were major victories – themes for brass and percussion

*Bonegate/Bradford Road, Brighouse, c1904*        (BM)

Never was she idle; never were her fingers still. She patched and better-patched our scanty clothing and household linen. I thought sometimes that she must knit in her sleep. She gladly accepted old stockings, whatever their condition. And you may be sure they were seldom discarded by the straitened, thrifty givers until apparently beyond redemption. But she undid them, and with the secondhand, faded wool – green-black, bluey-black, rust-black, anything but honest to goodness black-black – she kept us in leg gear more pleasing for its comfort than its aesthetic appeal. She taught herself to repair our clogs and boots, then taught me.

The street began to retreat and the home to resume its proper influence. She had no time for "neighbouring". She had four children with clothes, noses and morals to keep clean, and a lot of leeway to make up.

And she had to do it alone. My father, in his self-pitying indulgence, was more of a handicap than a help. Out of his earnings he gave her a pound a week for the feeding, housing and clothing of the six of us, but he often "borrowed" a quarter or a third of it back between paydays. Economy is a feeble word for the heart-searing scrutiny of every penny to which she was driven.

But she would never listen to any criticism of father. "He can't forget your mother", she said once in excuse for him. "He thought such a lot about her". And, on another occasion when I caught a glimpse of her in an unguarded moment, "I shall never be more than second best to him!" She spoke without jealousy, without even resentment, simply stating a fact with hurt, sad resignation.

We were all to climb out of the slough in due time, and she was to have some years of moderate comfort with a husband who had gradually grown sober, considerate and affectionate. She was also to see other rewards of her self-sacrifice and devotion. I wish I could say she enjoyed the moderate prosperity which crowned her struggle, but the years of harsh, intense economy left her incapable of any pleasure in spending – pennies never lost their scarcity value. And I very much doubt whether she ever fully realised what a grand job she had done. Many a statesman draws his thousands for less.[26]

---

[26] Lavinia Gregson died in 1944, aged 79.

# Chapter Six

The twentieth century was only three months old when I became a wage earner. [27] The day I was twelve – one couldn't start before – I began work as a half-timer in the spinning room of a cotton factory.[28] My wages were sixpence a half-day. I enjoyed every minute of the long working hours, but I preferred the shift when I went to the mill in the mornings, especially during the winter, for I could dash almost straight out of bed, out of the cold house and into the stuffy, greasy warmth of the mules. It was a wonderful luxury to get rid of my clogs and stockings, change into the thin cotton pants my boss had given me and thaw the chill out of my bones, lying flat on the oily heated floor. I grudged the half-days I had to waste at school- they really were wasted! – not because I could have been making a bigger contribution to the family exchequer, but because the factory was such a jolly, hearty world. A world in which I stood alone, free of family ties, unaided by family sympathy, an individual in my own right. A world with a harsher code than home or school, in which I had to make my own place, earn it and fight for it. Before my first morning was halfway through, I had fought the first of a series of cold-blooded, stand-up battles, taking on bigger and bigger lads, until I met my Waterloo. These combats were arranged by the older boys and always took place in the lavatory – a place so small that you could never get out of arm's reach of your opponent and could neither duck nor dodge a blow. I emerged victorious from that first fight, though with a black eye. I went home to dinner and to afternoon school with cubits added to my stature.

The spinners, or minders, were paid by the weight of the yarn they turned out, and they engaged their assistants personally and paid them out of their earnings. My first minder was a voracious reader of cheap publications such as *Heartsease Novels*, the *Police Budget*, *Famous Crimes* and various unnamed, crudely pornographic effusions, but one day, catching me with my nose deep in one of the latter, he gave me a clout that made my ears ring.

"Sethee!" he said, "If I can't stop thee reading, I'll stop thee reading muck! I'll bring

---

[27] The 1899 Education Act made full-time attendance at school compulsory until the age of twelve. The pupil was required to attend school part-time until the age of fourteen.

[28] H & J Sugden, George Street Mills, George Street, Brighouse.
Henry Sugden left Elland in November 1865 and took up residence at Canal Lodge, Brighouse. About the same time operations were commenced in regard to the erection of the present commodious George Street Mills. Spinning operations were commenced in the new premises in 1867. Since then extensions have been made to the structure until the premises are now nearly three times as large as when first erected. The premises contain no less than 60,000 spindles, and the mill ranks as the largest and most substantial of its kind in the district. About 400 workpeople are employed and work has invariably been plentiful at George Street Mills. Messrs. Sugdens are engaged in the cotton warp trade, principally for the Bradford Market. The cotton is purchased in its raw state, and after going through the various processes of manufacture is turned out in the warp ready for the loom. With very rare exceptions, Henry Sugden attends the weekly Tuesday Markets at Manchester and Liverpool, and also takes the Thursday Market at Bradford.
*Brighouse Echo* : December 15th 1893.
This large five story former cotton mill was destroyed by fire on July 5th 1940 ( not by enemy action). It had not been used for cotton spinning for many years and was tenanted by Universal Stores, Manchester, for storage. *Brighouse Echo* : July 12th 1940.

thee a right book, wi'stiff backs an' I'll see tha reads it right, an' all, becoss I've read it misen, an' I shall put thee through thi catechism on it! It's what they call a classic!"

He kept his word. The book was Charles Dana's *Two Years Before The Mast*. Apart from the Shakespeare at home, which so far was little more than a picture book to me, it was my first acquaintance with literature. I'm sure it was the only book of any quality he'd ever read. I still find his unlettered taste a matter for wonder.

Albert – I never thought of calling him "Mr Smith" – on condition that I "behaved misen", used to put threepence a week for me into the Work's Holiday Club, and promised that, when the Annual Holidays came round, I should spend a day with him at Blackpool . Again he kept his promise. He gave me a royal time, too, but I remember the day because of a very queer happening.

A crowd of us went to the Waxworks. On the first floor landing was a tableau from the Spanish Inquisition. A man, fastened to a heavy Maltese cross, was being beaten with iron rods. Long after the rest had passed on to other horrors, I stayed there fascinated, not by the blood or the signs of anguish, but by the figure of one monk who, a black crucifix in his hands, sat staring at me through the eyelet holes in the sack-like mask which covered his whole head. There was something about the fixed, cold scrutiny of those unseen eyes which made me try in my turn, to pierce the gloom beyond those empty sockets.

I was told afterwards that the party found me still there on their way out, that I had to be violently shaken to attract my attention, and that I came back to the present only to drop to the floor in a faint.

For years afterwards, I suffered from onsets of a sickening fear that I should come face to face with a creature with eyeless sockets. I knew it was ridiculous and groundless, but I couldn't rid myself of the loathsome bogey. It would lay dormant for weeks, waiting to spring on me when I was alone in the dark on a lonely country road or lying sleepless in bed. I had no fear of physical violence from the encounter, merely the horror of having to face such sickening disfigurement. The picture imagination conjured up was so agonizing, so revolting, that I often felt the reality would be a relief. Relief would have come, I suppose, if I could have talked about it, but I couldn't. I was thirty six, the father of two children, before the bogey was finally laid.

It was during my production of *Oedipus Rex*. I had devised a really gruesome make-up for the end of the play when I had to appear with my eyes gouged out. On the first night, after my final groping exit through the auditorium, I dashed to my dressing room and, as I turned into the unlit cubbyhole, there, approaching me, was an eyeless figure. The sweat prickled my face. But the shock lasted only a second. The next moment I was laughing – shakily, I confess! – at myself and at my own reflection in the full-length mirror on the wall. My bogy had come to life only to die the suddenest and completest of deaths. The obsession out of my system, I was able to cash in on it with a series of stories and radio plays, all with a cowled man as the central figure.

When I was thirteen and free of school I had two bosses. I still worked half-time for Albert Smith, but the rest of my time was claimed by his neighbour, Teddy Marsden. Teddy was a lovable, comical character; generous, easy-going, bawdy, and always ready for fun and a bit of fooling. He was something of a natural comedian, getting his laughs at his own apparent simplicity.

I asked him one day how he came to lose the first joint of his index finger. It appeared he'd been cleaning some sharp-toothed wheels whilst the mule was in motion.

"Yer" must have been daft!" I commented.
"Double daft!" he agreed solemnly. "I nearly lost my other pointer, an' all!"
"Nay, never!"
"Fact! Showing mi father how I lost this!"

Teddy had some deformity of the feet which made him waddle back and forth in the mule gate like a penguin. He was never silent. For the most part he whistled, sometimes halting on a long, drawn-out note, or to trill an intricate cadenza, before resuming his paddling. He had a trick, too, of suddenly breaking off in the middle of a phrase, whistling a command helped out by dumb show, like a shepherd to his collie, and then taking up his aria again with increased gusto. Now and then he would break into song – usually ribald – or into a mock recitation. His burlesque of a preacher appealing for a good collection was a real joy.

I loved being on the morning shift with Teddy. It meant being sent to his nearby home for his breakfast, and his mother, understanding soul, had always a hot bacon sandwich, or a bit of sausage-and-bread left over which "it seemed a sin to waste".

Teddy, like all the minders I knew, was hardworking to a degree, not merely because he was paid by the piece, but because of his innate independence and self-respect. In his more serious moments he would say, "never be obligated by anybody!" And again, "Nobody can dun thee if tha owes 'em nowt!" Time and again he would admonish me, "Always earn more than tha gets!"

Next to idleness the unforgivable sin was to be a "cry-baby". A "softy" was damned beyond redemption. We youngsters cultivated a stoicism that would not have disgraced a Red Indian. If we didn't profit by example it was knocked into us.

One day Teddy was trying to get a six-inch belt on to the main driving pulley. Perched on a narrow shelf, six to seven feet high, he tugged and wrestled with the stubborn thing which he'd made a shade too light. The strain finally proved too much. No sooner was the belt on the drum than it snapped at the joining, writhed in the air like a huge, vicious snake, and gave him a slap on the head which knocked him off his perch. He landed, backside first, with a resounding thud.

Then when he could get his breath, he silenced my noisy concern with, "Shut up! I'm making enough noise for both on us! Damn it! I'm singing at both ends!"

One morning, above the hum of machinery and the communal singing which rose above it, there came a piercing noise. We all rushed to see what was amiss. We found a new lad rocking on his bottom, nursing his foot, and blubbering over the bloody tip of his little toe. It had been nipped by a wheel.

"Where's mi toe-end? Where's mi toe-end?" he wailed. "I've lost mi toe-end!" He started grubbing about in the fluff, looking for the missing morsel. Nothing we could say or do pacified him. He made such a disgusting din that his minder lost patience with him, boxed his ears and said "Stop roaring, yer big baby! Damn it! Tha couldn't make more noise if it had cut tha hand off!"

Accidents, mainly of a minor character, were pretty frequent. They were mainly due to the lack of guards round dangerous parts of the mules and to the practice (contrary to regulations) of cleaning them whilst in motion. The most serious I suffered might have crushed my ribs, but I had sufficient nous to stretch myself on tiptoe when I realised I was trapped. Even then, there was an agonising five minutes before I was released, and I almost lost consciousness. I was brought to by someone dousing my belly with jugs of cold water, but I was quite content to lie there until my modesty was shocked by hearing a motherly creature lamenting the possible damage to my "well put together little figger".

My last memory of the cotton factory is of Teddy on the day I left to take up a new job.

"They tell me tha'rt going to work in an office?" he said.
I said I was.
"And tha knows there's such a thing as petty cash?"
I said I did.
"And tha knows tha'll have to handle that petty cash?"
I nodded.
"Well, just keep thi fingers off it! That's all!"

And with that characteristic exit line he passed out of my life – if anyone ever does.

# Chapter Seven

Somewhere towards the end of my happy five years in the cotton mill came an important turning point in my life. I suppose I must call it my conversion, though it was neither a turning from an old to a new faith, nor from one code of morals to another.

I already subscribed, in theory, and so far as I thought about such matters at all, to the creed proclaimed by the band of working class "missionaries" whose activities I've already mentioned. But although regular attendance at both Sunday School and Chapel was part of my stepmother's campaign for the family rehabilitation; although I gained book prizes for such attendance and won a bible for memorising certain psalms; although I took an active part as a reciter and actor in the entertainments; although I recognized the force of their moral teaching and could give, out of my own experience, unqualified assent to their diatribes against "strong drink"; although I could admire much that was really estimable and Christ-like in their characters and lives, there was something about their pulpit-thumping, fire-and-brimstone, hot gospelling which kept me aloof, critical and even faintly hostile.

I didn't object to their dramatization of Bible stories or their own experiences. Many of these lay preachers were born bards and storytellers. There was one whose sermon on the parable of the Prodigal Son was a masterpiece of homely histrionics. It consisted mainly of a vivid re-enactment of the story itself, himself taking all the parts in turn, with slight changes of voice and touches of homely humour, everyday phrases and allusions. As the younger son, gathering up his possessions, he would tie up the Bible and the hymnbook in his red handkerchief, and take his journey down the pulpit steps into the far country. He would feed the swine, crouching in misery on the "mourner's bench", then skip quickly into the pulpit again to become the father looking for the wayward boy, and so on.

His text on another occasion was "With joy shall ye draw water out of the wells of salvation". According to him, the wells were deep and the water not to be obtained without labour and effort. To illustrate the point he leaned farther and farther over the pulpit rail the hymnbook tied to his handkerchief for a pitcher. He ended by leaning too far, losing his footing and crashing down on to the communion table.

Another lay-preacher, I remember, used to dart out of the vestry, bound up the pulpit stairs two at a time, throw up his hands and open the service by declaring, with tears of joy in his eyes, "Hosanna! Hosanna! Our God is worthy to be praised with gladness, and let the redeemed of the Lord say so!" As a dramatic entrance it couldn't have been bettered by any actor-manager.

Not that all these preachers were actors who'd missed their real vocation. Not that all the sermons were mere frothy emotionalism. I remember one sermon – by a quietly spoken cultured man who was looked down upon as being "too much on the doctrinal side". I remember it because it did a great deal to resolve some of my difficulties in reconciling the various conceptions of the Godhead in the Scriptures.

The sermon was an apologia for the destruction of Sodom and Gomorrah; his explanation of the incident turned it from an act of jealous anger to one of merciful wisdom. The "fire and brimstone" said to have been rained down by God was, he said, natural phenomena in a land of volcanic origin with rich underground stores of oil and salt. Lot's wife, ignoring the warning to flee to the hills, was caught by the flood of molten lava, hence "the pillar of salt". And so on. We had to distinguish between fact and its interpretation by primitive man. So with the differing conceptions of the Deity; they were the natural result of man's widening enlightenment, the tribal god of Jacob becoming the Shepherd of David and ultimately the Father in the teaching of Jesus.

Commonplace as this may seem today, it came upon me like a blinding revelation, but even more impressive was the example of the preacher himself. If he could find his own explanation of the Scriptures, then anyone might. I might, or at least, I need no longer be bound to accept that of men who subscribed too literally to the interpretation of semi-savages groping in the ignorance and superstition of a long dead age.

I became even more restive under the "appeals" with which these sincere but old-school zealots ended their sermons. To "come to Jesus" to escape "the wrath to come" seemed a cowardly reason; to do it to "gain a crown of everlasting glory", a bit cheap. I had no use for this stick-and-carrot technique as I thought of it, secretly.

The climax came when, during a Revival Meeting, I was prayed for publicly by name. I scrambled out of the place, hot with embarrassment and anger, vowing never to go near it again. All the next day, as I followed the mules back and forth, I swung between resentment of their "antics" and longing for the real something which I felt gave them such a certainty and purpose in life, gave life itself a meaning it hadn't for me. Meaning. What meaning? Not the one life seemed to have for them.

Late in the day the solution came. I became conscious of a phrase which recurred with increasing frequency and significance. "The Carpenter of Nazareth". Carpenter. Working man. His hands rough with labour, bringing health to the sick, sight to the blind. I went over in my mind that quiet, heroic life of sacrifice, God-like in service whether or not it was God-like in origin. I thought of its tremendous honesty and its enduring courage. I knew there was no other pattern for me.

Having solved my immediate personal problem in my own fashion, I was at once faced with another. Should I join the Wesleyan community? Could I honestly do so holding views so much at variance with theirs, with so many reservations as to the significance I attached to terms such as "hell", "salvation" and the like, with such a shrinking from their exuberant, forthright hot-gospelling? I was young enough to want to be honest to the last detail about it all, sensitive enough to shrink from much self-exposure. But the alternative of cutting myself adrift was unthinkable. Wisely, if for motives I despised, I took the easier course, and soon found myself up to the ears in church activities.

One immediate benefit was the breaking down of a growing shyness and introspection. I was given the job of teaching a class of juveniles in Sunday School.[29] This meant

---

[29] "Also that the following be accepted on trial, Messrs. James Gregson, Edgar Neild and Norman Graves." Followed by : "Elected – School Secretaries J Gregson and C Haywood": Minutes of the meetings of Birds Royd Wesleyan Methodist Mission Sunday School, July 11th 1906 and December 14th 1907. West Yorkshire Archive Service (Calderdale) PA76.

not only a certain amount of regular reading and study, but steady practice in self-expression.

Left to myself, I should never have learned to speak without notes, but these "missionaries" were firm believers in prompt as well as plenary inspiration, and they lost no opportunity of forcing one into speaking extempore. I was not allowed to remain a modest wallflower, nor to limit myself to such indoor activities as conducting Sunday School prayers or announcing hymns and reading the lessons in Chapel. I was literally forced into the open, and with a kill or cure technique the first open-air pitch chosen for me was directly opposite my own doorstep. In the very middle of that long row of nineteen houses, all occupied by folk who knew me from A to Z, listened to by men who would later meet my father in the pub, watched by women who had "twelted" me for youthful misdemeanour, grinned at by old schoolmates who had leathered me for being a "softy", I had to raise a quivering voice almost choked by mortifying self-consciousness and invite them to God. Somehow I survived.

*Birds Royd Wesleyan Methodist Mission (c1905)*      *(Chris Helme)*

In due course I was put on probation as a prospective local Preacher, and what spare time was left from routine church activities was taken up with the study of sermon-building and theology.

The usual period of probation lasted a year. Mine lasted three. Instead of one trial sermon at its conclusion, I had to preach four before I satisfied the panel of local preachers before whom I had to appear.

The biggest ordeal of all was the viva-voce examination in theology and doctrine I had to undergo.  I never expected to pass, for, apart from certain dogma which struck me as little better than idle, foolish hair-splitting, there were certain doctrines, such as "Justification by Faith", which ran contrary to my youthful notions of logic, not to mention fairness and justice.  As I knew I should be subjected to a hot fire of awkward questions from the older, "hell-fire" group of lay brethren, I wasn't looking forward to the ordeal at all, but determined to go down all guns blazing.

The examination when it came proved to be something of an anti-climax.  This was mainly due to the dexterity with which the presiding minister, a liberal-minded "modern", steered the proceedings and deflected the more awkward thrusts.  This minister, as I learned later, was representative of the broader, less rigid outlook that was coming over the nonconformist movement.  He had his own difficulties with the old school – the difficulties of a paid propagandist with ideas in advance of those on whom he was dependent for his livelihood – difficulties which were to provide, later on, the main situation in my comedy, *T'Marsdens*.

Thanks to his sympathetic intervention I was elected a local preacher by a bare majority.  My troubles in this regard were, for the moment, over.  Some of my colleagues, no doubt, still questioned my orthodoxy, but as I never went out of my way to be provocative, and proved to be an acceptable speaker, it wasn't long before the idea of preparing myself for the ministry was suggested.

In the meantime I flung myself wholeheartedly into every branch of church work, especially the temperance side of it.[30] I formed a group of young actors who performed sketches showing the evils of intemperance, satisfying, I suppose, two subconscious urges – my dislike of drink for what it had done to my family, and my bent for the theatre which was taboo to the strict nonconformists of those days.  The sketches we performed were mawkish to a degree, the characters being mere lay figures mouthing uncolloquial moralisings.  I began to write sketches of my own, the moral being wrapped in as much humour and homely vigour as I could compass.  But the powers-that-were frowned on the use of our native dialect, and my efforts met with anything but encouragement.  I was in my twentieth year by the time I left the Mission and my native town; thin and slight, pale and mousy; a serious minded, not to say priggish, bespectacled youth; an easy, fluent, if somewhat frothy speaker; the rising hope of the Church, and so much the product of it that my Bible was little more than a text book.

---

[30] Glimpses of his activities can be gleaned from the newspapers, for example:  A paragraph about Birds Royd Wesleyan Methodist Mission – Band of Hope: Two cheery recitations from James Gregson and his sister Jane: …..Miss J Gregson recited *Only a woman drunk* …….Mr. J Gregson *The Widows plea*. *Brighouse Echo* : Friday, November 16th 1906.

# Chapter Eight

During these years of religious ferment matters at home had not made the improvement that might have been expected, in spite of the earnings which increased as the children in their turn grew old enough to work. My stepmother had two confinements, the baby in each case being stillborn. My father suffered a serious accident which kept him from his work for months. He was badly and extensively scalded by molten metal, and his recovery wasn't helped by the effect of his drinking.

There was no compensation in those days for industrial injury, and as he was not a member of any club, there was no sick pay either. It was a very thin time, but somehow or other, that quietly indomitable woman contrived to pull us through. If we didn't gain ground during that tight period we lost none. I had to suspend the violin lessons for which I was paying tenpence out of my weekly pocket money of one shilling, but as I was no musician, it was no hardship. And as I'd never had more than twopence to spend on myself, I thought myself, on the whole, better off.

I was just turned seventeen, and not as robust as I might have been, when our street was invaded by foreigners. An old disused foundry across the way was taken over by an energetic young German-Swiss.[31] He had a formula for making a steel which was

---

[31] Philibert Altenbach (a native of Switzerland) after having acquired a thorough commercial and general technical knowledge of engineering and foundry business in various countries on the continent and in Great Britain, commenced business on the first of November 1905, with a private capital of £400.

He took premises at 22a Westminster Palace Gardens, London, with a view of introducing and developing the process of the manufacture of Mild Steel castings without annealing. This process he acquired from a Mr. Carl Dornen.

This invention is the effect of what has been attempted many times before but with always unsuccessful results from a commercial standpoint. By its use the process of annealing steel, which takes many days to complete, and the consequent waste in labour and time is saved. The castings are supplied in a few days, which by the process at present in general use cannot be supplied under two or three weeks, and the quality of steel produced is actually superior to the steel annealed. The practical importance of the process is therefore, very great, and it follows that financially it is of the utmost importance. This process specifically applies to break down jobs. From the fact that other processes with the same object had turned out failures. It is disseminated amongst engineers in the profession in general a prejudice which it has taken hard work to eradicate. Mr. Altenbach, however, was successful in selling certain rights to Messrs. J Birch & Sons Ltd. of Walsall............

It was found necessary in order to do further business, to practically demonstrate this process, and accordingly a foundry was chosen in Brighouse, being favourably situated near Canal, Railways, and the centre of the Steel and Iron industries. The necessary capital for this was obtained from Messrs. Steinhart Vogel & Cloud, a well known firm of metallurgists of London, and from Messrs. Veithardt & Hall Ltd. also of London, an important firm of steel importers and merchants. On 1st March operations were started in Brighouse, and on the 15th the plant was ready....................Mr. Altenbach had practically no connections and had to obtain orders by appealing direct to the trade through the medium of the post.

Altenbach Ltd. Helvetia Steel Works.

Altenbach docs. West Yorkshire Archive Service (Calderdale) : HAS/C :23 – 193.

Those readers interested in early Twentieth century costing please refer to Appendix 3. The key to the enterprise was that the new process was able to deliver castings to its customers two to three weeks more rapidly than its competitors with no difference in quality.

The fact that the company only traded for a few years remains at present something of a mystery. Included in the collection are the above mentioned costing sheets, presumably prepared to attract outside investment; a list of customers, with their orders, again one feels, to impress potential investors and a brief history of the project and the principal.

mild enough to be turned or cut as soon as it was cast. It was unique at the time, and he took great pains to keep the formula secret.

A card appeared in the window of the cottage which had been taken as an office. The new firm wanted an office-boy. On the spur I went across and applied for the job, but I learnt to my dismay that what they wanted was a boy just leaving school at four shillings a week. I was getting fifteen at the mill . I turned crestfallen to leave, but the young foreigner, with his shaven bullet head said, "Halt! Not so, I mean to stop, to wait!" He eyed me sharply. "So. You have ambition. Then I shall help you. If you come to me, I will give you eight shillings each week."

I went back across the street with all my dreams behind me. I knew what the sacrifice of seven shillings would mean to my hard-pressed mother. But the unexpected happened. "We shall have to manage some road", she said quietly, after surprisingly little consideration. Then, as I started to speak, she cut me short with, "We've gone without before, an' there's more reason for it this time."

The new concern was quite a cosmopolitan affair. In addition to its Swiss director, a steel smelter from Germany and a moulder from Austria, it boasted an Irish bookkeeper and two Yorkshire labourers. I worked hard and long, running errands, entering the orders, keeping a register of the patterns that came with them, and teaching myself to type by serial – *The Invasion of 1910*.[32] Spare moments I filled in with odd jobs in the foundry, - shovelling sand or firing the crucible furnaces.

In the evenings there was night school, where I won prizes which paid for my text books and tuition. In short, I was the industrious apprentice, my progress in keeping with the best fairytale traditions. In a few months my wage was raised to fifteen shillings, and as the place grew, I was put in charge of the foundry office, checking both men and materials in and out and arranging the day's smelting programme.

There came a pay day when I took home my first golden sovereign. There came another when, with many injunctions to secrecy my employer took me into the locked cellar and initiated me into the mystery of mixing the special alloy which made all the difference between our steel and the ordinary kind that took two to three weeks to anneal. I was so thrilled that I wrote out the various formulae in a code of my own devising. I still keep the notebook hidden away, although I don't think the secret is worth a fig today, and I should have some difficulty in rediscovering my simple code.

The little venture prospered well at first, but it was dogged by misfortune and ill-luck, and in spite of all the owner's efforts, it lasted but two years in all.

The two years, however, were packed with excitement and thrills. The Irish bookkeeper absconded with all the cash he could lay hands on. Then there was a

---

[32] Invasion literature was a literary genre most notable between 1871 and the First World War. William Le Queux was perhaps the most prolific author of the genre. His work was regularly serialised in newspapers, particularly the *Daily Mail*, and attracted many readers. Le Queux's most popular invasion novel was *The Invasion of 1910*, published in 1906, which was translated into twenty seven languages selling more than a million copies world-wide. Le Queux and his publisher changed the ending depending on the language, so in the German print the Fatherland wins, whilst in the English edition the Germans lose.

furious, inexplicable row between the three continentals which resulted in the German steel-smelter and the Austrian moulder leaving the place. Then there was a more embarrassing occasion when all the loose cash in the office disappeared and all the clues pointed to only two possible culprits – the new partner-cum-manager (which on the face of it was preposterous) and myself. I was given time to clear myself and I set myself to a spot of amateur detection. I started with an advantage over most investigators. I knew there were only two possible suspects, and which one was innocent. All I had to do was to prove the guilt of the other. I took a chance shot at the nearest pub, knowing his habits, and discovered he'd been treating the company there the previous night, and had paid his shot with several sheets of postage stamps.

*The former Vulcan Inn, at the junction of Foundry Street and Vulcan Street closed as an inn in 1926. It is the only surviving Victorian building in Foundry Street, no houses remain. The licensees at the relevant time were Thomas Pendlebury (1905) and Charles Barnett (from October 1907).*

*Eileen Smith*

Sounds daft, I know. But he was like that. He'd found himself short of cash and without any more ado, remembering the stock in the petty cash drawer, had promptly prised it open with a file. When he turned up the following day with a black eye he admitted his guilt promptly and airily, and appeared quite puzzled at the fuss we were making about it. His apology to me was profuse, profane and most gentlemanly. When he found I was interested in literature he gave me the run of his library at home.

"You can borrow any book you like, my boy! Let me know when you're coming, and I'll try to keep sober enough to talk about them!"

This manager was by no means the only hard-drinking man in the foundry. He was almost a teetotaler to a steel-smelter from Sheffield who replaced the German, and who quickly became the bane of my life. He was nearest to being sober in the early morning, but even at that hour he moved in a fog of alcoholism. Frankly, I was scared to death of him. I hated him as I've never hated anyone else.

Every day his drunken humours followed the same unvarying cycle, keeping pace, I fancied, with the daily progress of his job, and the changing atmosphere of the foundry. In the early morning he seemed as cold, as dead, and as much an empty shell as the raked-out crucible furnaces over which he would become busy. He had little to say, and what he did say he barked - a dull, brooding savage with a too ready fist and foot.

As soon as he had seen the furnaces laid and lighted, he would go off to the pub (pubs in those days were always open in time to catch men on their way to work). When he came back an hour later he would be brisker, more talkative, but still morose and bitter. Under his biting sarcasm even the hardiest of us would writhe.

As the morning wore on and the furnaces warmed up, so did he. Step by step, between his recurring visits to the pub, his mood would mellow from searing bitterness to sunny ironic humour and then to Rabelaisian joviality. Like his furnaces he roared and sang through the middle of the day. By the time the furnaces were blue-hot and the crucibles were ready to be drawn he dominated the scene like Lucifer possessed. Straddling the flaring pits, enveloped in steam from the drenched sacking round his legs, he would pull out the pots holding over a hundredweight of molten metal with the ease and grace of a ballerina, screaming curses and blasphemies at the men who rushed to take them from him, but could never keep pace with his demonical speed and fury.

By this time, of course, his noise was mere theatricality. He was a natural, born actor, and this was his big scene. More than that. It was his justification. His proof to himself, no less than to us, that he was king of his job. For the moment he could forget his years and his talents wasted by debauchery, forget his thinning hair, his sagging belly, his pouchy face and the approaching day when he would be past his job.

But the moment the high spot of his working day was over, nagging self-knowledge would return. All his bombast would evaporate. He would weep and slobber over me, pouring out inconsequent memories of his youth, his many women, his squandered opportunities; would bore me with maudlin moralisings, disgust me with his drunken frankness. It was nauseating.

A queer card indeed. Tragic too, though I hated and despised him too much to see it then. Sprung from a well-to-do family, he'd had a good education, could speak several languages, and could quote the classics by the yard. I suppose I envied him too.

Our working life together was a constant duel, and our respective jobs provided plenty of opportunities for clashes. He made the most of them. I did my best to see that he got no satisfaction out of them. I might smart inwardly at some shaft that made me feel my inferiority, some phrase in French or Latin which he would gloatingly translate in pity of my ignorance, but I would thank him as gravely and sweetly as

I could. I might shrink secretly from physical violence, but I would suffer it silently. Sometimes he would order me to help him in drawing the crucibles and I would don tarpaulins and sopping sacks, trying my damndest to carry it off as a matter of course. Not even when he kept me crouching over the blistering fires, forcing me nearer and lower, would I give him the satisfaction of the slightest flicker.

One day, at the height of his big scene, drawing the crucibles, he ordered me to get back to my stool in the office. As I still had several pots to "doctor" with a dose of the secret alloy, I stood my ground. He repeated the order in coarser terms, and then, as I still stayed put, he started to swing the crucible he still held in the vertical tongs. I don't suppose he really meant to throw it at me - I shouldn't have stood my ground if I'd thought he would – but an alarmed moulder charged him and knocked him off his balance. The loaded crucible flew wide of me, spilt its contents on a pile of cold, wet pig-iron and filled the air with a myriad of scalding particles. Men shouted and yelled, brushing off the fiery sparks, the dust of ages was shaken from the beams above by the explosion, setting everyone coughing and sneezing, and the place was a pandemonium. With my clothes looking as though I had been peppered with buckshot, I staggered past the moulder who was giving my tormentor the thrashing of his life, found my way to the office sink and was beautifully sick.

I was to use that sink again a few months later when a grinding wheel in the fettling shed burst into fragments, tearing open a young lad's belly, and throwing him yards away with protruding entrails. Shocking as the sight was, it was nothing to the unconscious obscene ravings of the dying boy as the doctor stuffed him with piles of cotton wool and tied him together in a sack.[33]

---

[33] FATALITY AT RASTRICK  BURST OF AN EMERY WHEEL  A YOUTH KILLED  WORKMEN'S DANGEROUS PRACTICE
"A terrible accident, and one which aroused considerably alarm in the neighbourhood, occurred at the works of Messrs. Altenbach Ltd., Helvetia Works, Birds Royd, Rastrick, on Friday morning last, the victim being William Christopher Donaghue, a youth of eighteen years, who resided with his aunt at 5, Royal Oak Yard, Commercial Street, Brighouse. It appears that he was grinding an iron casting against an emery wheel, the former being held in position on the one side by the wall and on the other by a box, against which Donaghue had his knee. Somehow the casting became wedged between the wall and the wheel, and this caused the latter to burst, the result being that Donaghue received such injuries as caused his death seven hours later at the Huddersfield Infirmary whither he was conveyed. The workmen at the works rendered first assistance, and the Drs. Bond and Somerville treated the wound and ordered the youth's removal to the Infirmary." The report goes on to say that the inquest was held at the Huddersfield Infirmary, with both the firm and the family of William Donaghue being represented by solicitors. The solicitor for the firm stated that it was the first time a fatal accident had occurred at the steel works. He did not mention that the firm had only been in operation around eighteen months. The first witness was the surgeon who stated that the deceased had sustained a clean cut wound, four inches long and about the same depth, at the right side of the lower part of the abdomen, which had caused the bursting of the bladder. They did not consider any further examination necessary as the deceased was in an extremely bad condition, and died at six o'clock the same evening. His aunt, Mary Callery, said Donaghue had been employed at the Helvetia Steel Works for about three months. He had not done work as a grinder prior to that, being previously an engine cleaner at Brighouse station. Mr. John Law, H M Inspector of Factories at Halifax was present and questioned two witnesses from the steel works. The first was a Edward Hirst, 2, Heaton's Yard, Rastrick, repairing mechanic and engineer, the second, John Hartley Addingley, Bonegate Cottage, Brighouse, Manager. Mr. Law questioned both at some length about work practices in the grinding department, particularly the speed of the grinding wheel and the steam engine driving it. The Manager stated that he had heard of some of the grinders trying to pull up the engine by applying something to the wheel. Deceased was paid off a fortnight previously because of such an offence, but he was allowed to start again. After hearing all the evidence, the coroner stated that the accident appeared to be accidental, with no blame attached to anyone.
*Brighouse Echo* : October 18th 1907.

The comedy of life in that foundry was as broad and unsubtle as its tragedy. I loved to listen to the discussions of my workmates during the midday break. The bigger the issue the more flippant the tone. Gravity came with apparently trifling subjects, as one day, with the subject of flatulence, and the nicer behaviour of the female in the control of wind. Women, it was generally agreed, must suffer agonies through modesty. One man assenting, said "I'm sure my wife must. I've been wed to her nearly thirty year now, an' I've never heard her break wind once!."

"That's funny!" commented another. "My wife's a damn sight better looking nor thine, an' she farts like a trooper!"

My two years at the foundry passed swiftly. The crash came suddenly. There was an almost tearful farewell to the kindly alien whose English had improved as his fortune had worsened, and I had my first taste of unemployment.

For a fortnight I tramped the district looking for a job. There was no money for fares to the neighbouring towns nor for meals in eating-houses. It was a case of Shank's pony and a packet of jam or treacle sandwiches to be consumed furtively in shy corners. There was no unemployment benefit either. It was just sink or swim – or swim till you sank. It never occurred to me that things might, or ought to, be otherwise.

We still sang in Sunday school

> "The rich man in his castle,
> The poor man at his gate;
> God made them high or lowly
> And ordered their estate."

and I never thought of questioning either the truth or the equity of the statement. I knew, vaguely, that there were some people called Socialists who did, but as they were also reputed to be atheists, they were quite obviously neither fit to know or to listen to.

That fortnight of tired feet, of shabby boots wearing perilously thin and the heartbreaking feeling of being placeless and unwanted, ought to have made a rebel of me. I still wonder that it didn't. Its full impact was to come years later. I suppose I was immature for my years, a case of delayed development at this stage as later. I've no wish to enlarge on the searing experience. It was hellish.

A chance meeting with an old school chum ended it, and led to my being engaged as a clerk in the Civil Engineering Department of the then Lancashire and Yorkshire Railway. [34] The salary was £48 a year, a slight setback, but the work was light and I

---

[34] Quite by accident he met an old school friend who worked in the civil engineer's office on the Lancashire and Yorkshire Railway. He had obtained work in the Town Clerk's office in Brighouse, and had to find someone to take his place on the railway. Dick got the job at £48 a year, less 5% for superannuation.
*The Yorkshire Dalesman* : November 1956.

had plenty of time for reading. I read voraciously and indiscriminately, nothing but fiction, gulping at least one novel a day and keeping a notebook in which I jotted a précis of each plot with a paragraph or two of prentice criticism, with the sole purpose of improving my style as a speaker. If I looked to the future at all it was to see myself in a good safe job as a clerk or a bookkeeper with a prominent place in Chapel circles. I was still studying hard at the night school three nights a week, and the preparation for this, together with my Sunday School teaching and my preaching engagements, proved too much of a strain. I had my first attack of neurasthenia, the first and only real illness of my life. A distressing affair which not only made it difficult to speak or see, but so benumbed my brain that I couldn't grasp what I was reading or work out the simplest calculations. Subsequent attacks have been slight and much briefer in duration, little more than a vexatious interruption of enforced idleness.

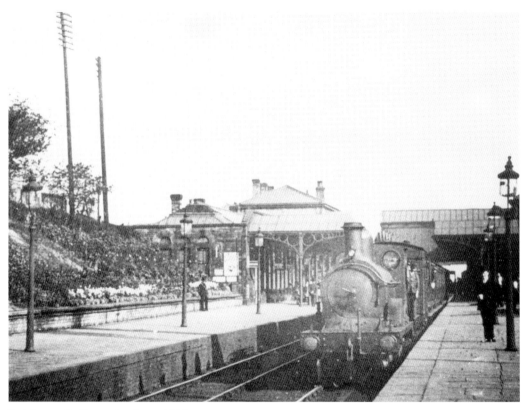

*Brighouse Railway Station, c1910*                    *(Lancashire & Yorkshire Railway Society)*

I have been singularly fortunate in the men I have worked for, and my chief at this time was no exception. He was a testy old gentleman (or old he seemed to me!) who distrusted profoundly my slick use of decimals and made crabbed comments on the state of my fingernails. I began by disliking him but before we parted company, years later, he'd earned my respect and gratitude. He stood by me in a crisis, did me a great service, although his breeding and traditions made it impossible for him either to agree with or to understand me. He was, in the words of our chainman, "a real old codger, but a thorough gentleman".

*George Corner, Brighouse (no date)*                                    *(BM)*

This chainman – a sort of labourer who carried the theodolite and other instruments used by the surveyors – was quite a character too. He spoke the rich, broad dialect of the Ryburn Valley, and his malapropisms were a joy. His best, I think, was his description of German as a "gluttonal" language.

He gave much advice on the management of women. "Keep 'em guessing – that's all there is to it, lad!" he told me. "They have to be given their head when you're courting 'em, in case they kick thee over. But as soon as t'weddings over, have a right row. A blazing row – on principle. Just to make her see she's only a boss with thy permission!"

According to him a woman's main flaw was her tendency to "take advantage". "So never let go of the reins lad, and the minute she gets the idea she's driving t'trap instead o' pulling it, tha checks her with a jerk that loosens her teeth!"

I saw him translating his theory into practice when, for a time, I lodged with them. He was a really good husband and took quite a large share of the household work and the care of the children, - the first workman I knew who wasn't ashamed of being able to do it. One evening, as we were finishing high tea, the wife said, "Yer haven't forgotten there's t'windows to clean, have yer?" That was his cue for a noisy dust-up ended by his banging off to the club. For days afterwards he wouldn't do a single job – not even chop the kindling.

It's nowt!" he assured me. "She'll unstiffen in time an' ask me to give her a hand. An' I shall oblige – as a favour. The minute she forgets it's a favour it stops – if tha gets mi drift!"

Soon after I was appointed, my new chief was given a job which suited his meticulous soul down to the ground. It was to prove the most unrewarding, needless and useless job I've known. It was to last the pair of us, off and on, for a decade. And the result was a settlement that a little give and take could have settled thirty years earlier on very similar terms.

About the time I was born extensive alterations had been made to Wakefield railway station. The cost was to have been shared by various companies, but for some unknown reason the proportions had never been worked out. So, twenty years late, we were faced with a glorious muddle of dilapidated, incomplete records and accounts. As the work had been in various stages, some portions paid for by the company, some by another, some items for purely maintenance work on their private lines, others for capital equipment to be used by all, the complications can be imagined. Before the investigation was over, we had reconstructed the course the whole job had taken, and uncovered, incidentally, one or two choice examples of sharp-practice. Looking for a three foot brick culvert we found a nine inch earthenware drainpipe, I remember.

At first the investigation was nothing but a job as fascinating and frustrating as a jigsaw; before it was completed it had become to me a telling instance of the fallacy that private enterprise and efficiency are synonymous. It was not to be the last, nor the most notable, revelation of incompetence and waste I was to enjoy, but it was the beginning of a process that left me with nothing but tolerant contempt for the system which couldn't efficiently serve its own narrow ends of profit making, much less efficiently serve the national needs.

The events which were to bring about this sceptical conclusion were, however, still

*King Street, Brighouse, c1900.* *(BM)*

in the future and, indeed, my chief and I were barely launched on our ten years investigation when the Brighouse office was closed and we were transferred to Manchester. For me it was not so much a transition as a translation.

I was then just turned twenty-one, legally a man, but really nothing but a diffident youth, provincial, even parochial in outlook; raw, inexperienced, with little education and less culture; the product of my class and generation, my horizon stretching no further than the office on the bread and butter side, no further than the chapel on the less material. My upbringing may have left much to be desired, though I didn't think it had then, but it had taught me to endure poverty, to make myself independent in the truest sense by earning more from the world than I was likely to get, and to look for the ultimate satisfaction in service rather than material gain. On the other side it had handicapped me with very poor teeth and a too-low opinion of myself and of my rights as an individual. If I'd been asked at that time for my code in life I might, after a pause in which to decide whether I had one or not, have quoted a line of Kipling's which I'd just come across –

> Help me to need
> No help from man
> That I may help
> Such men as need"

# Chapter Nine

Manchester began to play the very dickens with me almost the instant I stepped out of Victoria Station.

Almost the first thing I noticed was a verminous old crone shuffling along under a load of partly-made clothing. She was to lead me by my fastidious nose to Socialism.

A little further along my eye caught a theatrical twelve-sheet. That poster was to lure me into the modern theatre.

And soon after these two processes had got under way, Manchester gave me another cause for profound and lasting gratitude – my wife.

To say I was totally ignorant of politics when I left home to work in Manchester would not be strictly true. I knew that the Tories stood for the landlords and Tariff Reform which meant dear food; that the Liberals stood for Free Trade, Disestablishment and the Land For The People; that there were some queer women called "Suffragettes" who wanted to vote like men did, and that somewhere in the country there were folk called "Socialists" or "Labourites" who believed in some sort of impious revolutionary poppycock. I knew so much from what I'd been told by my Chapel friends. But I really hadn't a glimmering of the case for any political programme or party, and no idea of their importance, or their probable effect on my welfare. Nor was I sufficiently interested to find out.[35]

But just before moving to Manchester, in the course of my haphazard reading, I had come across Kingsley's *Alton Locke*. That dilapidated old crone with her bundle of clothing might have stepped right out of its pages. Hence the jolt she gave me.

I was to see her again and again as I explored my fresh habitat. To find others like her in the like occupation. I began to shadow them, during my lunch breaks, to find with dismay the slums which housed them and to learn that the sweat-shop was not a page in a novel but a very present reality. My first reaction was one of horror at the risks of contamination run by the buyers of cheap goods. But I soon found, by trailing these carriers from their workshops to the back entrances of stores in the city's most expensive shopping quarter, that high prices were no guarantee against infection.

I became aware of another disgusting phenomenon. All around our office were the premises of wholesale dealers in foodstuffs, where uncovered sides of bacon were transhipped from lorries into dingy, frowsy cellars by men whose cleanliness left a lot to be desired. There was nothing to protect the food they handled from their dirty clothes and hair. Very often the food was stacked on the greasy, grimy pavement, and dogs cocked their legs against stacks of bacon or cheese.

These shocks to my working-class notions of cleanliness inspired me to an indignant

---

[35] It is interesting to read in the *Brighouse Echo* (March 18th, 1910), of a debate held at Birds Royd Wesleyan Mission Hall on the subject of 'Should the House of Lords be abolished ? '. Gregson was one of the speakers who advocated its retention. The audience voted for abolition.

sermon on the un-Christian iniquity of selling tainted goods. The sermon drew from one listener the dry advice "to scratch a bit lower!"

I began to scratch deeper, to discover what my own experience should already have taught me, that sweating was not confined to tailoring, that the whole system of society was based on cash, not Christianity, and that this ape-and-tiger individualism, this conduct of business with an eye to Mammon and little regard for Man, had effects upon the producers even more to be deplored than those upon the buyers, or the goods that passed between them.

I was quickly on the way to becoming a Christian Socialist, though I'd yet to hear the term. Criticising the system, as its defects grew upon me, because it did not square with my notions of Christian morality and right dealing, and youth-like, doing my thinking aloud and often from the pulpit, I was accused of preaching socialism. My answer was that all I was trying to do was to ask what Christ would do, and if the answer was to be found in socialism, so much the better for socialism.

In this political conversion I experienced a glowing conviction which had been disappointingly absent from my religious one. At last I had a real purpose in life – a vital message to deliver. Reading, study and discussion were later to provide me with the economic case for my new creed, but the material argument was never as important to me as the moral. The passing years have brought me no reason to change my political creed, nor any better justification for it.

Although I had no longer any lack of themes for my sermons, nor any doubts about treating them, I knew well enough that Nonconformist Liberalism would never yield to a frontal attack. It was up to me to imitate Agag and walk delicately.[36] I must have been a poor mimic! The moment I descended from pious generalities to practical particulars I was suspect. Take for my text "Thou shalt do no murder", illustrate it with details of the latest sensational case, and I was safe. Take the same text and suggest it might apply to insanitary workshops, and I was sure to get it in the neck from some outraged chapel steward. I must not disturb young and tender minds. I must not offend some well-to-do church member. And so on, ad nauseam.

I kept on my course, as tactfully as I could compass, but I was gradually frozen out of every pulpit except one – that of a tiny chapel on the outermost edge of the circuit, the members of which were only too glad to get any preacher at all. I now had first-hand experience on which to draw for my first comedy, still some years in the future.[37]

I might have felt the loosening of my ties with the Chapel more keenly had I not at the same time been following a trail of sheer delight started by that striking theatrical poster I mentioned earlier.

Accustomed as I was to the tawdry, garish advertisements of the blood-tub at home, I had to look at it twice before its real nature dawned on me. Printed in two colours, panelled with a bold, rounded border, its plain lettering and restful use of space

---

[36] "Then said Samuel. Bring ye hither to me Agag the King of the Amalekites. And Agag came unto him delicately. And Agag said , Surely the bitterness of death is past." Samuel 1:c15,v 32. It didn't, however, do him any good – he was put to death.

[37] T''Marsdens: a Yorkshire dialect way of saying 'to the Marsdens', or 'the Marsdens', depending on the context.

*Gaiety Theatre, Manchester (1890)*                    *(MALS)*

made it at once arrestive and persuasive. There wasn't an adjective in it, much less a superlative, and all the emphasis was on the name of the play as though it said "The play's the thing!" It was as revolutionary as the theatre to which it drew my attention.

Not without an inward qualm as to my backsliding, for the theatre was still taboo to the chapel folk at home, I followed the pointing of this star to the Gaiety Theatre, where Miss Horniman was now running her now historic experiment in repertory. [38] I knew not the least thing about her nor her venture, was absolutely unprepared for what was in store for me.

I paid sixpence for a seat in the gallery and got my first surprise for, instead of the hen-perch I expected, it really <u>was</u> a seat, padded and separate from its fellows, and with a back to it. The curtain next caught my eye – a real curtain, not a painted act-drop; its dark red velvet folds had highlights and shadows in their own right, owing nothing to a painter's brushwork.

---

[38] Annie Elizabeth Horniman (1860-1937), a member of the Horniman family of tea merchants, was a pioneer of the modern repertory theatre movement. In 1894 she financed a season of plays at the Avenue Theatre, London. In 1904 she agreed to fund the opening of the Abbey Theatre in Dublin as a home for the Irish National Theatre. In 1907, after a disagreement with the Abbey, Miss Horniman moved to Manchester. Initially, she started a theatre at the Midland Hotel. However, in 1908 she took over the Gaiety Theatre and transformed it into what is generally regarded as the first full-scale modern repertory theatre. It was associated with writers of the so-called " Manchester School ". The theatre closed in 1921 and was sold to a cinema company.

Touring was an important aspect of their work from the start; there were sometimes two companies performing simultaneously, as the resident company fitted matinees at nearby towns into its Manchester schedule. Iden Payne, her stage director reported the comment of the stage carpenter at Oldham, which had proved resistant to all such opportunities: "It's only to be expected at Oudam. You wouldn't get folk to come to a theayter if you was to give 'em the Crucifixion with the original cast".

G.Rowell and A.Jackson, *The Repertory Movement; A History of Regional Theatre in Britain*, Cambridge University, 1984.

Writing this, I live again that ten minutes of trembling, delighted recognition of the rightness of the place. Those plain walls of cream, with mouldings innocent of gilt or florid colour; unmarred by pictorial panels of mermaids sporting on the backs of dolphins, or masks of Comedy and Tragedy hung by painted ribbons; those walls were right. Equally right was the strong yet quiet contrast between this creamy plainness and the rich red of the curtain and the upholstery. Marvellously right was the moulded inscription above the plain proscenium –

OUR TRUE INTENT IS ALL FOR YOUR DELIGHT

Rightest of all was the hushed traffic of the incoming patrons, and the warm, happy certainty that I belonged here. I was at home.

The play was to me as unknown as the theatre. Who or what *The Trojan Women* were, who or what Euripides was or were, except that he, she or they had written the play, I hadn't the slightest notion.

*Annie Horniman (1909)*

*(MALS)*

The lights went down, and the curtain rose in darkness <u>on</u> darkness. A voice became audible and light dawned faintly on a godlike head hanging in blackness. Another voice replied and slowly another face became visible in space. I clenched my hands to stop them trembling as the sonorous verse rose and fell, ebbed and flowed, in that chasm of listening emptiness, until sound and sight faded into the darkness from which they had emerged.

Out of that darkness now came other voices – the voices of women mourning – mourning for their dead and for the ruined homes in which they lay. And with a gradualness beyond the measurement of sense, the darkness thinned and thinned, the light quickened and quickened, shadows became slowly apprehended shapes and shapes became living creatures, full fleshed, warm and sentient with individual character and suffering. The tragic episode, paced by the mounting light, climbed slowly to its stormy crisis – the burning of the city – then slowly declined from passion to weeping nothingness as the flame-lit horror of the burning pile paled to cold ashy blackness and silence again……….

I walked home through streets that might never have been for what I saw of them. I walked in a blinding light – dazed by the glory of a revelation. I had glimpsed what real theatre could be and do. I was launched on another phase of my education, an enchanted pupil of the "Manchester School".

In quick succession I saw a series of plays such as *Arms and the Man, Candida, The Silver Box, Widower's Houses, Justice* and *The Voysey Inheritance,* presented with quiet realism, classic comedy staged with tasteful, spare décor instead of the fustian frippery I'd known at home, and all the plays, old or new, marked by a standard of acting I'd never dreamed of.

But the technical advances, impressive as they were to me, were not as important as my discovery of a drama which discussed present discontents and problems in an adult fashion; which took as its themes the wrongs of peasants as well as the rights of princes; which made the kitchen table a platform for reformers, the housewife a heroine in some social battle; a drama in which significant fable was matched by the manner of its telling, to which the name of the author was set boldly, both as a matter of right to him and a hallmark of quality to the public.

Even more significant still was the emergence of the new regional drama of Houghton, Brighouse and Monkhouse in which Lancashire idiom and dialect gave point to modern ideas, and to me, added the final touch of potency and poignancy to their work. [39]

All of which should have prompted me to write, but didn't. It wasn't until the end of that glorious era was approaching, and even then at the prompting of others, that I submitted some of my prentice efforts to the quaintly-dressed, eccentric Queen of Repertory. [40] I've no doubt they deserved the caustic rejection, on the famous mustard-yellow notepaper, that they invariably met with.

There were, of course, other theatres in Manchester, but they linger in the memory merely as foils to the glory that was the Gaiety. None provided a more startling contrast than the Shakespearean productions for which Richard Flanagan was responsible. The tradition of grandiose and spectacular mounting, often at the expense of the text, which was begun by the Calverts, developed by Irving and overdone by Tree, became, in the hands of Flanagan, a matter of lush, rococo pageantry – a Shakespearean pantomime, which was as popular as and ran even longer than the customary Christmas productions.

The first of these I saw was the The Winter's Tale. I watched it with amazement, which steadily deepened to amused resentment and jeering disdain. It began with an apparently endless procession of youths and maidens, accompanied by music, carrying dishes of fruit, ornate jars of wine, and all the pasteboard regalia of a banquet. The slow cavalcade sang as it passed – words which owed nothing to Shakespeare and would have given him the belly-ache. Then, at very long last, and almost as an afterthought, or so it seemed, came Camillo and a Gentleman to start the play.

---

[39] William Stanley Houghton (1881-1913). Together with Allan Monkhouse and Harold Brighouse, formed what became known as the ' Manchester School ' of dramatists. Houghton's connection with the Gaiety Theatre began with the production in 1908 of his one-act play *The Dear Departed*. His first popular success was *The Younger Generation* , produced by Miss Horniman in 1910. With *Hindle Wakes* ( 1911 ) he leapt into fame. His early death from meningitis cut short a career of much promise.

Harold Brighouse (1882-1958). A prolific author of more than seventy plays, many of which are set in his native Lancashire and show, in a comic way, the attitudes and character of the working and trading people. His most famous play, *Hobson's Choice* was written during the First World War, in his spare time, whilst seconded to the Air Ministry Intelligence Staff.

Allan Noble Monkhouse (1858-1936). A novelist and dramatist in his own right, several of his plays were produced by Miss Horniman. He is best remembered as the dramatic and literary critic of the *Manchester Guardian* from 1902 to 1932.

[40] Tall, slightly angular, she had a decisive, suffragettish manner and was very modern in her outlook. She wore the most wonderfully characteristic clothes. The only time Dick Gregson saw her in person she was lecturing in a local hall, clad in a dress that was partly purple and partly black, with pointed bodice and skirt, and there was a richly coloured shawl round her shoulders. On her head was a bonnet, with tapes that tied under the chin. *The Yorkshire Dalesman* : November 1956 .

The pastoral scene of the Fourth Act was described as "a masterpiece of theatrical stagecraft". Like Crummles on another occasion, Flanagan had decided to use his full stage. We gazed on a clearing in a valley complete with grass, trees and flowers, a stream tumbling over canvas rocks into a pool which apparently had no outlet yet never brimmed over. The whole of the forestage was crowded with pigeons, doves, sheep, poultry, goats and dogs. The sight was impressive by its very prodigality, and the cleansing of the stage cloth must have been quite a problem. The audience rose to it. Round upon round of applause rolled and returned until, in response, on walked a red-faced, bald-headed man in evening dress, flourishing a shiny top hat as he bowed and gesticulated his thanks for the tribute. He came back again and again before the play was allowed to proceed.

There was one curious lapse from the general magnificence. The bear hunting scene was played before a frontcloth which showed a very stormy seascape with a ship fixed in immobile distress. There was a real bear, of course, but it was as shabby as the scene, and it tore across the stage as though chased by fiends instead of humans.

Actually, as I learned years later, the poor thing was making a beeline to the artists' bar for its nightly carouse when it ate pork pies and guzzled bottled beer until it passed into a coma. Rehearsals of the scene had been most disappointing until the producer realised he was asking the poor animal to run in the wrong direction, and reversed the whole business, to the delight of the bear but the dismay of the actor who played Antigonus and who found it difficult to dodge the charge of the hungry creature.

Manchester, in those last few years before the 1914-1918 war, was the best place in England for a dramatic apprentice, offering a choice of every style and school of writing, acting and production. Besides the Gaiety with Miss Horniman and the old Queen's with Flanagan, there was the Royal and the Princes where all the London stars could be seen on their provincial tours, and in the near suburbs at least a dozen humbler theatres housed the old-fashioned stock companies in the melodramas I now looked down my nose at. But in spite of the glamour of the Irvings, the Bensons, the Terrys, the Martin Harveys, Forbes Robertsons, Lewis Wallers, Wilson Barretts and many other historic names, Miss Horniman's venture had my undivided heart. I've always regretted that my tardy development prevented me from being anything more than a mere spectator in it.

A terrific burst of reading followed naturally upon the new interest I'd found in politics and the theatre. I began to devour all the plays and political pamphlets I could lay my hands on. Henry George, Blatchford, Morris, Bellamy and Wells jostled Shaw, Galsworthy, Barker, Ibsen and Barrie for my greedy, uncritical attention. The immediate result of this feverish study was another attack of neurasthenia, during which my eyes began to trouble again. I went to the Royal Eye Hospital in John Street, in search of relief – and found my wife.

# Chapter Ten

As I waited my turn in the large, dingy out-patient department of the hospital, I became aware of a fair haired pale-faced girl at the reception desk. She appeared to be in difficulties with a column of figures. I watched her failures and her increasing exasperation as long as I could, then asked if I might do the little job for her. She gave me a look that ought to have withered me, but as I didn't wilt, she finally passed me the pencil without a word.

It was now my turn to become flustered, but I got through the job somehow and faded into the semi-obscurity of the waiting crowd feeling curiously out of breath. Feeling mad, too. Mad at myself for sticking my neck out; mad at her for being so up-stage, even though I was a patient getting cheap treatment. I got madder every time I caught her eye on me. It was obvious I'd made more impression on her than patients usually did. It was equally obvious that the impression wasn't favourable.

It ought not to have mattered a ha'porth to me. I told myself it didn't. But it went on nattering just the same. I reminded myself that I'd bigger things to think about than a stuck-up piece who couldn't add a column of coppers.

I was still fuming when a shaft of sunlight streaked the gloom of the prison-like place. It caught the minx's fair hair and turned her pale face to warm ivory. She'd taken off the gold pince-nez which had made me so conscious of my shabby steel rims. The officious female was transformed into a creature who made me feel drabber and less significant than ever. The next moment the sunlight faded, but the mischief was done.

From then on I began to take extra care of my celluloid collar, my shiny suit with its double-breasted waistcoat and my buttoned boots. The effect on her as far as I could judge was nil. Fortunately for me, my eye trouble persisted for some time. So did I.

There came a never-to-be-forgotten evening when, the true son of my father, I blued half a week's wages on a couple of stalls and etceteras at a music hall, and we both settled ourselves in the seats of the wealthy trying, not altogether successfully, to act as though we had never been used to anything else. For the next two hours life had no more to offer me.

Our courtship was brief but far from smooth. Apart from mutual attraction we had very little in common.

Florence Hine was of working-class stock, as I was. Her parents were caretakers at the Eye Hospital in John Street, and little better off than mine. She herself, assisting in the work, was little more than a household servant, getting in return, her keep and five shillings a week, out of which she had to provide her own clothes and incidentals. But city breeding had given her a poise and independence which I still lacked and a carefree attitude towards religion and politics which I could not help thinking deplorable. I was dashed to discover that she was a churchwoman, dismayed to find she was a Conservative, and utterly dumbfounded when I realised she had no real convictions about either or thought they mattered much. Instead of writing sonnets to her eyebrows I set about her political education with results that may be imagined.

The Hines were a musical family. Florence had a good but untrained voice and played the piano passably. Her father could manage several instruments, was leader of an amateur orchestra and made violins as a hobby. One of her brothers was a professional violinist. Although I thoroughly enjoyed the family concerts and the new world to which they introduced me I couldn't help feeling something of an outsider; and although I always accompanied Florence and her concert-party friends freely, even eagerly, to the public entertainments they gave, my pleasure was always tinged with the feeling of being a mere hanger-on. I wished I could do something more than talk, and envied the easy camaraderie in which I found it so difficult to join. And yet I jibbed at coming to terms with this careless, more sophisticated world in which I'd found myself – a world whose facile, city manners made me feel awkward and loutish – as I've little doubt I was.

I suppose that all this mental and emotional turmoil was the natural result of my slow development. I was making up the leeway too rapidly, sprouting in all directions at once, and making heavy weather of it.

But growing pains don't encourage tact – not that I had much then – and the result of all this ferment was a courtship that mixed argument with adoration, exasperation with ecstasy. I must have bored, teased and maddened Florence beyond all bearing. But neither then nor since, thank goodness, have we ever had a difference about money. For one thing, we've never had much of it to quarrel over.

We certainly hadn't then. My salary was £60 a year, and I had to sell or pawn my fiddle to help pay for the engagement ring – a magnificent affair which cost every penny of three pound ten. We hadn't a penny saved, and were still rubbing the corners off each other when the prospect of a coming child plunged us, without preparation, into hasty marriage.

We married and furnished distinctly on the cheap. There was a modest ceremony at the Church a few yards from my wife's home.[41] We walked there. The Vicar, with whom Florence was a favourite, refused to accept his fee. I borrowed £10 from my parents, and with that and some oddments supplied by our respective families, we furnished our first home – a tiny, four roomed house in Heaton Park.[42] There was no

---

[41] Gregson was married at St. Johns, Deansgate, Manchester on January 31st 1912.

[42] A Lancashire Playwright (sic)
Mr. James R Gregson ............once occupied a clerical stool in the engineering office of the Lancashire and Yorkshire Railway Company in Trevelyan Buildings, Corporation Street, Manchester. On his marriage he took up his residence in Heaton Park, where he formed an amateur dramatic society, called the Heaton Park "Mummers". Many of his early plays and duologues were produced at the Congregational School, Heaton Park, and the rehearsals took place at his own house. He has been a voluminous writer, and four of his most successful plays when at Heaton Park were *Sybil*, *Breezes*, *Ashes*, and *Liddy*, and he generally played the leading role. He offered *Liddy* to Miss Horniman when she controlled the Gaiety, but she desired to make an alteration in the opening stages, which did not meet with Mr. Gregson's approval at the time. While at Heaton Park he produced a monthly typewritten journal called the *Mummers*, which circulated amongst his friends. He edited and typed about sixty copies each month, and they were often to be seen in the hands of the passengers travelling to town by the 8.30 train.
*Manchester City News* : May 5th 1923.
The rent for the Heaton Park house was 4/6 a week.

honeymoon. I got half a day's leave for the wedding, and after a quiet little party in John Street we went straight to our new establishment to begin a partnership which was to prove I'd found a wife in a million.

Ten pounds didn't go far in those days. By the time we had bought four secondhand chairs at five shillings apiece, a deal table for seven-and-six, a square of coconut matting, some lace curtains (which I never saw from outside without being impressed by the splendid lie they gave to the nakedness within), a wickerwork table to carry the aspidistra which nobly backed up the curtains in hiding our poverty, a bed and two basket chairs, there was little left for pots and pans and such refinements as knives and forks. Upstairs, one room was absolutely empty and the other contained only the bed and an old cabin trunk, so there was plenty of room for the dancing lessons Florence began to give me.

Our straitened circumstances worried neither of us unduly. We were both used to short commons. We were both young and determined to better ourselves. We had plenty of differences to bridge, a hard struggle in front of us, but absolute confidence in each other and the love between us.

And here and now let me set down my gratitude to the woman who proved herself as good and loyal a mate as any man could desire – a comrade who has shirked no sacrifice and often borne the major share; a shrewd critic; something of a slave-driver when necessary; a rival-cum-partner in our stage careers; a generous lover; not to mention such odds and ends as a devoted mother, a capable housekeeper and genius of a cook. Open-hearted to a fault, independent to the point of mulishness on occasions, fearless and outspoken, much more jealous for my reputation and interest than her own and, above all, blessed with a keen and lively sense of humour. Heaven knows, she's needed it in her life with me!

Our early economic difficulties helped us more then anything else to bridge our difficulties. Politics and religion became unimportant against the novelty and drama of a joint existence in which a burnt tin of parkin was a tragedy and the emergence from debt as a theme for brass and percussion.

On the day I was married I drew my first month's salary of £68 per year. By the time I had drawn it six times, we had repaid the loan of £10. How we lived for six months – or rather, how Florence kept us going for that time on £24 - I don't know.

But I do know that towards the end of each month things got pretty tight. I remember one month-end when they were really desperate. Pay day fell that month on a Friday. On the Sunday prior to that day of deliverance, we had either fourpence or fivepence in the kitty. Lying in bed to save breakfast and food we held an anxious Committee of Ways and Means. It was interrupted by the postman's knock. (In that faraway era we had Sunday deliveries.) There was a parcel for me from an acquaintance in Oldham. I had done a spot of reciting for him at a Chapel Concert. Returning a book I had left behind, he also enclosed a postal order for two-and-six to cover my travelling expenses. We both, unashamedly, wept in relief. It was the first, and the richest fee, I ever received.

Whether it was her hard grounding in these practical economies, or my forgetting to hammer her with my theories, or whether it was due to some of our new friends who turned out to belong to the Left wing in politics, I really don't know. Perhaps something of all three. But, Florence, I soon found to my rueful amusement, was more of a rebel than I was. When I taxed her with her change of politics she came out with the characteristic defence, "It isn't politics at all! It's what's right"

"Well, wasn't it right when I said it?" I asked, just a bit nettled.

"It might have been, if you'd said right!" And she left me to ponder over her womanly logic and her gift for repartee.

The difficulty as to which Church we should attend solved itself almost as easily. The trouble I was experiencing because of my sermons made me indifferent as to where we went. I was quite honestly prepared to settle in one of the Established Churches in the village, but after trying them both for a week or two, Florence decided quite firmly that she'd never be comfortable at either. "Then we'll try my lot!" I said.

The following Sunday evening we went to the Wesleyan Methodist chapel. It was fairly full, we went towards a half empty pew. A steward headed us off. "Excuse me!" he said, "That's a private pew!"

It appeared there were only about half-a-dozen pews in that "House of God" which weren't rented and reserved for those with more pence than piety. We stood redfaced in the sight of God and that congregation whilst the steward found an individual who was willing to share with us his particular little corner in the fold. We never went again.

There was only one other place – the Congregational Church. It proved a happy compromise for both of us. Florence joined the Choir, and I found jobs in the Sunday School and the Band of Hope. I resumed my habit of writing temperance sketches, turning out and rehearsing one a month, writing with an eye to the idiosyncrasies of my players, of whom Florence was one. With a view to improving our standards, she and I joined an elocution class run by the W.E.A.[43] The fee was two-and-six for the winter's session.

We lasted with the Congregationalists until 1914. Then, just before the outbreak of the First World War, a well-to-do widow, offered to install new seating in the church in memory of her husband. The cost of pews made by a local firm proved to be a little higher than the woman was either able or willing to go. It was decided to buy chairs from High Wycombe. The workers at High Wycombe were at that moment striking for a minimum wage of twopence-halfpenny an hour. I barged into the argument in the magazine I was then editing, typing and circulating, asking questions, such as "Would Christ sit on sweated chairs?"

The affair ended with me resigning, and taking one or two others with me into the wilderness. The chairs were installed to the Glory of God and the memory of a nobody.

---

[43] The Workers' Educational Association (WEA) was founded in 1903 in order to support the educational needs of working men and women, to provide access to higher education and learning for adults of all backgrounds, and in particular, to those who had previously missed out on education.

On the first anniversary of our wedding day my salary was raised to £80. By that time a baby was really on the way and economy was still the order of the day. By cutting down our projected new clothing programme, we became the proud owners of a dressing table and washstand, new and of "real" oak, at a cost of five pounds. The bedroom floor was covered with a cheap oilcloth, thin and limp enough, as Florence said,"to wipe your nose on!" We also acquired some secondhand carpet for the stairs.

Our first daughter was born about five am on July 7th, 1913. None of us really rose to the occasion. Florence had made a bilberry pie for Sunday. We were just sitting down to it when her first pains came upon her. I ran like the devil a good mile and a half for the midwife, arriving back home again drenched in sweat and summer rain, to find Florence, not in extremis as I expected, but coolly finishing off that outsize bilberry pie! I knew she was passionately fond of that particular fruit, but felt this was carrying liking to the point of idolatry, but she replied with calm, devastating logic, "I'm having it whilst I can! It'll be nothing but gruel for me tomorrow"

Before the midwife bundled me out of the house to spend the night with a friend, I was allowed to go upstairs for a last look at my wife. She was twisting in agony, holding on to a towel fastened to the bedhead. At the height of the spasm she demanded, indignantly, "Is this going on for ever?"

Soothingly the midwife replied, "Yer'll feel different when yer holding a bonny little babby!"

I don't care if it's a ninepenny rabbit!" came the reply through gritted teeth, "so long as this gets over!"

We couldn't afford a nurse, of course, but neighbours found time to look after Florence whilst I was at work. The night nursing and housework devolved upon me. I shall never forget that first night when I changed the baby's nappy, sitting in nothing but my shirt, balancing the tiny mite precariously across my bony knees and trying to unplait her legs. She wriggled like a politician explaining away an awkward past.

We bought little Florence a gorgeous pram, a seeming extravagance which proved a first-class investment. It cost three pounds ten, but we got more than full value out of it even as first user. At weekends we pulled and pushed it on long tramps over the countryside, hoisting it over stiles and walls. When the child was too big for it, we sold it for thirty shillings. I don't know how many babies it served before we bought it back again, in its seventh year, for fifteen shillings, but it served our second child as nobly as it had served the first. We last saw it, at least ten years old, being used to cart firewood, and apparently going as strong as ever.

That pram might stand as a worthy symbol of the age which produced it – an age of sound and honest workmanship, in which the gimcrack and the cheap were recognised and despised, an age in which men expected to get value for their money and to give it, and those who failed in the latter, whither statesman or craftsman, expected no honour; an age in which "moving pictures" were still a novelty, the slavery of mass entertainment, mass communication and mass production unknown. Life left more to be desired by the majority, it is true, but it also left us freer to make the most of what we had in our own individual fashion. In spite of its shortcomings and our discontents, life then was a challenge to be accepted, a flesh-and-blood drama in which we had to take our part. We were actors, not spectators watching its flickering shadows on a screen.

That age, seemingly as eternal and leisurely as the hills, ended for me on the morning of August 4th, 1914. A lovely, quiet, sunny morning, in a still drowsy street. The calm shattered by the excited shouting of newsboys. A paper tossed onto my lap as I sit on the warm doorstep, nursing a baby still smelling of sleep. Before I've time to take in the leaded headlines, the street is alive. Women are scurrying to the shops in a panic rush to collar food supplies. Florence joins the stampede and comes back, hours later, with fourteen pounds of flour.

I was a conscientious objector. I believed, firmly and sincerely, that it was wrong to shed blood under any circumstances. I could not, by any stretch of imagination, see the Carpenter of Nazareth taking up arms.

Mixed with this ethical objection to war in the abstract there was my political objection to this war in particular. I was a socialist, an internationalist, and Sir Edward Grey's excuses stank in my nostrils. This was a capitalists' war – the outcome of a system that allowed dogs to befoul bacon and the chair and chain makers of High Wycombe and Cradley Heath to sweat for twopence-halfpenny an hour.

I wasn't blind to the fact that I really couldn't keep out of things, and that if I refused to serve my country I should, willy-nilly, be helping the enemy. I couldn't stand aside no matter how I tried, short of committing suicide. No one could do the right thing in a world gone wrong. But right or wrong, I felt it was imperative for all who thought and felt as I did to make a gesture, if necessary to be martyred for that gesture. Somebody had to make it, whether the time was out of joint or not, if war was ever to be outlawed.

But though I had no doubt as to the rightness of my attitude, I had about my courage. Knowing how I always shrunk from physical violence, I wasn't sure whether I wasn't sheltering behind my ideals and convictions.

In the end I decided that the only thing, illogical as it was, was to try to enlist. If I were accepted, that would be that. If I was turned down, then I should be free to fight the battle of conscience with a clear one.

Before the war was a fortnight old I was in the queue at the recruiting centre, without a permit from the railway authorities, wondering how I could get over the snag. I need not have worried. Things were in such a muddle that it was easy to join the men waiting to be medically examined. The only other snag I anticipated was the sight test, and whilst I waited my turn, I carefully memorised the letters on the wall chart.

"Very nice!" said the doctor, after what I thought was an artistic performance. "Now let's see your glasses!"

"What glasses ….?"

"Pincenez!—and too tight by the marks on your nose!"

I ran mother-naked, the focus of every draught in a long chilly passage for the glasses. When I got back, I saw that the test card had been changed. The game was up. I was dismissed with a grin and the advice to think up a better trick next time.

Until the Conscription Bill came into force I was merely a passive member of the No-Conscription Fellowship, but in due course the time came when I had to go through the farce of appealing before a tribunal.

My chief, as crabbed and cantankerous as ever, fretted over me like a father over a misguided son.

"Why run your head against a stone wall?" he wanted to know. "It's only a matter of form! Even if they pass you with your poor eyes, you'll be exempted because of your job. You've got intelligence! Why don't you use it intelligently?"

He became more and more concerned as I withstood threats of dismissal from our higher-ups and my exemption card was withdrawn. He was almost tearful when he begged me to behave circumspectly in conducting my appeal before the tribunal. He was like a man bereaved during the fortnight after my appeal was dismissed and I received my calling-up papers.

*Fenner*
*Brockway 1959*
National Portrait Gallery, London

I can't say I enjoyed it myself. It was no joke to try to put a reasoned case to a bench of prejudiced, stupid men too old to have to fight in any case. I couldn't tell them, as I told respective tormentors on the morning train, that I wasn't sheltering behind my son, that I wasn't evading service on the grounds of hardship in business. I couldn't tell them that they would stop a bullet or fill a hole in Flanders with more justice than the youngsters who were paying for their fathers' past political muddling. Nor did I enjoy the strain of the daily goodbye, wondering each morning whether I should be arrested before the day was out. Florence, needless to say, acted like a brick, from beginning to end.

The end came when I arrived at the office one morning to find on my desk, a new red card exempting me from military service on the ground that I was indispensable in my railway job. It didn't say that the job was merely cleaning up a bookkeeping muddle, thirty years old!

I showed the card to my chief. "Thank you!" I said.

Thank me for nothing!" he muttered in crabbed confusion. "I hope you're satisfied with yourself!"

Apart from the shortages of food due to the inadequate rationing system, and an open-air meeting in which Fenner Brockway, then editor of the *Labour Leader*, and I were roughly handled by the crowd, the rest of the war period was unremarkable for us. [44] Almost idyllic.

We were living in a very tiny house in Derbyshire, surrounded by sweeping hills whose heavenly loneliness was a rare solace. It was here, in November 1919, our second daughter, Joan was born. During the months she was on the way our family life was at its most peaceful and promising. I had an easy job, I was dreaming of success through the writing I was launched upon; my wife was equally well and happy in her own spot of creation; we were living in modest comfort amongst simple, friendly people who regarded us as the lions of the village; and we were looking forward to the new job which was looming on the horizon for me.

Before Joan was a month old, I was back in Yorkshire – in familiar surroundings but a novel atmosphere – that of the theatre.

---

[44] Fenner Brockway (1888-1988). Journalist and politician, Brockway played a heroic role in the Independent Labour Party's opposition to the war of 1914-1918 as a journalist, and then through the No Conscription Fellowship as an opponent of military conscription. On four occasions he was sentenced to gaol and in total served 28 months. Brockway was a frequent recipient of white feathers, handed to him by indignant young women keen to demonstrate their disgust of his "cowardice". Unabashed, Brockway merely remarked that after a while he had collected enough white feathers with which to construct a fan.

# Chapter Eleven

On our moving to Derbyshire I forswore for a time all activities of a public nature except those connected with the No-Conscription Fellowship and the I. L.P.[45] I'd had more than enough of what I called religious hypocrisy, and the amateur dramatic society with whom I'd made my Shakespearean debut (a disastrous essay at the part of the Prince of Morocco) had folded up for lack of male players.

I had besides conceived a most ambitious project, if "conceived" is not an erroneous term for my slow and tardy growing awareness of a gradually dawning notion. Tired of writing sketches for indifferent amateurs such as myself, I found myself struggling with a play – a real one-act which would be so good that I might be justified in offering it to Miss Horniman.

The result was *Youth Disposes*, and my first rejection from that redoubtable critic, who put an unerring finger on its major, damning weakness. I had evaded the obligatory scene. The denouement demanded the appearance of a character, instead of which I had made him send a letter.

I was still very much in the dumps about this, when, just as I was dropping off to sleep one night, the idea of *Liddy* came to me – a situation, theme and characters, all leaping upon me, as it seems now, ready-made.[46] The impression was so vivid that I simply had to get up and make a brief sketch of what I had seen and heard and lived through – the first and only time it has happened to me. Even then it wasn't really necessary, for next morning the play was waiting on my pillow, ready to pounce on me as vividly and as complete as before. Although I kept a tight rein on myself, determined not to allow the play to burn me up or run away with me, it was written in three days. It is perhaps the most completely satisfying piece of work of which I have been the medium – the only suitable word for a process in which I was so possessed and driven. It is certainly the best of my one-act plays and the result of my sole experience of what I can only describe by the theological term, "plenary inspiration".

Miss Horniman turned down *Liddy* as promptly and as curtly as usual, telling me with some asperity that a coffin on the stage would upset her players.

Still smarting under this rebuff, I asked Fred Pennington to read the play. Pennington was a schoolmaster in Marple with whom I'd struck up a friendship.[47] He was one of the founders of the Stockport Garrick Society, the first of the experimental "Little

---

[45] Independent Labour Party.

[46] In my own belief, the finest of Gregson's plays is Liddy, a short one act play. It is a gem which sparkles as well in the daylight as in the limelight. In the room of an ordinary workman's cottage there rests a coffin – a pauper coffin. It is round this coffin that the various characters move, and by James Gregson's art, we look upon their naked souls. *The Worker* : December 25th 1920.
For the full article, including part of the dialogue see Appendix 4.

[47] At the time of the fiftieth Anniversary celebrations of the Stockport Garrick Society, Fred Pennington was reported to be living at Camden, Gloucestershire but had still retained his membership of the Society.

Theatres" – at the time a lonely herald of the coming post-war renaissance in amateur drama. I expected very stern treatment from this able producer and actor who had achieved the dizzy height, to me, of appearing in plays by Ibsen and Shaw.[48]

We were walking over Werneth Low, I remember, on our way to an I.L.P. meeting in Hyde, when he took the wind out of my sails. In his usual deliberate fashion, he said." I don't suppose you need me to tell you that *Liddy* is little short of being a masterpiece?"

Is it really as good as that?" He scared me.

"Surely you know yourself that it's the real stuff?" he countered, turning his dark, thoughtful eyes on me.

I stammered that I thought it was good.

"It's better than that. It's proof to me that you're what's called a discovery. It's the work of a genuine dramatist – some might say, a genius."

It was some time before I could breathe naturally. He left me late that night almost paralysed with awe at myself. I've long since lost the awe though I still have my periods of paralysis.

Encouraged by Pennington, I launched upon my first full-length comedy. The early summer of 1917 saw me happily up to the eyes in the sunniest-tempered of all my plays - *T'Marsdens*. It was prompted by and based upon my experience as a local preacher. Fortunately for me, some sixth sense prevented me from taking sides in the conflict between my characters and allowed none of the resentment I still felt to tinge the comedy. I laughed at, and with, both sides – and, though maybe a shade wryly, at myself. But though my preaching experience had lost most of its sting, it had left me with the profound conviction that all propaganda, whether religion, politics or art, should be amateur, that for any propagandist to accept pay was to accept compromise, crippledom and all too often, complete defeat; that professionalism spelt shackles for the paid propagandist, whether called painter, player, parson, politician or merely a damned nuisance; that in a world where he who pays the piper calls the tune, no true artist can afford to go round with the hat, and that his only way of salvation and to keep his self-respect is to prove himself as good as the next man by earning his bread-and-butter by doing some job without which the world couldn't move, and thus earn for himself absolute freedom to follow his special job of moving it. I was then and, confirmed by experience, still am, the incorrigible amateur.

Something of this I set myself to say in *T'Marsdens*. (I felt still young enough to believe

---

[48] The Garrick gave private performances, for members only, of such plays as Bernard Shaw's *Candida*, with no admission charge. *The Manchester Guardian* praised the venture, while Shaw himself, who was usually rude about amateur drama, waived his normal fee of five guineas stating "In the case of a society such as yours I have no desire to press my rights". However, when the Garrick performed *Candida* at Buxton, raising £100 (mainly for a convalescent home for poor children) and sending only five guineas to Shaw, the indignant playwright launched a barrage of angry letters at the Society. Fortunately, peace was restored in time for the Garrick to produce Shaw's *Arms and the Man* a few month's later.

Stockport & District Heritage: Spring 2001

I had something worth saying.) In it my parson-hero leaves his frustrated ministry and goes back to the factory to be, like Paul with his sailmaking, free to "tell folk they're sinners, free gratis and for nowt!" But I knew so little of my job, or my gift of creating character, that it wasn't until the play was produced that I realised my "propaganda" was swamped by the "comedy" which carried it – that the pill was lost in the jam. It came as a bitter pill to me!

Miss Horniman had evidently lost patience with me. The play came back with something of a snort. She "employed her actors to act, not to talk dialect!" And that was that.

Pennington pressed the play upon The Stockport-Garrick Society. It was accepted, and I found myself directing players who knew their job better than I did.[49]

This is not the place for a history of the Stockport Garrick, nor could I do it justice. It had, even then, a great tradition and a deservedly high reputation, and in its poky little garret was doing grand pioneer work, with both restricted facilities and finance. Its semi-private productions were supported by subscriptions and eked out by collections. The aim was high, the conditions austere. The audience sat on hard chairs in an L-shaped upper room which was reached by narrow stairs. The tiny stage was only a foot above the floor – had it been any higher the actors would have bumped their heads on the ceiling – and the proscenium opening was divided by a pillar.[50]

It was in this modest cradle of the English "Little Theatre" that I took my first curtain

---

[49] The play was first performed on Monday, October 15th 1917.

[50] The place: Stockport. The time: October 1901. The result: The formation of Stockport Garrick Society, which this month enters its 75th season of plays as the borough's leading amateur theatre group.

Edwin Heys and his friends had been connected for three years with the production of plays at Stockport Unitarian Sunday School. Teddy, as he was affectionately known, was distressed by the fact that it was impossible during productions at the Sunday School to get from one wing of the stage to the other without undertaking a tortuous journey through the church on the floor above.

For years everyone had thought it an impossible problem. But young Teddy decided that if they didn't want to go over the top of the stage, and it was impossible to go round the back of the stage, the only alternative was to go UNDER the stage.

And so, with the help of his head-strong colleagues he started the molework and tried to dig a passage under the stage. Of course discovery was not far away, as prisoners of war found 40 year's later, there are a lot of problems involved in trying to hide a hole in the ground and disposing of several cubic yards of earth.

The elders were furious and the spadework was forbidden. The lads were indignant and decided to quit. But they were already heavily involved in their next production, which was to be *The Merchant of Venice*. Parts had been cast, props were under construction, the whole production process was underway but they now had no theatre at which to perform.

And so from his home at 31 Tatton Road North, Heaton Moor, on October 16th 1901, Edwin T Heys – signing himself Hon Sec pro tem, and appending the names of 16 of his Unitarian fellows – wrote to a selected band of enthusiasts throughout Stockport, setting out his aims and hopes for a 'proposed new Stockport Dramatic and Literary Society'.

.........The response was greatly encouraging and the society was formed. Fred Pennington remembered that his father had, 40 years earlier, been a member of the Stockport Garrick Society, a short lived group with similar aims to Teddy Heys. Fred suggested the name be adopted, and it was accepted. On February 27th 1902, the curtain rose on Stockport Garrick Society's first production, *The Merchant of Venice*, at the Mechanics Institute. Unusually, the programme asked ladies to remove their hats. Edwin Heys played the Duke. Portia was played by schoolmistress Josephine Gaul: parents of her pupils objected loudly and wanted her sacked for the 'immoral behaviour' of appearing on stage, but Miss Gaul was a determined character and kept her job. *Stockport Advertiser* : October 1975.

call as author. It was not the Gaiety, but the next best thing, and at the moment I could almost have pitied the Queen of Repertory for missing the success the play proved to be. It set new records for the society – its run had to be extended, and it raised the average collection per head an infinitesimal fraction of a penny.

Flushed with triumph I launched on the heart-breaking process of submitting the play to managers. It was nearly seven years before it got a professional production.

Before the end of the First World War and my return to Yorkshire I had one more full-length comedy to my credit – *Young Imeson*. This came at the end of a vexatious period in which I made my first abortive attempt at a drama with my old antagonist, the drunken steelmelter, as its central character. But he defeated me then as in later attempts, and the most persistently nagging theme of my life still remains to be mastered. In despair at my failure I turned to a very trivial idea for a light "society" comedy, another, and a deserved flop, for I ought to have known better than to try my hand at something so foreign to my experience. I called it *A Democrat From Debrett*, and one of its very few productions led to the formation of the earliest West Riding Little Theatre group, the Huddersfield Thespians.

I persevered, mulishly, with the *Democrat* long after I realised it wasn't my cup of tea, then went through an agonising fallow period when I feared I should never write again. This was ended by *Young Imeson*, a comedy-drama about a strike at a jam factory, and a return to my natural vein of Northern humour. Technically superior in every way to *T'Marsdens*, it lacks the latter's sense of fun. I was taking myself too seriously, I suppose, writing consciously and watching all my ps and qs. It has never proved as popular as its better known predecessor, and has, indeed been an unlucky play – at least every production of it in which I have been concerned has been marked by some disappointment to me or some accident to one of the cast. The only performance I've ever missed was during one run of it.

It was rejected by the Stockport Garrick, but taken up by the Marple Dramatic Society and performed for the first time in a Primitive Methodist schoolroom.[51] Two men had a great place in the writing of it – Arthur Lealand and Joe Harrison.

---

[51] The play was performed on March 29th 1919 at the Primitive Methodist School, Compstall.
MR. GREGSON'S NEW PLAY
The title of the new comedy written by Mr. Gregson, who by the way, though a resident of or near Mellor, is in business in Manchester and is Yorkshire by origin, but may we think be reckoned a cosmopolitan............
Young Imeson (the name by the way of a well-known theatrical family who, in old days, were located in a big town bordering on Yorkshire). No doubt the reason why the initial performance was given at Compstall, and especially why the Primitive Methodist School there was chosen as the modest venue for an event of some importance in the annals of local amateur theatricals was that Mr. Gregson is intimately associated with the Methodist Churches in Compstall, Marple and Holly Bank (near Mellor)
*North Cheshire Herald* : April 5th 1919.
Also in a later paper, presumably the *North Cheshire Herald (no date)*, a "news" item
A SCARE
On Wednesday evening, the revived Marple Amateur Dramatic Society gave a performance of Mr. Gregson's new play Young Imeson in the Girls Institute. Early in the evening it got out in the village that the play was in some way connected with the Conscientious Objectors, and everyone had it that a number of discharged soldiers were going to the hall to make a vigorous protest. This story went the rounds of the village as something in the nature of a scare, but the play was produced without interruption.

Lealand was a dynamic, ugly little man – one of the livest and most voluble I've known. Beginning life as an agricultural labourer, he'd risen from an unskilled job to that of manager of the C.W.S. jam works at Middleton. He'd worked his way through Ruskin College, was a very keen socialist, speaking and writing for the Labour Party with fiery fluency. He was also something of an inventive genius – had, in fact, invented the labour-saving machines I gave to my hero with his permission. Before beginning the play I wanted to get the technical details of jam-making absolutely right. Lealand replied to my list of forty-odd questions on a sheet of paper two feet wide and three long. I ought to have used the man himself as a model for my strike leader and hero, but I was afraid he'd split the play down the seams.

But *Young Imeson*, to me, will always be Joe Harrison's play. We first met in the W.E.A. elocution class and became fast friends from the start. We were in the Shakespearean company together. He was the most generous of men, but had too low an opinion of his own abilities. He identified himself completely with my ambitions and hopes – rejoicing and grieving over my ups and downs as though they were his own. He'd a tactful, quizzical way of sharing any windfalls that came his way. Heaven knows we both needed them badly. I remember he gave me my first overcoat. It was one he'd been given by a well-to-do relative who'd just presented him with a second, and better one he'd no further use for. Joe was a picture of comical apology when he explained that he would have liked me to have had the newer coat but he had to wear it himself in case the giver, not seeing him in it, would think he'd no use for secondhand clothing! His commonest way of helping was to buy some article of clothing for young Florence. Even the proudest, most independent Yorkshire parents will fall for this face-saving device. His kindnesses were legion.

As we worked in fairly close proximity, it became our habit to meet daily during our weekday lunch breaks, and I began to talk over difficulties in my plays with him. When I toured my own amateur production of *T'Marsdens* around the wartime hospitals, with Florence as "Anne" and myself as "Ezra", he played "Sim Umpleby" with a depth and sincerity I've never seen equalled. [52]

It was during this tour that he fell ill and was laid up for months with sciatica and heart trouble. But although he grew slowly frailer, he was always serene and cheerful during my lunch-hour visits.

During one of these visits I outlined the plot of *Young Imeson*. Before we knew where we were, we had begun to work out a scenario. Day by day we hammered out the details, and soon I was taking each day's instalment of dialogue for his comments and suggestions. I don't think I ever worked so consistently as during those two or three months. I simply couldn't face his disappointment when I turned up empty-handed.

It was no empty collaboration. The day I took him the last pages of the script were

---

[52] *T'Marsdens* – the theme is unconventional and deals with the proposal of the Borough Council Arts Committee to introduce a 'life model' into the art class studio of a small and unenlightened West Riding town (presumed to be Brighouse). This daring innovation shocks the mock modesty and disturbs the prejudices of the inhabitants. *Hyde Reporter* : May 3rd 1919.
Sim Umpleby – the most indignant and uncompromising leader of them all, an ernest but rather narrow-minded Christian bursting with righteous indignation at the "scandalous proposal" of the Arts Committee.

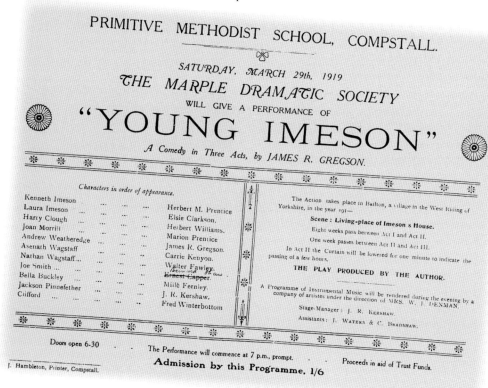

*Programme: Primitive Methodists, Compstall (1919)* (CA)

*Programme: Middleton I.L.P. (1915)* (CA)

Programme:
*Sons of Temperance (1914)* (CA)

**The Order of the Sons of Temperance**
Wesley Division No. 868.

# PUBLIC MEETING

IN SUSSEX STREET WESLEYAN SCHOOL
ON WEDNESDAY, DECEMBER 2nd, 1914

## PROGRAMME BY THE HEATON PARK DRAMATIC SOCIETY ::

| | | |
|---|---|---|
| Song | " Roses " | Miss Daisy Hawthorn |
| Recital | "The Dandy Fifth" | Mr. Jas. R. Gregson |
| Song | "Love the Pedlar" | Miss F. Gregson |
| Humorous Selection | | Mr. C. Ramsden |
| Recital | "The Taming of the Shrew" *Act II. Scene I.* | Miss F. Chadwick & Mr. Edgar Watterson |
| Song | "Happy Summer Song" | Miss F. Gregson |
| Recital | "Uncle Podgers" | Mr. J. R. Gregson |
| Song | "When Jack and I were Children" | Miss D. Hawthorn |
| Humorous Selection | | Mr. C. Ramsden |

**Comedy** "Clear Proof" **The Mummers**

| | |
|---|---|
| Mr. Merton | Mr. J. R. Gregson |
| Servant | Mr. E. Watterson |
| Miss Wheeler | Miss F. Chadwick |
| Mrs. Merton | Miss F. Gregson |

*Scene : Mr. Merton's Study.* *Time : Present*

**Chair taken at 7-45 by Coun. J. P. McDougall, G**

## ADMISSION FREE.

"Sons" offer best Benefits. Men, Women and Children ma
Apply at the School any Wednesday Evening.

## Marple Dramatic Society.

# T' MARSDENS

A COMEDY IN THREE ACTS
BY JAMES R. GREGSON,

will be presented by
Mr. Gregson and friends, in the
: : Girls' Institute, Marple, on : :
Wednesday, October 16th, and
Saturday, October 19th, 1918.
Doors Open at 6.30 p.m.   Commence at 7.0 p.m.
Carriages at 9.30 p.m.

Invitation:
*Marple Dramatic Society T'Marsdens (1918)* (CA)

This invitation will admit one person only.
on WEDNESDAY, October 16th.

typical. I read the closing scene. He listened, as always, with closed eyes. I had to pause in the reading whilst he endured an attack of pain. When I came to the end, he repeated the curtain tag to himself once or twice, then said, "Ay, Dick. It'll do. I think we've pulled it off."

Another pause as he thought it over once again, then a shocked look of dismay came over his wasted features.

"Hey up! We've made a right mess of it! We have that! Do yer know we've made Laura Imeson commit bigamy?"

"What?"

"We haven't killed her husband off!"

We hadn't. We promptly set about repairing the omission. It meant remodelling the whole middle act, incidentally improving the construction considerably and incidentally presenting whoever would play "Laura" with a great opportunity for a piece of quiet, emotional acting.

Joe didn't live to see the play produced. During the early Autumn of 1918 he was back with us in *T'Marsdens*, but one night we had to find a substitute for him at short notice. He was down with 'flu and pneumonia.

He died on the first Armistice Day. I saw him for the last time that morning. Just as I got up to leave him, the bells began to ring. I went back to the office, dazed and stricken through gathering crowds whose almost demented antics meant nothing to me.

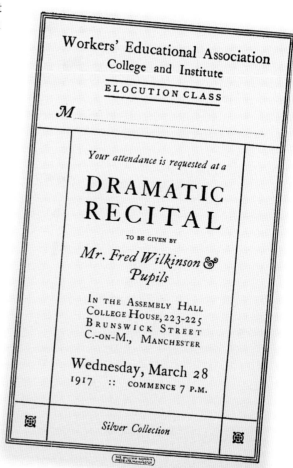

Programme:
*Worker's Educational*
*Association (1917) (CA)*

# Chapter Twelve

Early in 1919 I read in the *Manchester Guardian* that a Mr. Alfred Wareing proposed to launch a Yorkshire Repertory venture at the Theatre Royal, Huddersfield. [53] Up to then I had had no luck in hawking *T'Marsdens* and, indeed, although the play had already had some forty performances, I had not drawn any royalties, had not earned a penny from any of my writing.

Thinking that here if anywhere was my heaven-sent opportunity, I hastily retyped *T'Marsdens* and posted a copy with speed to Wareing. I heard nothing from him, beyond the usual formal acknowledgement, for some months. Then, just when I'd abandoned hope once again, came a most enthusiastic letter. Could I go to see him?

He met me with flattering courtesy and charm. He took me to his club for a meal – a meal with a bewildering variety of courses – tactfully ignoring the inexperience which made me fill myself with hors-d'oeuvres and rolls and plunged me into confusion with the knives and forks, though he seemed surprised that I refused all drinks. He praised my play even to my satisfaction. It was evident to him, he assured me, that I was a born

*Theatre Royal, Huddersfield*
*(Noel Spencer: Scrapbook of Huddersfield, 1941)*
Image courtesy of Kirklees Museums and Galleries

playwright with a sure sense of the theatre. But that was not enough. What I needed was a thorough, practical knowledge of it – by working in it. He was prepared to help me to get it. He was willing to engage me as his assistant acting-manager with a few

---

[53] Alfred Wareing (1876-1942). After his apprenticeship to Herbert Beerbohm Tree and Benson's Company, he went on to found the first Scottish National Theatre in 1909, and subsequently the resident company at the Theatre Royal, Huddersfield.
A PENNINE MALVERN
During the years that Gray pioneered Continental ways and plays in Cambridge, a pioneer from the earliest days of repertory, Alfred Wareing, attempted on a modest scale something similar in the less congenial setting of the Theatre Royal, Huddersfield, of which he had become manager in 1918. The theatre was part of a commercial circuit with companies for the greater part of the year, but Wareing introduced an annual summer 'repertory season' between 1921 and 1931. Frequently this was provided by an established Shakespearean company (Benson, Baynton, Doran and on one occasion the Old Vic), but Wareing favoured a more contemporary and Continental programme, billed as 'International Masterpieces', which included several of Pirandello's plays, notably the world premiere of *Lazzaro* in 1929. Wareing's 'incredible gallantry' in trying to make Huddersfield 'a Pennine Malvern' (Ivor Brown's verdict) was at least ten years premature. Pirandello and International Masterpieces were still caviare to the general playgoer at Huddersfield or elsewhere, and the owners of the Theatre Royal decided to turn it into a 'twice nightly' house, provoking Wareing's resignation.
G.Powell and A.Jackson, *The Repertory Movement; A History of Regional Theatre in Britain*, Cambridge University Press, 1984.

light, almost nominal front-of-the-house duties.  But my real work would be to learn every job in the theatre, tackling each one seriously a week in turn, scene-shifting, lighting, stage-management, selling programmes and chocolates even.  As he was really creating a job for me, in order that I could really learn my craft, he couldn't offer me more than a modest salary, say, three pounds a week.

I felt this was a wonderful, a most generous offer.  The only snag was that I was already earning more than five pounds a week.

He told me not to decide anything in a hurry.  My decision wouldn't affect his determination to produce the play. It would be one of, if not the, first he would put on.  As a token of this, he drafted a simple agreement which I signed there and then, giving him a twelvemonth's option on the comedy, in return for which he gave me a cheque for five pounds.

Florence and I could hardly sleep that night.  We gloated over that cheque – my first earnings as an author, the first cheque that had ever borne my name – scarcely able to believe our eyes.  We began adding noughts to that five, and, still dazed by our dreams, we decided that an "Irishman's rise" of two pounds a week was a small, and would be a temporary, sacrifice.

So, in due course – December 1919 – to be precise – I stood in the foyer of the Huddersfield Theatre Royal in all the glory of a secondhand, made-over dinner suit which had swallowed two weeks salary, receiving my first lesson in managerial tact and salesmanship, and feeling horribly raw and provincial by the side of my suave, polished, cosmopolitan mentor.  As I watched Wareing "doing the lah-di-dah", as I called it privately, fussing around and almost fawning upon the more expensive patrons, I wondered whether I should ever learn the mannered tricks and shallow insincerities of my brave new world – whether, indeed, they were worth learning.

Up to that day I had met no professional actors except Wareing, and their theatrical extravagance of speech and manner, their gushing endearments and so forth came as something of an unpleasant shock, causing me to curl up inside.

Another shock that day had been the painful discovery that the theatre was not the simple palace of pure delight I had, in my green innocence, imagined, but a place of business. That the public didn't clamour for admittance but had to be tempted, cajoled and even tricked into coming in, and once in, had to be persuaded into spending as much as possible on chocolates, cigarettes, programmes and drinks; that the money taken at the doors barely covered our running expenses and that our profit depended as much on double whiskies as on drama.  This elementary lesson in theatrical economics was underlined by the ledgers and stock books, the handling of which would be part of my various "nominal" duties. To bookkeeping was added the job of shopkeeping.  I had to study the taste of the clients who frequented the theatre's four bars and to keep track of their womenfolk's fickle fashion in chocolates.  I made the discovery that the presence of an opera company would send up the sales of Guinness in the stage bar a dozen times over, that melodrama fostered the consumption of draught beer, and musical comedy that of gin and short drinks generally.

During all my time at the Theatre Royal I was a strict teetotaler and as I had to take visiting managers and favoured patrons for drinks and had to take something myself for politeness sake, I had an arrangement with all the barmaids. They would ask, "The usual for you, Mr Gregson?" and I would nod and be served with green peppermint and soda. One seasoned toper, in whose company I was forced to swallow three or four of these innocuous concoctions, solemnly warned Wareing that his young manager was an absinthe addict!

But I had not only to sell the etceteras. I had to sell the weekly attraction, too; to draft the newspaper adverts and daybills, to write the preliminary puffs and reading matter for insertion in the programmes, and correct the printer's proofs.

In fact it seemed to me at that time that the least important job, and last to be thought about, was the presentation of the play itself.

But, as Wareing had promised, I tackled every job in the theatre in turn, taking spells in the box-office, the various pay-boxes, serving behind the bars, acting as usher, programme-boy and chocolate-seller. I put in a week with the charwomen, and I carried bottled beer (four dozen at a time) in place of the handyman, from the street level to the gallery bar almost in the roof of the theatre. And so that art might be served as well as commerce, I took turns as call-boy, scene-shifter, property-man, fly-man and electrical assistant. There was one blush making flying matinee when I worked the "star spot" on Pavlova, and almost ruined her famous

*Anna Pavlova (MM)*

Swan Dance, getting so interested in what she was doing that I swung my "spot" through the proscenium, nearly blinded the Upper Circle, and was only recalled to actuality by the furious, muttered imprecations of the great ballerina. [54] I was to have been presented to the great lady after the matinee, but decided I shouldn't be too popular, and kept well out of the way.

It was a hard, full life. On the go six days a week from nine-thirty in the morning

---

[54] Anna Pavlova (1881-1931). The Russian-born ballet dancer Pavlova trained at the Imperial Ballet School in St. Petersburg. From 1912 she made London her base, living at Ivy House, Golders Green. In 1907 she created Folkine's "Dying Swan" which became her signature role.

until eleven at night. It was all the more difficult because when I'd been there less than a fortnight, Wareing's acting-manager walked out on him, and I was forthwith promoted to full responsibility in a job of which I really knew nothing. As Wareing often went away for days or a week at a time, I should have been in a bad way over and over again but for the help of a staff who not only knew their job but had a real interest in it and, like most West Riding workers, so long as you respected their ability and independence and didn't patronise them, took pride in giving you a square deal.

But arduous as my job was it had its compensations, not the least of which was being able to watch a play, night after night, for a whole week, very often with Wareing at one's elbow to point out a virtue here, a flaw there in writing, production or acting. He had a real flair and love for the theatre. He never stinted criticism or advice. With his long experience and unerring judgement he was a superb teacher.

*Francis Benson: on the way up (MM)*

*Francis Benson: arrived (MM)*

Wareing had other claims on my gratitude and loyalty. One was his ambition to raise the status of the Huddersfield Theatre Royal which was then a number 3 touring date. Besides offering higher percentages to number 2 managements, he made use of any personal pull he had with his fellow Old Bensonians, many of them now stars and actor-managers in their own right. [55] He never minded being a beggar for the theatre. Another idea of his was to induce some producers to give their new shows a try-out week with us, as a kind of extended dress rehearsal, before putting them on in London. He was the first to press this revolutionary idea of "trying it on the dog" and the result was that Huddersfield saw number 1 London companies at number 3 prices.

And another result, even more valuable to me, was that I was able to watch first class producers and actors at close quarters and study their methods and their "vehicles",

One notable occasion was the visit of Henry Ainley in a play called *The Jest*. [56] It was a fine production and gave me my first glimpse of the then new directional lighting

---

[55] Sir Francis Robert Benson (1858-1939), commonly known as Frank Benson or F R Benson, was an actor and theatre manager. He founded his own company in 1883 and produced all but two of Shakespeare's plays.

[56] Henry Hinchliffe Ainley (1879-1945) was a Shakespearean stage and screen actor. He made his professional stage debut for F R Benson's company of actors and later joined Herbert Beerbohm Tree's company.

being used with imagination. Ainley, in fact toured all his own lighting equipment, even travelling his own switchboard. I watched with amazement the setting of floods and spots at various angles, some of them on the ceiling.

But in spite of its effects and wonderful stage pictures, the play didn't appeal to our public, and I grew more apologetic with every nightly return of our receipts I took to him. But nothing seemed to disturb his sunny serenity. One night he said, "Well, you like it, Mr. Wareing likes it and I like it! That's three of us happy!" Another night when I wondered aloud why he'd chosen a play he felt must lose him money, he said, "Well, I made so much money out of that pot-boiler, *Quinneys*, that I felt I ought to spend some of it in justifying my existence!"

*Henry Ainley*
*(MM)*

There was another thing puzzled me. The two leading parts were of equal strength, but Ainley was playing against the audience all the time, and Claud Rains was getting all the sympathy.[57] But when I asked Ainley, "Rains' part is the actor-manager's part – why did you give it to him?, he smiled and said "Well, you see, Claude's a good boy. He's always done his best for me in poor parts. It's time he had his chance!"

This real generosity, so rare in the theatre was typical of Ainley. He also had the integrity and humility of the true artist. Careless, boyish, all too easy to approach, he treated everyone with the supreme courtesy of one who recognised no inferiors. I learned much more than stagecraft from him.

*Claud Rains*
*(MM)*

The first play to have its first ever performance at the Theatre Royal was *The Heart Of A Child* – a dramatic version of a novel by "Frank Danby", made by her son, Gilbert Frankau.[58] As part of my education I was to make notes of anything which struck me as wrong at the dress rehearsal and report to Wareing.

*Gilbert Frankau*
*(MM)*

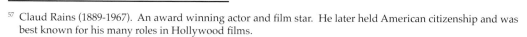

[57] Claud Rains (1889-1967). An award winning actor and film star. He later held American citizenship and was best known for his many roles in Hollywood films.

[58] Gilbert Frankau (1884-1952) was a popular novelist. His mother Julia Frankau (1864-1916) wrote under the name Frank Danby. His novels, while having conventional content, also contained material from his own conservative politics, and meditations on Jewish identity in the climate of the times. His political ambitions were frustrated by the fact he was a divorcee (he married three times), which was not acceptable in the Conservative party of the time. He wrote a 1933 article "As a Jew I am not against Hitler" for the *Daily Express*, shortly after Adolf Hitler had come to power in Germany; he later retracted his position.

I thought the play the most utter tosh, but Wareing had prophesied it would be as big a success as *Peg O'My Heart*, so I wasn't unduly disappointed by its quality, nor was I surprised when it broke all records during the week I had to watch it.

Frankau travelled from London with the company, and almost his first question to me was about the advance bookings. He was a lean, hungry-looking creature, bursting with a self-confidence I secretly envied. He was neat but shabby; his suit well-cared for but shiny at the seams, his boots neatly patched, his linen collar carefully darned. It was evident he'd been passing through a lean time.

How lean I was to learn before the week was out. When the curtain was up on the Thursday evening performance, he came into my office and insisted that I went with him to look at the "house". Reluctantly, I followed him to the back of the Dress Circle.

"I'm going to give you an object lesson!" he said, as we looked through the glass weather screen. "Look at that house!"

I looked at him instead. I guessed something of what was coming.

"Isn't it a lovely sight?" he asked. I agreed.

"A gorgeous house – a record house – for this theatre, isn't it?" I agreed again.

"And the play's tripe, isn't it ?"
"Bloody tripe!" – I couldn't help it.

*Matheson Lang* (MM)

"Bloody tripe, as you say! Now listen, highbrow! But keep your eye on that house. For ten years I've tried my damnedest to earn a living by writing the best that was in me. I've written my guts out – written good stuff, too. For ten years, mind you! And for what? Damn all! You saw the boots I came in! For ten years I've written and written, sponging on my family to keep going. So at last I decided to give the public what they want. What you call tripe! But tripe pays, Gregson, as you'll learn when you stop looking down your nose!"

As graciously as I could, I told him I knew it already. "You think you do! But you'll know it a damned sight better when you've been through it as I have!"

Matheson Lang was another Old Bensonian whom Wareing persuaded, for old times' sake, to give the theatre a lift up. [59] The visit proved another most instructive week, for he was rehearsing a new play called *The Phantom Ship*, and Lang was a much better producer than an actor – one of the six best in the world in my estimation – and I found

---

[59] Matheson Lang (1879-1946) was a Canadian film actor and playwright. In 1916, he became one of the first major theatre stars to act in a silent film, by playing Shylock in the *Merchant of Venice*, with his wife as Portia. Lang, in 1913, created one of his most memorable roles, the title character in *Mr. Wu*. He reprised this part in a 1919 silent film, and became so indentified with the role that he titled his 1940 memoirs *Mr. Wu Looks Back*.

him very ready to explain his reasons for this move, or that trimming of a line. Routine work went by the board that week, I'm afraid. He was much taken by my idea of a play based on my steel foundry experience and my feud with the smelter, and I was encouraged by him to have a second shot at writing it. Somehow I squeezed it into my crowded schedule and completed a first draft although I realised I was beaten long before I reached the final curtain. I sent Lang the draft, but only to prove to him that I'd failed again.

All was grist to Wareing's mill, and when a film company wanted a theatre for the location shots in a back-stage story called *Nothing Else Matters*, he made no bones about renting the Royal to them, and our patrons who'd come to see *Candida* that week, were invited to stay and take part in the film's "crowd" scenes. As the star of the film was Betty Balfour, we had bigger audiences that week for Shaw than we'd any right to expect. [60]

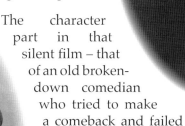

*Betty Balfour*
*(MM)*

The character part in that silent film – that of an old broken-down comedian who tried to make a comeback and failed – was played by Hugh E. Wright a sensitive, intelligent artist who never got the public recognition he deserved, possibly because his work was too subtle and his characterizations so true to life that the public couldn't see the artistry. [61]

He was thin and bony, with a wrinkled face and the dark, tragic eyes of a monkey. He had the most beautiful and most expressive hands of any actor or artist I've known. He used them to wonderful effect in the shop where he was doing his music hall turn only to break down and get "the bird". Through the whole of one long afternoon I watched him trying to give the producer all he asked

*Hugh E Wright*
*(MM)*

---

[60] Betty Balfour (1903-1978) was the only international star of the British silent cinema, the most popular actress in Britain in the 20's and in 1927 was named by the Daily Mirror as the country's favourite world star. Balfour's sound debut , The Brat (1930), was only moderately successful, and her popularity waned in the period of the talkies. Britain's 'Queen of Happiness' was anything but happy in her private life. Her marriage to composer Jimmy Campbell ended in divorce in 1941, and after a failed comeback in 1952 she attempted suicide. Sadly, she was a recluse for the last twenty years of her life.

[61] Hugh E Wright (1879-1940) was a French born, actor and screenwriter, who spent all his career in Britain.

for. The scene grew richer and richer in detail, more and more poignant in effect as rehearsal followed rehearsal. It was a marvel how that frail figure stood up to the incessant, increasing strain – a marvel, too, how exacting and insatiable the producer grew. I ached with the strain of merely watching the strain, and I wondered when that taut, keyed-up spirit would snap under it. But it didn't, and the actual "shooting" began. I wanted to weep at such superb artistry. Then the producer announced that the next "take" would be the last. Hughie was even better than ever. Then, just half a second before Hughie should have shrunk away from an imaginary orange, a real one came hurtling down from the producer in the gallery. The aim was marvellous; the orange landed between Hughie's feet with a sickening squelsh. The effect was brilliant but cruel – Hughie's start and look of reproach were something that no art could ever have compassed. And, somehow, the tragedy of that broken-down, red-nosed comedian had become Hughie's own. The tears he was shedding were no fake.

I felt the producer had gone too far. The showman had insulted the artist. The producer must have felt something of the same, for he turned to hurry away, saying over his shoulder, "Be a pal! Take Hughie to the bar and get him anything he wants!"

It was two hours and eight Guinnesses later that I bundled Hughie into a cab, soothed if not consoled.

The following Christmas he came to us for Pantomime. He tore *Aladdin* in two, playing "Abanazer" as carefully and meticulously as a character in a modern comedy. He took his share in all the routine gags, but he had one entirely his own which began on his first entrance and grew, scene by scene, into a perfect sequence of serio-comic invention. For this gag he had a silent stooge – a local girl who, dressed in rags and munching an everlasting apple, followed him through the show like a dog, throwing him out of his stride whenever she appeared. Every such interruption was the cue and occasion for a heart-to-heart talk with the urchin, full of wise fun and touched at times with genuine pathos. His patter was inimitable and the whole thing had the wistful quality of the mature Chaplin. I watched every bit of his scenes, two shows a day, for seven weeks.

*Herbert Lomas (MM)*

Another actor who had much to teach me during the week he was in Huddersfield as well as later was Herbert Lomas.[62] I had seen his debut with Miss Horniman in

---

[62] Herbert Lomas (1887-1961), born in Burnley, Lancashire, appeared in 40 films in a career lasting from 1931 to 1955. His first film appearance was in *Hobson's Choice* (1931). He first made his name in Annie Horniman's company at the Gaiety Theatre, Manchester.

a tiny part in a curtain-raiser by Harold Brighouse. I had seen him as "Nat Jeffcote" in *Hindle Wakes* after storming London in the part. That week I saw him as the finest "Abraham Lincoln" that the most exacting could desire; a performance as finished and convincing as the make-up over which I watched him take such pains. Later he was to give some of my own creations that same quality of life and truth. Not all Wareing's "brainwaves" came off. One comical fiasco was a performance of *Elijah*

*Allington-Charsley Opera Company (c1920) at the Stockton Hippodrome: Note the billboard – 'One of the Largest Touring Opera Companies in the World'.*
*Photograph courtesy of www.picturestockton.co.uk*

by an opera company who shall be nameless.[63] Wareing knew that Huddersfield folk were fond of oratorio, but I doubt if he realised how much they knew about it. His idea that a dramatised treatment of it might be popular was sound enough; what he didn't foresee was the scrambled treatment it got, almost inevitably, from a touring company with perhaps insufficient time for rehearsal. The settings were makeshift. The fire from heaven missed its cue, and when it did fall, did so with a speed and

---

[63] The *Elijah* given by the Allington-Charsley Company at the Theatre Royal last night was a qualified success. The principals were satisfying, the work of the chorus was shaky, and the production itself had points both good and mediocre..............The chorus was augmented by members of the Huddersfield Choral Society, but there was apparently little unanimity between the company and the Huddersfield singers. The choruses were often spoiled by false openings, and the Baal choruses, from which we had naturally expected a good deal, were very disappointing performances. Yet despite these faults the work of the principals was so good that it was, after all, a very enjoyable performance.
*Huddersfield Examiner*: December 17th 1919.

punch that crushed the gimcrack altar absolutely flat. To help out with the choruses, Wareing had enlisted the aid of the local Choral Societies. They knew those choruses backwards; the company didn't. From the stage came uncertain bleatings; from the wings the glorious, thundering music of some of the finest choirs in England. True, the amateurs had copies and the professionals had to sing from memory – obviously sketchy and incomplete. The two sections got out of step – the amateurs a couple of bars ahead at least. Then, from some disgruntled local, a copy of the score came hurtling from the wings. There was a scramble for it amongst the professionals, whose need was greater than their pride. They clustered round it with relief.

The leading tenor of that company had been sacked the night before, after singing *Faust*. At the morning run through of the score, he had had an argument as to the singing of some passage or other. When they reached this point in the performance, the conductor tapped a signal to remind the tenor to follow his lead. But the singer went on regardless, drew his property sword, leaned over the footlights, and tried to decapitate the conductor.

The education which Wareing had promised me certainly proved both valuable and varied, but after a year of it, I began to feel that I was paying pretty dearly for it, was both overworked and underpaid. I had really no time for writing, and the repertory project, with my chance of a professional tryout, seemed to have faded into limbo. Things came to a head early in 1921 over some trifling point of routine. I was feeling the strain of a month of twice-daily pantomime in an understaffed theatre, losing my temper, and, like those who do not lose it quickly but bottle it up, I lost it thoroughly and said some rather bitter things. He reminded me I was talking to my employer, whereupon I promptly wrote out my month's notice. Whilst working it, we communicated in writing.

The breach lasted two years by which time I was in sight of my first London production. There was a touch of comedy about our reconciliation. Taking the family to a matinee and wishing to avoid meeting him, instead of using the foyer, I went in at the Pit Entrance, and, of course, it had to happen that he should be there. Thinking we had booked for the Pit, naturally, he insisted we should wait a moment, dashed to the Box Office and returned with four stalls tickets. He ushered us personally to our seats – we might have been Royalty. The joke was that the seats were always the most difficult to sell – near the front, and too close to the drums – goodness knows how often I'd tried to sell them in the past and failed! He took the tickets we'd paid for without looking at them – they were for much better seats – and Florence and I had a quiet laugh, wishing we could see his face when he realised how he'd put his foot in it. But he turned the tables on us neatly. He was back in no time with two splendiferous boxes of chocolate for the children worth much more than we'd paid for our seats.

In the years that followed we had many happy times under his management. He starred the pair of us in a variety bill which my one-actor, *Liddy*, tore in two as thoroughly as Hugh Wright's "Abanazer" had torn *Aladdin*. Florence's performance in the title part was as good as any acting I've seen by a woman, and her get-up so true and convincing that one artist mistook her for a dresser and asked her to get her something to drink! After this Wareing often gave us special weeks in which we appeared in my plays. He also paid me a very great compliment by putting my portrait in the company of Shaw, Galsworthy, Bennett, Barrie and Pinero, in the mural painting which spans the proscenium of the theatre.

Like too many in the profession, Wareing was a better actor off the stage than on, but he brought to the theatre both fine taste and a great devotion. His service to the drama was not flawless – whose is? – but it was ungrudging and sincere. He did great things for me, and I like to remember that he called me his "sea-green incorruptible".

The day after I left Wareing I began a six month's spell as manager of a new cinema in Huddersfield.[64] It was not a happy experience, in spite of the six pounds a week salary, for I missed the warm pulse of the theatre, and I found I had nine bosses instead of one. The nine put together hadn't as much artistic sensibility as Wareing had in his little finger, and all but one knew much less about films than I did, which was precious little. They were all worthy tradesmen I have no doubt – I remember they included a dentist, an ironmonger, a tinsmith and a drysalter – but they'd very little faith either in me or each other. They'd sunk more of their hard-won pennies in the venture than was comfortable and they were inclined to be cheeseparing, and to grudge the ship its ha'porth of tar. The worst of the lot was a miserly creature who smoked the cheapest of cigarettes, nipping each one neatly into two halves to make it go further. There were always a couple or more of them hanging about the place, counting the house or reporting shortcomings on the part of the staff. Then, late one Saturday night, as I was preparing for home, I was told they were dissatisfied with the discipline, or lack of it, and I was asked to take a week's salary in lieu of notice. In short I was sacked.

It was a sickening blow. I think that seeing poor Florence's face whiten as I told her the shameful news was the worst moment of my life. Her loyal, warm-hearted indignation was no comfort. I've never been so near to utter despair. For the life of me I couldn't see where I'd failed my nine cheeseparers. I'd grudged them as little as I'd grudged Wareing, with far less reason, moreover.

But there was no time for post mortems or self-reproach. We had to consider the future. It looked black enough in all conscience. We were not only on our backsides – we were in the basement – heavily in debt to my parents and friends.

We had moved into a small, dark house near my family in Brighouse. It was in a cul-de-sac with communal privies at its blind end. Unsatisfactory as it was, we had felt ourselves lucky to get it on condition that we bought the tasteless, heavy furniture it housed, at an exorbitant price. We'd been paying back our borrowings at the rate of two pounds a week, but we still owed over a hundred pounds.

The prospect was bleak enough, but the actuality of the next few months proved worse. Try as I might, I could get no regular job of any kind. Sinking what pride I had left, I made myself a nuisance to anyone I thought might help, but it led to nothing. In desperation I even tried hawking soap and washing powder from door to door, a disguised form of begging which went down badly and met with disheartening result.

Coming home footsore and hopeless one evening, I saw an old schoolmate pushing a

---

[64] The Grand Picture Theatre, Manchester Road, Huddersfield opened in 1921, with seating for 878. It was then taken over by Union Cinemas, followed by ABC Cinema, closing in 1957. Adapted then into a night club. Its more recent reincarnation is, perhaps inevitably, as a supermarket. (See illustration p98).

The Grand Picture Theatre

handcart loaded with timber up a slight rise. I gave him a hand. He was a joiner in a modest way. The encounter led to his finding me part-time work as his labourer at a shilling an hour. I averaged about a pound a week. Thanks to Florence's miraculous economy, we managed to exist on this, eked out by various occasional fees I drew from amateur performances of my plays.

Fighting desperately against the feeling of being utterly unwanted, I filled in my time between chasing will-o'-the-wisp jobs, by sending my plays round the managers and writing articles and stories for the newspapers. The job still eluded me, the managers showed no interest in my plays, and editors returned my offerings with unfailing regularity.

It was a hell of a time for me. What it was like for Florence I don't care to remember. Our second child, Joan, wasn't too well – as difficult and fractious as young Florence was amiable and quiet. The strain of those days was to take its toll of my wife later, but, at the time, the struggle brought out every fine, fighting quality she possessed. But for her I think I should have gone under completely.

But the thing that worried Florence most was not the hard labour of nursing two children, nor washing, cooking and cleaning for the family, nor the grind of poverty. It was the dingy, stuffy house itself with its florid dark wallpaper, and she didn't rest until she'd thinned out some of the ugliest furniture and given the walls a new look with brown packing paper. The change was a tonic to our morale, summed up by her in characteristic fashion, "Taste is cheap enough if you have it!"

One other glowing spot in this dreary period I must recall, if only to record my gratitude. One of our creditors demanded sudden repayment of the fifty pounds we owed him. At my wits' end I approached a man I'd met only once and for a very brief moment in connection with a film. His name was George Jesson. He heard my story and without hesitation took me to his bank, cashed a cheque and handed me the fifty pounds. He refused to take my I.O.U. for it, explaining, "I know you'll pay me back when you can, but in case anything happened to me before you could, there'll be nothing to show and you won't find yourself faced with the job of having to meet it before you're ready!" Much as the money meant to us, the manner of its lending meant a great deal more. It restored something of my self-respect.

Apart from my unsuccessful attempts at journalism, and the second attempt, for Matthew Lang, at my foundry play, the only product of this dismal period was a one-act play which I called *Melchisadek*, though it didn't see the light until 1923. [65] It is haunted by the pessimism and bitterness of those months; its humour, such as it possesses, is grim and harsh; it has not the faintest gleam of hope. It was one of the plays which insisted on being written, but it came slowly and with many attempts to cast it aside. I hated every

---

[65] J R Gregson speaking at the Garrick Theatre, Stockport. Mr. Gregson called Melchisadek the grimmest and saddest and most despondent play he had ever written or hoped to write, and his descriptions proved to be in no way exaggerated. *Melchisadek* is a well wrought character study of Yorkshire life, but hardly a play for polite drawing-room production. It is terribly grim and is only saved from utter sordidness by the threads of warm humanity which runs through the play and characters.
Unattributed newspaper cutting, Gregson Scrapbooks, West Yorkshire Archives, Calderdale, GRE2.

It should, therefore, come as no surprise to learn that Melchisadek has been translated into Russian. Melchisadek was a king of Salem (Jerusalem) and priest of the most High God. The name means 'King of Righteousness'.

moment it stole from my life, though it ended a practically barren stretch of six years. What few performances it has had have been at my own hands.

One other person and one other development claim their places in this Huddersfield chapter.

The first evening I donned my made-over dinner-suit and stood beside Wareing in the foyer of the Royal, I was introduced to Sidney Crowther, a local journalist, with a great interest in drama and music.[66] He was a year or two younger than I, slim, fresh-coloured, fair-haired – and as shabby as I was in my day clothes. When he grinned at me, "So this is the Yorkshire Ibsen?" I guessed that Wareing's enthusiasm, or keen scent for publicity, had given me a lot to live down.

But Sidney and I had much in common – a modest, meagre start in life; our way to make in the world; very much the same views on art, literature and politics. It wasn't long before we were firm friends and he'd appointed himself my unpaid publicity agent, and set himself the job of building me a local reputation.

After an accident in the factory which had lost him two fingers and months of employment, he'd made a fresh start on the *Huddersfield Examiner* as junior reporter, and had just reached the stage when he could afford to pay for a little domestic help for his widowed mother. She was an arthritic cripple for whom he'd had to be both breadwinner and nurse. A true journalist, he knew Huddersfield inside out, every phase of its workaday and leisure life and a great deal about its domestic drama and comedy. He'd a keen eye for the quirks of its many "characters", and an inside knowledge of every event of any consequence. His memory for detail struck me as little short of miraculous.

Very early in our acquaintance, Sidney introduced me to his old schoolmaster, Robert Montgomery, a teacher too true to his profession to make a career of it.[67] He still kept

---

[66]  Mr. Sidney Crowther (1895-1981 ).
Mr. Crowther was a leading figure in the cultural life of Huddersfield. The small, pipe-smoking man who invariably wore a Basque beret, was music critic of the *Huddersfield Examiner* and never missed a Huddersfield Choral Society concert in 60 years. For 20 years he wrote notices of Huddersfield musical events on a freelance basis for the Yorkshire Post over the initials S H C. During his long journalistic career, he wrote the histories of the Huddersfield Choral Society, the Philharmonic, the Glee and Madrigal, the Colne Valley Male Voice Choir and the Huddersfield Thespians, of which, with the playwright James R Gregson, he was the founder 60 years ago.
*Yorkshire Post* : November 7th 1981.

[67]  Pen-Pictures of Important People
No.10.Mr. Robert Montgomery B.A.by 'Ariel'.
It was not merely the camaraderie of the home, but the culture which, without a touch of priggery, mingled so freely with it, that made a visit so delightful an experience.......Discussions sometimes waxed furious, and the most unorthodox opinions were allowed expression, but even in the heat of debate tempers were never lost and comradeship reigned supreme. To spend an evening in that domestic 'school' was in itself an education, quickening the mind, kindling the imagination, and provoking thought even where one disagreed.
Mr. Montgomery is a Highlander. Born in 1859 near Campbelltown, he was educated at the village school, and subsequently went on to Glasgow University. He studied there for some time, but took his degree at London University, beginning his career as a schoolmaster while he was still working for it. He taught mathematics in the Alan Glen School (now the West of Scotland Technical College), but English has always been his favourite subject, and when he came to Huddersfield in 1894 it was in this that he specialised.
From 1894 to 1909 he was headmaster of what was then the joint school in New North Road. When this school was divided into two, and the Huddersfield College was formed, Mr. Montgomery was made headmaster of the new joint school at Hillhouse, and there he has been ever since. He will complete his fifteen year's service at Hillhouse next July, when he intends to retire, and I understand he will remove to London.
*Huddersfield Examiner*: April 15th 1924.

in touch with any of his old pupils who desired it through an Old Students' Union at the school, and by keeping open house every Sunday evening. He was not unlike Chesterton in build and appearance – humourous and kindly, with a wise, almost infinite tolerance.

Those Sunday nights were grand affairs of earnest, amusing, sometimes elevating, occasionally Rabellaisian talk on any and every topic under the sun. The first night I was there, they were debating the choice of play for the next production by the Old Students' Union. The only play I was at liberty to offer them was the abortive attempt I'd made at a "Society" comedy.[68] It was given two performances on a makeshift stage in the schoolroom.

On the Sunday evening following what was described respectively on the programme as "The first and last but one" and "The second and last" performance on any stage, the "Monty" house was crowded for the inquest. I told the story of the Stockport Garrick Society and they were all agog to start a similar "Little Theatre" in Huddersfield. Montgomery, Sidney and I were appointed to call a public meeting to get things going. Wareing gave the venture his blessing with one of the best speeches I ever heard him deliver. We called ourselves "The Huddersfield Thespians", made Montgomery our first president, and became, by a short head, the earliest amateur experimental group in Yorkshire.

During the venture's first season I scored with a performance of the comedy part in Moliere's *Doctor In Spite Of Himself*, and came a flop as "Valentine Brown" in Barrie's *Quality Street* and appeared with Florence in my one-acter, *Youth Disposes* – the only production it has had.

That first season, in spite of a "private" performance of Shaw's *Mrs. Warren's Profession*,[69] then still under the Lord Chamberlain's ban, didn't set Huddersfield on fire, but it gave various budding actors and producers a chance to try their prentice hands; some of them later to appear in New York as the first English amateurs to take the American stage. The second season, which coincided with my out-of-work period was as trying for the Thespians as my private worries were for me. The major production was *Richard II*. It was notable for the fine work of Lloyd Pearson, about to take the plunge as a professional, in the name part, and the appalling gap between receipts and expenses. A loss of over £80, and no means of meeting tradesmen's bills until the following season, made the following summer something of a nightmare to sensitive members of the committee. Dodging creditors – especially outspoken Yorkshire creditors – is an over-rated occupation.

---

[68] *A Democrat from Debrett* performed on April 16th 1920 at Hillhouse Elementary School, Hillhouse, Huddersfield.

[69] *Mrs. Warren's Profession* was then "banned". Any performance had to be private, and the Thespian production must have been one of the first half dozen. The occasion created some mild scandal. Many in town heard of the Thespians for the first time because they were putting on a banned play in private and those who knew nothing of the play were often loud in condemnation of the Thespians for "dabbling in muck". None the less and perhaps naturally this brought in many new members. Those who turned up at Broadbent's Canteen "on spec" of getting in, were told that they had to be members, and the committee sat at the doors writing out membership cards, while a policeman in uniform was standing near by!
S. H. Crowther, *The Huddersfield Thespians – A Jubilee History* : 1920-1970.

By the time the third season began I was busy elsewhere and my work with the Thespians had to be curtailed, but for several years afterwards I still acted as producer and actor from time to time, developing my own particular line of "Little Man" parts, such as "Androcles", "Lob" and "Zero", and taking my share in the fierce arguments between the more advanced wing and those members who wanted to do nothing more but the pretty-pretty stuff of Barrie and Milne.

My contract with Wareing being at an end, I was free to produce my own plays again at my own discretion. The modest royalties I began to draw eased our troubles somewhat and the profit the plays made lightened the Thespian burden. Not calling for elaborate staging, *Young Imeson* and *T'Marsdens* could be touted without much difficulty around the neighbouring village and chapel halls, and the income from these tours made all the difference in those early years, (until our pioneer productions of modern drama were being rewarded by "House Full" notices), between the Society's remaining solvent or going bust.

Incidentally, it was one such production which paved my way to London at long last.

# Chapter Thirteen

Late in 1921, the Huddersfield Thespians, still going through their teething troubles with years of pioneer work ahead of them before they were to achieve social success, attract a less devoted membership and lose their experimental impetus, my personal circumstances took an unexpected, slight turn for the better.

I received a letter from a Mr. W.D. Dow.[70] From the heading I gathered that Mr Dow ran a factory in Hunslet which manufactured "perambulators, baby carriages and large wheel toys".[71] From the letter itself I learned that he was running what he called "The Leeds Industrial Theatre" – his idea being to interest his workpeople in drama, not merely as audience but as actors. Membership cost twopence a week for a show a week. The provision of the shows was the snag. Until his workpeople were ready to put on shows of their own, he was appealing to amateurs all over the county to provide them. Would the Huddersfield Thespians help? He could only guarantee bare expenses, etc.

This was a thin chance, but one I could not afford to miss. After promising to put his request before the committee I made one on my own behalf in return. A request for a job. I told him that I was a thoroughly competent clerk and bookkeeper, could take shorthand and could type, but in addition that I had a thorough knowledge of the theatre as actor, producer and playwright. If he could find me a job in his office at, say three pounds a week, I should be more than willing to put my theatrical experience at his service for nothing.

Dow replied that he didn't believe in mixing things. He employed clerks as clerks not as theatrical producers. He had no vacancy for a clerk, and in any case didn't pay three pounds a week for them. But if I was interested in earning a pound a week for an evening's coaching a week – plus travelling expenses, of course – he'd be glad to see me.

I went to see him. The only cash we had in the world was a ten shilling note. My fare to Leeds took exactly half of it.

Dow was a talkative, energetic, volatile man; young, but with hair grey from some illness; well built, with a plumpish face and upper teeth which suggested he'd been a thumb-sucker as a child. He was a new type of business man to me, frank and ingenuous in manner, generous both in appreciation and cash; he'd a lively, cultured mind; kindly and tactful, he was also shrewd enough not only in business, but in making the most out of his non-commercial experiment. I'd an early example of this.

---

[70] Warrender B Dow, died at Worthing, 1951, aged 65.

[71] Simpson, Fawcett & Co. Ltd., Hunslet, Leeds, was established in 1859. By the middle of 1921 the Leeds and allied factories employed over 1000 work-people. The Book of Simpson, Fawcett & Co. Ltd. The World's Largest Baby Carriage Factories. 1921
V & A Museum of Childhood, Lines Bros. Archive, uncatalogued.

Fired by his story of what he was trying to do, I said something about being pleased to find a business man so keen on his worker's welfare.

"But it pays!" he retorted. "I should do it, perhaps if it didn't, but seeing I <u>do</u> it, I see I get the returns! – see these?"

He riffled a pile of newspapers. "In those papers there's thousands of pounds of the best publicity in the world! The publicity that's in the news columns – no displayed "ads" – just human stories that the public falls for, pictures of our actors at work in the factory and then on the stage – and into every story and every caption our firm's name comes with the fact that we make prams. So far I've spent about five hundred pounds on the experiment – the advertisement I've got from it from the *Daily Mail* alone is worth five thousand!" Then he explained with a grin, "That's why I'm paying for the venture out of my publicity accounts!"

We walked over to the "theatre" – a bare, gaunt hall attached to the local Club. The stage was too high and too small – about eighteen feet across and nine feet from back to front. He had installed some lighting – primitive and inadequate – the tableau curtains had no centre overlap. I made my first real impression when I drew his attention to this flaw.

I made a deeper one when the work's dinner hour struck and I was taken to watch a dispatch clerk as "Othello" and machinist as "Desdemona" make an appalling botch of the smothering scene. I then gave them a demonstration rehearsal. It was just pie. The actors had hardly a vestige of technique and the few simple hints I gave – such as telling "Othello" to play behind the couch, so that the audience could see the faces of himself and "Desdemona" instead of his backside – were listened to with flattering respect.

"You've earned your lunch at least "said Dow, and he carted me off in his Daimler to the Queen's Hotel. I broke my teetotal pledge and had my first taste of wine. When the bill was presented, Dow put a pound and a ten shilling note on the tray. Enough to keep the family, as we were living then, for a week at least. One of life's bitter jokes I still can't laugh at!

After the meal Dow suggested we got "down to brass tacks". They proved to be almost golden. When we parted about four that afternoon, I was engaged for three evenings a week for three pounds a week and my expenses. I didn't remind him he could have had a clerk thrown in for the price. "So much for his so-called business acumen", I thought, but kept it to myself.

I went home; Dow made a beeline to the nearest newspaper office, pursuing his policy of getting back with one hand what he'd given away with the other; but I'm certain the hard-boiled journalist didn't respond to his story as satisfactorily as Florence did to mine. The only fly in the ointment was that I was only engaged for four months.

I began my job the following Monday evening with a sketchy audition of my players. Our first production was to be *The Merchant of Venice* and this was to be followed by *Diana of Dobsons*. Forty or fifty would-be actors crowded the tiny room – managers, machinists, joiners, fitters, blacksmiths, painters – all the many trades were represented, and every age, shape, size and colouring.

Before putting any of them through their paces, I asked how many of them had seen a performance of *The Merchant*. Not one. Had any of them seen a performance of any Shakespearean play? – Two. Two men. They'd both seen one play only. In both cases, *Richard III*.

As the audition proceeded, my heart sank. Dow had stipulated that everyone who wanted to act was to have his or her chance. He was concerned with the welfare and education of his worker-players, not with the entertainment of the audience. It was a hard doctrine to a young, unfledged producer with ambition and an eye on the probable press-notices. What reputation could I hope to make with these people, most of whom found difficulty in reading at all and none of whom showed much ability or taste?

When we got down to actual rehearsals I found myself facing a bigger snag than their inability to read – their terrible self-consciousness which made them giggle at each other's efforts whilst resenting the amusement they aroused in their parts. Coupled with a rough shyness which made them chary of any display of emotion and made them afraid of "looking soft" when attempting speech a little nearer English than their Leeds dialect, this self-consciousness made the going very hard at first. Unthinking laughter would provoke quarrels, and I had much ado to preserve some sort of discipline without a display of authority which I knew would be fatal. My only chance was to get them to take me as one of themselves, not there to teach or hector, but to lead them in a game which I knew a little bit more than they.

It needed all my patience and tact, but progress was heartbreakingly slow, and I think that, but for the thought of that three pounds a week, I should have thrown up the job in despair and disgust. The nervous strain was considerable too, for the only way to get anything out of any of them was to go through their lines for them, myself, over and over again, trying to mesmerize them into self-forgetfulness. I felt like Svengali with a tribe of insubordinate Trilbys.[72] The early rehearsals were continually being held up for the pronunciation of some unusual or difficult word. I found it quicker in the end to spell it phonetically in the margin of their copies.

But even then it was obvious that few of them had much idea of what they were supposed to be saying, especially in the case of any classical allusions. I found myself retailing the Greek myths to help them. This was much more to their liking than rehearsals. They listened entranced and asked for more.

Dow was delighted! "Just what I wanted!" he declared.

"But the show!" I objected. "It'll never be ready!"

"Never mind!" he chuckled. "We'll put it on unready! These people are getting more out of it than any audience will, even if it's perfect!"

There were compensations, of course – moments when one got a heart-warming glimpse that one's efforts were not being entirely wasted. At the end of one rehearsal one actor grinned and said, "Ee! I've been miles away from Hunslet to-neet. An' I feel pounds lighter for it!"

---

[72] Svengali : Fictional character in George du Maurier's novel *Trilby* (1894). Svegali transforms Trilby into a great singer using hypnosis, but she cannot perform without his help.

Another time one of my actors came to me with a grave face, and said, "Yer'll have to tell "Shylock" not to waste that line!"
"What line?"
"For sufferance is the badge of all our tribe! He doesn't seem to see there's thousands o' years o' history, in that line!"
Not all the teaching was on one side.

My difficulties with Shakespeare were as nothing compared to those I met when rehearsing Cicely Hamilton's shop-girl comedy, *Diana of Dobson's* and my players found it much easier to mouth blank verse than to speak modern comedy lines. Later experience has only strengthened my conviction that the best thing for beginners is a course of Shakespeare. Shakespeare with an occasional dash of good, old-fashioned melodrama, in short something to encourage them to be larger than life, something on which they can cut their teeth and loosen their jaws, something in which they have to act, not merely behave. As to the counter-argument that masterpieces should not be botched, my answer is that beginners botch everything, but if they botch something not worth much to begin with there's nothing left: botch a masterpiece, there's still plenty.

We botched both in that first season, but Dow laughed at my anguish. He laughed even more at my difficulties with my stage carpenter, an excellent man at his job in the factory but unsophisticated in the theatre. And all too enthusiastic! Very early in the proceedings he came along, straining at the leash. "I've been thinking about this gondola you'll be wanting," he began. "I'll put it on wheels and then it can sail across the canal, like!"

I made him see that we'd no room for it on a stage nine feet by eighteen.

"Not even if I make it flat, cut out of three-ply?" he asked hopefully. "Things won't seem right if we haven't a gondola passing across the back!"

"Without a gondolier?"

"Oo,gow! I'd forgotten it'll want a driver! – Well, we shall have to make do with one painted on t'scenery. Billy Wilson in t'paint shop'll make a reight go of it. He's a real artist, Billy is. Paints fruit in oils! An' he says he can manage perspective, an' all!"

He was almost heartbroken when I told him that all I wanted were plain cream flats and arches and a blue skycloth.

"Eh? No palaces?"
No palaces
"No watter?"
No water.

"Then where are yer going to have them things like barbers' poles that stick up in it?"

He went down fighting right to the end. Even Dow was sceptical about my idea for a simple, composite set, light and cheerful in tone, but susceptible to changes of lighting. Apart from the fact that the size of my stage would make any attempt at realism a farce, I wanted something that would throw our gay costumes into relief and that could be changed quickly and easily with the minimum margin for errors and hold-ups. I was not too sure it would come off, myself, but this was the first show in which I'd been able to start from scratch, as it were, and not had to "make do" with properties already in existence, and I felt like having a flutter.

Dow, whatever doubts he might have about my "revolutionary" ideas, saw at once what a story they would make. Work in the factory, as well as rehearsals, was interrupted by eager pressmen who took photographs of our actors at their anvils and their sewing machines in workaday attire to be published side by side with pictures of the same persons in their Venetian costumes on the Rialto and at Belmont. A score of journalists came to see our joiner-actors building flats alongside pram bodies, our upholsterers covering the flats with obsolete leather cloth, our machinists making costumes out of cheap linings, our painters stippling and stenciling them, our nickel-platers dipping our swords into their vats with batches of pram handles, and so on. In return they were mercifully uncritical in their notices.[73]

Dow, who kept strict tab of all time and materials we absorbed, charging it all to his publicity account, told me that my first professional production of Shakespeare, complete with new scenery and costumes, two baby spots and a small dimmer, had cost just over £100. I felt both guilty and pleased at my extravagance. [74]

---

[73] Blacksmith Thespians

In the staging of an amateur theatrical performance for which only a small space is available, attempts at verisimilitude are often wasted. It is generally beyond the skill of minor scenic artists to produce a scene which shall give the impression of being what it pretends to be, without being either out of perspective when viewed by the audience, or out of scale when compared to the stature of the performers.

Some of our modern theatrical designers have attempted simpler methods. Something of their style was to be noted in the staging at the Leeds Industrial Theatre last night, of *The Merchant of Venice*. Mr. J R Gregson, who was responsible for the production, may or may not have seen *The Beggar's Opera*, but there is some kinship, at any rate, between the late Mr. Lovat Fraser's designs for that production and Mr. Gregson's variable arrangement of white flats, arches and doorways, which made a far better background for Shakespeare's play than if the usual futile makeshifts and compromises had been patched together.

The scenery, it was stated, had all been made by employees of Messrs. Simpson, Fawcett and Company, of Hunslet, and their play was acted by the No.2 dramatic section from the works of the same firm, consisting almost entirely of workers in the blacksmith's shops.

The costumes, too, designed by Mr. Gregson – a man of ideas, and a considerable asset to the Industrial Theatre scheme – had all been dyed, cut and made by the workers themselves. Apart from the economy of such a method, the result was far better than could have been secured by hiring a probably ill-assorted collection of garments from a theatrical costumier. There was nothing sumptuous or costly-looking about the costumes, but they were well conceived, and they suggested the period.

The acting of the play, as might have been expected, betrayed constantly the inexperience of the players, most of whom had never acted before. But at least it showed that the Industrial Theatre is producing an audience that will give a careful and attentive hearing to good stuff, and will support the efforts, however inexpert of fellow-workers. Audience and players may well develop appreciation and ability together.

The best work in this production was the Bassanio of a player named in the programme as G R James – not an impenetrable alias for Mr. Gregson – but Mr. Jack Priestley's Shylock was also good, and his attempt at a modern Jewish accent, though unusual, lent colour to the rendering.

*Yorkshire Evening Post* : February 21st, 1922.

[74] Extract from interview with J R Gregson

"How do you cover your expenses?" I asked, immediately coming to the rock on which most theatrical enterprises founder. "We have from 1200 to 1500 members who each pay 3d a week whether they attend the performances or not," he answered. "This covers the hire of the hall for two nights a week and the material we need. We make all our own scenery and dresses. Each night we could fill the hall, which holds 600, but that would take up too much of our time. We do a play ourselves every month, and the other weeks local amateur societies give us a show."

"May the public come to see?"

"No" he said grimly, "but sometimes we allow students from the University"

*The Daily Herald*  1923 (no date).

The £100 Dow refers to is, as Gregson says, probably factory labour costs in making the scenery, costumes etc.

It would be idle to pretend that the performance was anything but indifferent, but the press, grateful, I suppose, for past favours and anxious to keep what they thought a good story alive, made a great deal of it. The staging and costumes were praised for their ingenuity and novelty and I was greeted as a discovery. Our players were invited to neighbouring towns by groups anxious to start "worker theatres" of their own, and I was called upon for lectures and talks by literary societies, Rotary Clubs, and the like. It would all have been even more gratifying but for anxiety as to the future.

My contract with Dow was nearing its end, and *Diana of Dobson's* proved something of an anti-climax, due partly to rehearsals being interfered with by the Spring rush of work in the factory. The approach of Easter, 1922 brought with it the dread of another spell of unemployment, and I began to cast about in earnest for another job.

I need not have worried.

A day or two before Easter Dow said, "I've a fortnight's money here for you! I'm having a fortnight's rest and so are you!"

"Only a fortnight?" I stammered.

"That's all. Then I start exploiting you again, Ramsay MacGregson!"[75] He grinned. "I'm booking a row of spouting engagements for you through the summer. We're going to take "The Merchant" to various schools – it'll be an infliction on the kids, but all for their better grace, let's hope.[76] That'll give us time to plan our next season's programme. And it's got to be a knock-out!"

I murmured something about it not being much to do for my salary and he gave me a lecture on the folly of giving way to my Nonconformist conscience and not knowing my value, ending with, "Still, I suppose I've got to act the slave-driving capitalist, or you won't be happy! You can price out the stock sheets for us, and a few things like that, but don't kill yourself!"

He saw that I didn't. At least once a week he would carry me off for a day's outing in the Dales to discuss our plans without interruption. When he entertained notabilities such as Sir Frank Benson I was always included in the trips and the luncheon parties. There was one exhausting fortnight when he booked a box at the Grand Theatre, Leeds, and dragged me to every performance by the National Opera Company.

---

[75] Presumably a dig at Ramsay McDonald (First Labour Prime Minister) and Gregson's left leaning sympathies.

[76] Performance of *The Merchant of Venice* at Brighouse.
The Industrial Theatre Movement is making important developments and is being linked up with schools. The first experiment in this direction was made at Brighouse yesterday, when a highly-critical audience, numbering nearly 2000, assembled at the Albert Theatre, which the directors had placed at the disposal of the promoters. All the students at the two secondary schools in Brighouse were present, as well as the elder scholars from all the elementary schools in the borough.
The theatre was much larger than those in which the players had previously displayed their histrionic abilities, and some time elapsed before this fact seemed to be realised by the performers, but in the later stages almost every player made a considerable effort at adaptation to the newer and more trying conditions.
*The Yorkshire Post* : May 30, 1922.
*The Brighouse Echo* report gave the two secondary schools as the Girls Secondary and Rastrick Grammar. They also stated that 'over 1000 children 'attended, which is probably nearer the mark than the nearly 2000 given by *The Yorkshire Post*.

It was a happy summer, though I felt a trifle guilty at the thought of how much Florence, tied to the home and our still narrow budget, was missing. Almost before we knew it our next and most exciting season was upon us.

We had decided to open with our own production of *Peer Gynt* and to follow this at intervals with *Romeo and Juliet*, a pantomime, *The Cenci*, *Measure for Measure* and a revival of *The Merchant of Venice*. For the weeks in between our own productions we had booked visits from amateur groups all over the county, and our full programme included no less than nine plays by Shakespeare, two by Ibsen, two by Shaw, a Galsworthy, a Tebakov, a Sudermann, a Maeterlinck, a Strindberg, an alloy of modern comedies and two ventures into opera – *Il Trovatore* and Ethel Smythe's *The Bosun's Mate*. We raised our price to threepence a week and threw open our theatre to workers from other factories.

The standard of plays and productions varied considerably from the first-class offering of The Leeds Art Theatre – they brought their entire season's programme, using us for a super dress rehearsal – to performances by new beginners which were a weariness to the flesh. But our theatre that season was the throbbing, heart-warming centre of a new movement, the epitome of the "Little Theatre of the North".

I was no sooner launched on the production of *Peer Gynt* than I began to regret my

*Simpson Fawcett:*
*Leeds Industrial No.1 Theatre (1921):*

*The above is the outside of the famous Leeds No.1 Industrial Theatre, run by the firm for their own and the employees of surrounding works. New plays are produced week by week on a large stage with the latest lighting, the membership being at present 960.*

*"The first 'Industrial Theatre' in this country caters for the masses in the same way as the 'Old Vic' in London, but it really goes farther, and aspires to produce plays for working men, performed by working men, and even in some cases written by working men."*

*TIMES, London, November 19 1921.*

*Simpson Fawcett publicity (VA)*

No mention of working women!

ambitious folly in tackling it. The only thing I felt sure would be right about it was the music, for which we'd recruited a first class amateur orchestra, imported the full score from Germany and had the stage directions translated for us. I decided to sacrifice none of this and cut the play accordingly, but even then it ran for four hours. With a ballet drawn from a local dancing school and my trolls selected from the firm's three football teams. I had a company of eighty-odd crude but all too enthusiastic performers to support me in the name part.

The three nights of the play's run were easily the most exhausting I've known. The part itself is quite enough for any actor, making formidable demands on his technical and physical resources, with many quick changes of costume and make-up. I had to make all my changes on the stage, supervising the stagehands in the changing of the many scenes, marshalling my crowd of eighty actors on a stage eighteen feet by nine. By the time I had to weep in Solveig's arms during the lullaby which ends the play, real tears were trickling down my cheeks – tears of sheer exhaustion. The most effective scene in a very ragged affair was that in the hall of the Mountain King where the trolls used me as a football; the most disastrous was that in which, with no ear for pitch, I had to serenade "Anitra". Florence nearly went frantic in her attempts to teach me the air, and I still cringe when I remember the pity on the conductor's face when I slid off key.

The hit of the evening was scored by a young troll who, in the hurly-burly of the scrimmage, was tossed over the footlights into the percussion. My most abiding memory of that harum-scarum three nights is of the smart of my many abrasions in hot water. [77]

*Romeo and Juliet* was a cake walk after *Peer Gynt*. I went back to my composite set idea though with a less "arty" décor, I made as much use as possible of the costumes designed for *The Merchant* and of the actors who had appeared in it. It took its place as a companion "touring" piece with the earlier production and proved the more popular of the two. I remember it mainly for one performance which drew the tears to my eyes. That night, during my duel with Paris before Juliet's tomb, I lost my dagger. Poor "Juliet", groping for it, broke off her last lines to ask me in a whisper where it was. I told her. She started her last speech again, only to break off and ask me, still

---

[77]  Leeds Industrial Theatre's Ambitious Effort
The acting members of the Leeds Industrial Theatre at Hunslet have a difficult task in a production of *Peer Gynt*, but although there was very much to be desired in the niceties of elecution, especially in some of the smaller parts, last night's performance was interesting, and in its way enjoyable. The chief fault in most of the players is monotonous delivery, a defect which practice and experience may remedy. This does not apply to Mr. James Gregson's work as Peer, which in the early scenes especially, was excellent and vigorous. Miss May Ellis, as Ingrid, a relatively small part acts well, and her diction is good. The ballet, with Miss Muriel Clarke as Anitra, present the Eastern scene very pleasantly……………In conclusion, it may be said that Ibsen, if above the players as yet, is also above the audience, judging by their occasional ill-timed mirth.
*Yorkshire Evening Post* : Wednesday, September 27th 1922
Excellent as were the dramatic performances last winter at the Leeds No.1 Industrial Theatre the improvement at the opening of this is obvious at first glance. *Peer Gynt*, Henrik Ibsen's 'dramatic poem' was the choice for the opening of the season on Monday night. Mr. J R Gregson of Brighouse, in the title role, was extremely good in spirit, elecution and gesture, and received whole-hearted support from the company. Greig's incidental music was played by the Leeds Symphony Society with taste and feeling.
*Brighouse Echo* : Friday, September 29th 1922.

*Simpson Fawcett: Lowfield Works (1921): These works were opened shortly before the close of the war. Intended for the building of aircraft originally, they were diverted by the rapid end of hostilities to an additional pram and toy factory, and equipped with the latest machinery and fittings. We have, in addition, works at Manchester, Birmingham, London and Reading, devoted to the manufacture of perambulators.* Simpson Fawcett publicity (VA)

in a whisper, what she had to do. I told her to turn her back on the audience and stab herself with nothing. She did. But the poor thing was so bemused by this time that instead of falling across my face downwards, she threw herself backwards, the back of her head giving me a real sock on the nose. Hence the tears.

The outstanding success of that hectic season was Shelly's little known *The Cenci*.[78] It had had only one English performance when we attempted our three, and just about the same time, Lewis Casson and Sybil Thorndyke put it on for a few matinees. I doubt if it's been done since. I don't know what effect the play had on other audiences, but on ours, and on us who appeared in it, it was devastating. Structurally it's an indifferent play with wonderful passages of lyric description interspersed with odd lines cribbed – subconsciously, no doubt – from Shakespeare – paraphrases which are certainly no improvement on the originals. Yet the play has great, almost uncanny emotional power. Even at rehearsals we felt it taking possession of us. In performance it proved to be almost unbearably harrowing and horrifying. As one critic described it privately, it was "a real belly-scourer!"

There was one detail in my last scene as Count Cenci which teased and nattered me

---

[78] *The Cenci* : a verse drama by Percy Bysshe Shelley written in the summer of 1819, and inspired by a real Italian family, the Cencis (in particular, Beatrice Cenci). The play was not considered performable in its day, due to its theme of incest, and was not performed in London until 1922.

*Simpson Fawcett: Leeds Town Hall (1921): PRESENTING THE PRIZES: Miss Spencer (National Opera Co.), Mr. Fred Duprez and Mr. Bert Errol. Above:- Mr. Pindar (Works Manager), a lady friend and Mr. W B Dow*   *Simpson Fawcett publicity (VA)*

*Unfortunately, it doesn't say whose lady friend she was!*

right up to the first night. In this last scene of mine I had to send my servant, Andrea, with repeated commands to my daughter. Each time she refused to obey me. Each repeat of my command was couched in stronger language. Then, on her last refusal, when one expected the servant to be dismissed with some terrible imprecation, came the bare stage direction, "Exit Andrea". It all seemed terribly lame, especially as I then had to kneel down and begin a prayer-curse which mixed a distorted, superstitious piety with the most debased human hate and lust. One of my stagehands, hearing that speech for the first time, said,"If I'd said a quarter of what you've just said, I should be freetened o' summat happening to me!"

What I was frightened of was that Andrea's exit would fall flat and give me nothing to mount on for my final curtain speech. But think as I could, no solution came until on the first night, fingering my dagger all through the scene, I took two steps up stage and flung it, apparently, at my servant. Had he stayed put, it would have flown harmlessly past him. Instead, he moved right into the line of its flight. It landed between his feet, fortunately, sticking upright in the stage, quivering. I watched it fascinated for a moment, then lifted my eyes to see "Andrea" turning green under his olive-skinned make-up, and falling backwards through the wings in a faint.

Naturally, next night, our stage hands collected in the off-stage well, waiting for the

*Simpson Fawcett: Leeds Industrial No. 1 Theatre – Interior (1921): The above is a flashlight photo of the No. 1 Industrial Theatre with audience. The stage is about 30ft long and 20ft wide, and in addition to amateur dramatic companies of workpeople there are held concerts – choral and orchestral work – a new production being given each Monday throughout the Winter. The stage is equipped with blue, red, amber and green electric lights, and there are spacious dressing rooms and a large refreshment room attached to the building.*

*Among the plays produced this Winter have been:-*

*SHAKESPEARE – Scenes from Winter's Tale, King John, Henry VIII, Hamlet, Macbeth, Othello (twice); complete production of Merchant of Venice, Othello, As You Like It, Midsummer's Night's Dream, Taming of the Shrew.*

*LOCAL PLAYS – (Mostly by local playwrights): Collingham Ghost, Landlord's Share (Mr. T R Dawes); Heptonstall Hoax (Mr. Sutcliffe); The Key (Rev. Mr. Witham); T'Marsdens (Mr. J R Gregson); Jack and Jill (Pantomime), several nights, by Mr. Eric David.*

*OTHER NIGHTS – Scenes from Masefield's Good Friday, Diana of Dobsons, The Little Stone House (Calderson), Mother of Pearl (G Jennings), Playgoers (Sir Arthur Pinero), The Will (Sir J M Barrie).*

*DANCING – Classical, Ballet, Period and English Dances, Choral Nights by the Industrial Theatre Choral Union of 40 picked voices. Orchestras by the two String Orchestras in the group, and Dance Music on Dance Nights by the Jazz Band.*

*Any firms interested in this movement would be given full information free on application to Miss Jones, at our firm, who is the permanent secretary of the movement, and a limited number of complimentary tickets can be issued to customers for admission on Monday nights.*

*Simpson Fawcett publicity (VA)*

*Leeds Industrial Theatre: Publicity Shot (c1921), with James Gregson to the fore.* (CA)

*Simpson Fawcett: A Works Theatre (1921): The Simcett Theatre is an institution unique in Europe and has been visited by many notable people. In it the firm's workpeople play to an audience of their own fellows with perfect stage equipment. Such plays as Peer Gynt have been produced, with a cast of 160 and an orchestra of 42 players. Romeo and Juliet brought forth the praise of the local Press that such "exquisite rendering" of the spoken lines was a joy to listen to.* Simpson Fawcett publicity (VA)

*Simpson Fawcett: Catalogue cover (1892): The full title is intriguing. Why manufacture perambulators in conjunction with pails and tubs? Another booklet I have seen in the V & A archive mentions that James Simpson first manufactured perambulators at the Thomas Cross & Co. Leeds Pail Works in 1852 by cutting a bucket in half from top to bottom, and fitting the two sides together with board lined with cloth. By doing so he produced the first perambulator that children could lie down in, which consequently meant that much younger babies could be pushed around outside. Although the company's claim that, in so doing, they introduced the biggest factor in the subsequent decline in infant mortality, in teaching people the new gospel of taking very young children out into the open air is perhaps exaggerated, it's obvious from the speed and extent to which this style of pram was adopted by the public that this innovation was an important one.* (VA)

*The New Movement in Industrial Drama (c1921)* (CA
*W B Dow, on back row (4th from left), next to the policeman. J R Gregson on front row, smoking a pipe*

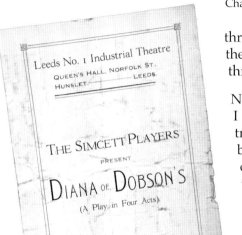

*Leeds Industrial Theatre –*
*Diana of Dobson (1921)  (CA)*

thrill.  We all got one we weren't expecting, for the dagger, instead of sticking in the floor, flew through the wings, and six heads ducked as one!

Not content to let the play create its own horror, I added an unseen torture scene.  Before the trial in the last act, I lowered the house lights, brought up dim footlights, but kept the curtain down.  The audience heard curt commands, the sound of a creaking rack, the groans of the tortured man, and their imagination did the rest.  We had seven faints one night.

And every night, hard-bitten theatre-goers would come round back stage, with haggard, drawn faces, the women often with the traces of unmopped tears channelling their powder, to assure us, though we didn't need it, of how they'd been moved.  This production was not strictly an Industrial Theatre affair.  Neither Dow nor I felt our own players were to be trusted with the play, and so we interested various members of the Leeds Art Theatre in the venture.  Amongst these were Muriel Hague – better known by her stage name of Muriel Essex – and Charles F. Smith, with both of whom I was to work for many years in the Leeds Civic Playhouse.[79]  But that was still some years ahead and in the meantime I had made my debut in London.  Had, in fact, gone up like a rocket and come down like a stick!

---

[79]  A Dubious Experiment
In a general way we have understood and sympathised with the aims of the promoters of the Industrial Theatre, but it must be confessed that we are totally at a loss to understand the reasons which led to the production this week of Shelley's long banned play *The Cenci*.  It is true that the ban has been now removed and that in November last the play was produced in London.  In the capital it has been regarded chiefly as a literary curiosity.  It is one thing to produce such a play in London for people whose education enables them to view it from the only point of view which it should be judged; it is quite another matter to thrust it upon (by comparison) shallow literary culture of the factory lads and lasses of industrial Leeds.  Perhaps no more severe criticism could be passed on this misguided effort than the inane laughter of a group of young girls who filled the Queens Hall during the intervals last night.  And when the curtain went up on one scene and there were 'noises off' indicating a storm, the girls shrieked with mirth as if it were one of the funniest effects in a pantomime.
Shelley's treatment of the awful story of the unspeakable Count Cenci is gloomy and depressing in the extreme, and breathes throughout the dismal atheism that led to his being sent down as an undergraduate from Oxford.  It has no uplift whatever.  Throughout the whole orgy of sin and madness and gloom runs the thought that perhaps there is 'no God, no heaven, no earth in the wide world'.
The acting, for amateurs reached a very high level, and Mr. J R Gregson, the producer is entitled to high praise for his selection of players and for the way in which he has trained them.
But when all credit is given to the acting and production, one cannot help hoping that the desire for novelty or scope for strong acting  will not in future lead to the production of plays so unpleasant as this – if they can be found.
*The Yorkshire Post* : January 17th 1923.

# Chapter Fourteen

Although the Industrial Theatre had become a full-time job, though still with my original part-time salary, I found time somehow, in the Autumn of 1922 to produce *T'Marsdens* for the Huddersfield Thespians, and my six-year-old comedy had its first native performance. Florence, after her long spell of unrelieved and harassing domestic strain, celebrated our brightening fortunes with a grand, fully-realised portrayal of "Ann".

On the second night of the week's run, Will Foster came round to see me, excited and enthusiastic. I had met him several times at the Theatre Royal. He was one of Wareing's co-directors, had been responsible for Wareing's coming to Huddersfield in the first place and, had things gone as he hoped in his financial affairs, would, by now, have been the owner of the theatre. The Yorkshire Repertory project had been his in the first place, but a disastrous fall in the price of flax after the First World War had compelled him to withdraw his backing. Now, apparently his affairs had taken a more promising turn, and he was putting money into the Everyman Theatre, Hampstead, where Norman Macdermott was attracting considerable attention as producer.[80] Some of the new plays he had put on had been transferred to the West End. I must, Foster insisted warmly, send my play to him.

Somewhat grimly I told him I'd done so some time ago, and that it had met its customary rejection, though a shade more promptly than usual. Then I must send it again! Not on your life!

"Then there's only one thing for it!" Foster declared. "I must get him up here to see it!"

Will Foster was an odd but admirable mixture. He had a cultured, volatile mind and an incurably optimistic outlook. A deeply religious man with a book of poems and some verse plays to his credit, he brought to his theatrical ventures something of the evangelistic spirit he put into his work as a lay preacher. He had high and genuine ideals for the theatre of his dreams and to the end of his life retained the high spirits and hopefulness of a boy.

Knowing his over-sanguine temperament and the dilatory ways of managers, I had no great expectations from the encounter, but before the week was out Macdermott was in Huddersfield and I found myself shaking hands with a slight, dark, somewhat cadaverous man, much younger than I expected, with the quiet, precise manner and speech of a scholar or a superior civil servant. Anything less theatrical I couldn't have imagined.

Florence gave the show of her life that night. Macdermott quietly but freely admitted his judgment on reading the play had been wrong. Florence dashed home to relieve

---

[80] Norman Macdermott (1890-1977) founded the Everyman Theatre in Hampstead in 1920. He ran it until 1926, then in the 1930s he had the tenancy of the Royalty Theatre before being appointed, in 1938, Director of Entertainments at the Empire Exhibition in Glasgow. During the war he joined the Department of National Service Entertainment and became the Controller of the Scottish Region. From 1947 he worked for St.Dunstan's and the Royal National Institute for the Blind. In 1951 he was appointed General Manager of the South Bank Exhibition during the Festival of Britain.

whoever was sitting in with the children and to wait anxiously for my return. I went to the Foster's for supper and to discuss the terms of a possible contract.

The terms were not, as Macdermott frankly admitted, all I might have desired, or might have got if I'd been lucky enough to sell the play to an established management in the West End, but they were the best he could offer in his somewhat precarious position as director of a small and experimental theatre. For my part I had to admit that I'd hawked the play for six years without success and might hawk it another six without being offered better, if any, terms. Heaven knows what fantastic ideas I'd been secretly cherishing, but they withered quickly at this touch of frosty reality, my one consolation, and no small one, being the realization that the suggested contract meant that I should not be thrown aside if my first play proved to be a flop, and that I should certainly have a second, probably third chance to make good.

I swallowed my disappointment and sensibly, if a little ungraciously, accepted the offer. Macdermott promised to send the contract as soon as it was drafted, and with Foster's delighted good wishes, I made my way home through the darkened town, in a mood of sober elation.

There followed six months of weary waiting, of constant postponements, before the call finally came and, as spruce as Florence could make me, I was in the train, speeding towards London for the first time in my life. Besides the suit I was wearing, and the made-over dinner suit of my Wareing days, I had little besides a pair of pyjamas and a toothbrush. But I ate my cheese sandwiches with no envy of my fellow-travellers who made their way to the unknown luxuries of the dining-car. My ambition had plenty to feed on. I had still to learn that ambition should be made of sterner stuff than I could boast, and that the success I dreamed of would turn out to be as hollow as Dead Sea fruit.[81]

London, when at last I found it around me, proved disappointingly and reassuringly ordinary. Euston was merely a railway station after all. Even the legendary tube train to which I found my way easily without a word to anybody was only a string of comfortable coaches. I had constantly to remind myself "You're here! At Mornington Crescent! London is all round you. These are some of its teeming millions. Camden Town! Chalk Farm! There was a murder there once. You're where things happen. Where things have always happened".

Nothing seemed to be happening at the Everyman Theatre when I arrived. The Hampstead people passed it and me without a glance. The tiny foyer was dim and empty, hushed by its cloistral atmosphere, I whispered my name to the gentleman in the Olympian quietude of the microscopic box-office.

He spoke aloofly through the discreet telephone to some remoter Jove, and informed me that Mr. Macdermott was at rehearsal and not to be disturbed. He would be free in thirty minutes. I was too abashed to remember it must be my play he was rehearsing.

---

[81] Dead Sea fruit: something that appears to be beautiful or full of promise but is in reality nothing but illusion and disappointment.

I murmured something about calling again later and escaped into the open-air to lug my case round Hampstead for an endless thirty minutes.

When I ventured back to the foyer it was occupied by a jovial, thick-set fellow who introduced himself as Forster Bovill and Macdermott's business manager. He was highly amused when he heard how I had hung about the village instead of barging into the theatre as I might have done.

As he led me to Macdermott's room he paused a moment to say with a twinkle, "Look here, my boy. You keep up that simplicity touch. D'ye get me? Shy fellow from the provinces - blushing and awkward - overpowered by London and its wonderful ways-bashful and shy - it'll go down well with the press boys I'm going to let loose on you!"

It did. A few nights later I met a batch of them in the bar of the Duke of York's Theatre and created quite a sensation when I asked, in all simplicity, for a peppermint-and-soda. Some of them rather overplayed the incident I thought, in their stories, but Forster Bovill was delighted and declared my request to the barmaid was "sheer inspiration". He laughed all the more heartily when I explained it was sheer habit.

Rehearsal was over for the day when, on my arrival, I was at last ushered into Macdermott's room. He gave me some precise, quiet instructions as to how I should comport myself with the players the following morning and some details as to timetables and the living allowance I was to receive. He then ushered me into my first London taxi and saw me installed in my modest but, to me, overpowering Bloomsbury hotel. After a long letter to Florence and supper at a coffee stall - plain and cheap as my allowance dictated - I had the freedom of London's dusky, lamplit magic.

As soon as possible the following morning, after making the most of the hotel breakfast, again with an eye on my allowance, l set out on foot to explore London, or rather let it reveal itself to me. Neither then nor subsequent mornings did I ask my way. What did it matter which street I took, seeing every one had a name with its thrill for me? What did it matter how I got there when I stumbled upon an open place with a tall column and fountains? It was enough to realise I was in Trafalgar Square, that the long tree-lined avenue was The Mall, and that the building at its far end, not unlike a rather handsome silk factory at home in Brighouse, was Buckingham Palace. I still can't understand anyone wanting to ride instead of walk in London.

My first impact on the cast of *T'Marsdens* had the same effect that it had on Forster Bovill. I'd hardly spoken six words before Reginald Bache, who was playing "Ezra", threw down his script in comic despair of ever copying my accent.

There was difficulty about the use of "Squire" as a Christian name for one of the characters - Londoners would expect him to appear in breeches and leggings - could I think of another name for him?

Yes, I could. What about "Ceecil"?

Everyone laughed with delight. Nadine March who was to play "Olive" cried, "Isn't he lovely? I suppose he means "Cecil"! It was a pronunciation new to me.

Every evening I was captured by one or another of the company for lessons in dialect.

Bache collared me for the week-end. He wanted more from me than dialect. I couldn't give him too much detail of our life at home - the ovens we baked our bread in, our Chapel services, our factories, the streets we walked, anything and everything that helped him to build a background for the character he was to play. "I must know where I'm going when I make an exit!" he explained.

But even in that first ecstatic week I got a glimpse of the underside of theatrical life in London which disturbed me - glimpses of a struggle for success, of rivalry; hints of a grim conflict behind the glitter and glamour, of malice which edged the gossip and allusions which went over my head.

I soon realised that this envy, this malice, was spiced with fear - that even Bache, with all his ability and industry, didn't feel secure, and that the fact that he'd climbed so far up the ladder was no guarantee that my play might not see him slipping down a few precious rungs, if not to the bottom. In spite of their surface bonhomie, their facile courtesy and compliments, these charming people were steel beneath their velvet.

My first glimpse of this seamier side came to me during one of the dialect lessons I tried to give to Nadine March. When I told her that, in her part as one of the younger generation her dialect should not be as strong or as broad as that of the others, she was aghast. "But it must be!" she said. "If it isn't the critics will say it's because I can't do it! I shall never have another chance of another part like it!"

Before the dress rehearsal was upon us I had become ill at ease in this world of spit and polish, of airy graces and easy compliments, of seemingly fragile, friendly creatures who nevertheless turned out to be tough enough when it came to fighting for themselves, and ruthless enough in pursuit of their own interests. I didn't blame them. One had to be tough to succeed. I was ill at ease because I'd begun to suspect I should never be tough enough. No more than that at this stage, and nothing like so definite a feeling as setting down in words must make it appear. Those pre-production days remain in the memory as days of hard study, of happy comradeship in a common purpose, and of constant kindness by the company generally to the unsophisticated provincial who had strayed amongst them.[82]

And of all the happy memories of that happy ten days that of Frank Pettingell is supreme.[83] I found him a joy from the first moment with his buoyant humour and his habit of dramatising everything. To Frank a broken bootlace can be high tragedy, the catching of a bus a triumph to be marked with fanfares, a recalcitrant button a malignant Fate's diremost unkindness - a theme poignant as the woes of Hecub and calling for the same tears and "horrid speech". Frank cannot tell you about a dispute with a taxi-driver

---

[82] One of the actresses who is appearing in *T'Marsdens*, Mr. Gregson's Yorkshire play at the Everyman Theatre, states she had great difficulty in procuring clothes suitable for her part as the daughter of a nightwatchman in a Yorkshire village. At one carefully selected shop in populous but aristocratic Camden Town she got a portion of her costume, but incautiously remarked that the skirt was "too smart". "Smart?" said the indignant shopman, "Of course. Everything we sell is smart!"
*Bradford Daily Telegraph*: May 2nd 1923.

[83] Frank Pettingell (1891-1966). A character actor on stage and screen, born in Liverpool, educated at Manchester University. Before becoming an actor he worked as an artist and journalist.

without playing all the parts in that (for the moment) overwhelming drama. He cannot praise or criticise another actor's work without illustrating his points with flashes of brilliant, revealing mimicry. He cannot tell a yarn without embroidering each character into a thing of rich delight, and funny as the point of the yarn may be, it doesn't matter whether you arrive at it or not. In fact, with Frank, it's often much more enjoyable to travel than to arrive.

The first time we fed together he told me of a benefit performance of *Hamlet* in which he'd figured. But before he'd reached the side-splitting denouement, he'd given me a full–length account of his early days in a portable Theatre - wages a pound a week and find your own wardrobe - and he'd followed his own progress there until, instead of drawing a pound a week and sleeping under a caravan, he was earning twenty-five shillings and sleeping in one. Incidentally, he'd given me a whole gallery of cameo portraits of the company, every man-jack and woman-jill of them in their humour as they lived. My eyes were red with tears, my muscles ached - my lunch was stone cold.

*Frank Pettingell (MM)*

I annexed that story promptly and have used it shamelessly ever since. It's appeared in at least three different printed versions, I've broadcast it and told it on T.V., and it's the tailpiece to one of my most popular lectures - and the main reason for its popularity.

I place Pettingell amongst the ten best actors I have known. He acts as a bird sings, or a duck swims, or those of us without chest complaints breathe. Acting has been more than a career to him. It's the very reason for his being. That's why, even after he'd made his mark on the West End, he would depart for some God-forsaken twice-nightly repertory company, putting on two plays a week, rather than remain not acting in London. The years have brought inevitable mannerisms and cramped his versatility, but they've also brought a ripeness and certainty which still make him a joy to watch - especially to his fellow players. And his stories still make our occasional meetings a delight to me.

The great day found me in a despondent, almost despairing mood. The dress rehearsal had plunged me into the deepest gloom, although, I suppose, it was neither better nor worse than a hundred others.

I dashed up to the theatre early, spent an hour or two helping to make the kitchen set a little more lifelike, then dashed down to Euston to meet Florence.

She was wearing the same shabby costume she'd had for five years, but she'd plunged on a new silk jumper, and treated herself to her first lunch on the train. Sidney Crowther was with us, and we gave her a hectic afternoon's bus-top tour of London.

After a sketchy meal which we were too agitated to enjoy we got ready for the great toss-up of our lives. I put on my shiny dinner suit, wrapped up my evening pumps (complete with bows) in brown paper, and got into my shabby raincoat.

Sitting opposite us in the tube to Hampstead was a most splendiferous creature correct in every detail from the crush hat and silver-topped stick to his patent-leather shoes. [84] He eyed us curiously as we did him. He seemed fascinated by my battered felt hat, a little puzzled at my wrinkled, laced boots.

"I'll bet he's a critic!" whispered Florence in something like panic. "Look at that silk-lined cloak!"

I did. And felt smaller and shabbier than before.

"I'll bet he's going to the Everyman!" Florence whispered again after an agitated silence. "He ought to slip on some orange peel!"

He didn't. At the theatre we found him in the seat next to Florence. Beyond the merest flicker of recognition he paid us no more attention, until, as Florence reported with glee, I appeared to take my curtain call. "His face was worth seeing then!" she said.

But there were ages of agony and apprehension to be endured before that moment came. Never in my life have I seen such a shaky, halting performance of any play, nor so many sure-fire laughs fumbled or missed. I felt like drowning myself.

I stood it for two acts, but at the second interval slunk out of the theatre to find what composure I could under the stars. Macdermott had warned me to stand by in the Green Room for a curtain call, but I was still in the night when I heard rolling waves of applause. I dashed to the stage door as Foster Bovill came looking for me, panting, "Upstairs, my boy. Upstairs! Can't you hear 'em calling for you?"

He pushed me up the corkscrew, iron staircase, and Macdermott yanked me up the last three steps, hissing, "Where the devil have you been?" He gave me a push that sent me stumbling on to the set. The applause swelled and rolled, sending chilly, prickly ripples all over me.

"I must be a success", I told myself and tried to feel elated about it. But I knew it wasn't all me by any manner of means. I thought of all the friends who had helped me - my step-mother, Joe Harrison, Dow, Foster, Crowther - a host of them - foremost of all, Florence, whose pale face was lit like an angel's. I felt more like weeping than smiling - so much effort and self-sacrifice from so many so that I could master such a modest summit.

I bowed to the actors; I bowed to the audience; I bowed to Macdermott in the wings. I bowed to them all again, ignoring the cries for a speech. Catching sight of Macdermott's

---

[84] Most London playgoers were accustomed to wait until a play had been running for a week or two before bestirring themselves to keep up with the Joneses and "go west" to see it. The Everyman could count on its regulars but needed also bookings by other playgoers. There was no passing traffic at Hampstead. In the West End, failing to get into a play of choice in Shaftesbury Avenue, one could hurry to half a dozen other theatres within a stone-throw; but it took half an hour to get to Hampstead. The weary tube journey, finishing with the deepest and slowest tube lift in all London, called for real courage and determination. The alternative, taxis, at that time had almost to be bribed to grind up Fitzjohn's Avenue or Haverstock Hill.
N. Macdermott , *Everymania*, London, The Society For Theatre Research, 1975, p.27

furious signals in the wings, I stepped forward and murmured something modest about "my little play" and my gratitude to those who had made it seem better than it was (God forgive me!) and to the audience who had received it so kindly.

As I left the stage Forster Bovill clapped me on the shoulder. "You know your onions all right, my boy! That was the best bit of acting on this stage to-night!"

Try as I could and did, I couldn't shake off my melancholy. I went through all the necessary, usual motions, receiving congratulations, thanking the actors, and so on, feeling I was playing an unreal part in a shadow show. The feeling persisted at the party thrown by Macdermott after the performance. Florence and I were bundled into our shabby outdoor clothes and taxied to his flat somewhere in St James. We found it swarming with well-wishers.

We sat together on a divan, feeling lost and out of place. I was tired out and would have given the world to be somewhere where we could talk things over quietly by ourselves. We hardly spoke except when one of the party remembered us. There were coffee, drinks and speeches. Toasts to the author who they believed had conquered London; to the producer who had discovered him; to the cast who had so ably presented the little masterpiece, and so on, and so on.

I stammered a few more words of thanks: Macdermott replied quietly and fluently. He was proud to have been the means of bringing Mr Gregson to London. He was looking forward to a long and successful partnership. He knew they would all like to be witnesses of the formal ratification of that partnership. The contract which I'd already seen was produced and they were handclaps and more congratulations and good wishes as we signed it. At long last it was all over and we were allowed to go to our hotel, leaving the party in full swing.

Our mood changed next morning when we bought the papers and scanned eagerly what Macdermott described as "the press of the year".[85] The notices – "eulogies" Foster called them - were unanimously favourable. I really began to feel that I had arrived, especially when a Bond Street photographer rang up and begged me to give him "the honour of a sitting". We fitted it into the crowded morning, bought the first editions of the evening papers, and boarded the train for home. The evening notices were as enthusiastic as the morning's and a good deal of space was devoted to my "romantic" career and gossip about the players. But the most amusing evidence of my "success" was supplied by the local press. Editors asked me for contributions. I fed them with the articles they'd previously rejected.

Foster returned from London a week after us with the news that several West End

---

[85] A Brilliant Comedy
Good work, that otherwise might not be staged has become a speciality of the Everyman Theatre, and one of the most meritorious achievements is the production of *T'Marsdens* by a new dramatist Mr. James Gregson. This comedy of life in a small Yorkshire town is a gem of wit and characterisation and is permeated with a systematic humour and faithful observation. As the author knows his subject, the story rings true, is naturally told, the characters being real life people. Apart from a few easily remedied faults of construction, Mr. Gregson's first attempt promised a brilliant future.
*Glasgow Bulletin* : March 8th 1923.

theatres were "clamouring" for the play to be transferred to them, and touring managements were angling for the rights. He seemed surprised that we were carrying on as usual and that I had gone straight back to the factory where, to keep me going through the summer, Dow had given me a job usually held down by an office girl. But repeated disappointments had made us cautious and we felt, as Florence put it, "This may only be a flash in the pan".

As it proved to be.[86] There was not an item of news direct from Macdermott, but the negotiations which Foster reported as in progress came to nothing at all. After a month's run the play was withdrawn. There was nothing for it but to hope for better luck with *Young Imeson* which Macdermott planned to put on as soon as practicable.

He did so a twelvemonth later and, on Foster's insistence I was engaged to play my original part of "Andrew Weatheredge". Foster and I also wanted a local amateur, Tom Denham, to play the broad comedy part of "Nathan" – a part which fitted him like a glove, and in which he'd have swept London off its feet. Tom had a deservedly high reputation in local dramatic circles, a born actor who had refused various offers to turn professional. In *Young Imeson* he was superb. Unfortunately for us, Tom's commitments in business made it impossible for him to leave Huddersfield for an indefinite period. It was a thousand pities for I'm sure he would have made all the difference to the play's fate.

The cast included Louise Hampton, Frank Petley, Dorothy Holmes Gore and Phillip Wade who was later to make his name as a radio actor and playwright. We rehearsed five weeks for nothing and played two for minimum salaries. We were engaged on "sharing" contracts with a guaranteed basic salary and a share in any profit until our various maximum terms were reached.

It amazed me to find that actors of the calibre of Louise Hampton, Petley and Wade were not only willing but pleased to take jobs on those terms until I learned that Louise had had only eight weeks work in eighteen months and that Philip Wade, after years of experience as a Shakespearean clown with Benson and Baynton, had spent over a year trying to get his first West End part. Others had similar illustrations for me of the hardships behind the glamour to re-enforce the doubts and fears I'd first felt twelve months earlier.

They were a grand crowd to work with, loyal and hard-working. They were not only determined to make the play the success they believed it ought to and would be, but they did all in their power to help me with my part. I learned to my surprise that

---

[86] The third experimental new play was put on between two forthcoming Shaw productions. It was *T'Marsdens* by J R Gregson, a Yorkshire writer. The main part of the company being at the Royalty in *At Mrs. Beams*, additions were necessary to fill the gaps. This allowed recruitment of three well-known character actors most suitable for the type of part in the play; Charles Groves, Edward Rigby, Frank Pettingell. Good though it was, and with such skilled comedians as added attraction, London showed it could not care less how Yorkshire lived.
N.Macdermott, *Everymania*, London, The Society for Theatre Research, 1975, p.56
One problem may have been the title. Even in Yorkshire there were misunderstandings.
Leeds took to Mr. Gregson's *T' Marsdens* very kindly – although both printers and playgoers were very shy about the title. On one poster it was 'The Marsdens', on another just 'Marsdens'.
*Huddersfield Examiner* : May 3rd 1923.

they had no doubt I would bag the acting honours. Even Macdermott unbent so much as to say that he was glad he'd given me the part. Like the rest of them he felt sure we were on to a winner and that the play was a great advance on *T'Marsdens* in every way. On the Friday evening before *Young Imeson* was due to open he called me aside in the Green Room where I was chatting with Athlene Saylor and Franklyn Dyall, who were starring in *The Mask And The Face*, to tell me he had just refused an offer for the American rights of my second play. When I asked him why, he said he'd be refusing twice the figure they'd offered the following Tuesday morning when they'd read the notices the play would get.

The only snag was that it didn't get the notices we'd all anticipated. We met disaster. The morning after Macdermott told me of the American offer, Frank Petley didn't turn up to rehearsal. He was down with pneumonia. The part had to be taken at cruelly short notice by George Merritt. A fine actor, working against time, he did all that could have been expected of him in a part outside his own natural line. The cast plunged loyally into a hectic weekend of continuous rehearsal and forgot their personal interests in their efforts to save the play. But worse was to come.

On the morning of the first night London found itself in the grip of a bus strike. There were rumours that the tubes would be stopped in sympathy. We opened to a very thin house. It saw a careful but tame performance. We'd had it![87]

EVERYMAN THEATRE
OPPOSITE HAMPSTEAD TUBE STATION
LESSEE AND DIRECTOR · · NORMAN MACDERMOTT.
Telephone : 7224 Hampstead.

Mr. NORMAN MACDERMOTT presents his compliments and requests the pleasure of your presence on Tuesday, March 18th, at 8.15 p.m., to witness the first production of a new Comedy by J. R. GREGSON, the author of " Marsdens " entitled :

## YOUNG
## IMESON

Should you or your representative be unable to be present, will you kindly return the enclosed ticket to

W. B. FORSTER BOVILL,
*Manager.*

*Invitation: Everyman Theatre, Hampstead (1924)* (CA)

---

[87] ....numerous plays were offered with down payments towards the cost of production. Such arrangements as were accepted were dissociated from my productions by special wording on posters and programmes....... In the first half of 1924 too many of these were agreed in the effort to keep losses from sinking the ship. The *Morals of Vanda, Love in a Village, The Painted Lady, Young Imeson, Monica, In and Out, The Tropic Line,* and *Her Daughter* which was thankfully announced as "the last of the productions under special contracts". Most of them were described by the authors as farcical comedies and it was a grave disappointment that the effort and money provided to encourage new playwrights brought no better results.
N.Mcdermott, *Everymania,* London, The Society for Theatre Research, 1975, p.61
Macdermott wrote his book in 1975, over fifty years after the event. The inclusion of *Young Imeson* in the list of plays which gave financial inducements to be performed is rather puzzling. Gregson didn't have any money. Either Macdermott got his facts wrong or Will Foster, unbeknown to Gregson, put some money up front to have the play performed.

The notices were tepid but not damning.[88] The only one I care to remember is that of James Agate who wrote, "*Young Imeson* is easily the best play of the week. It would be a good play in any week".

The bus strike went on too long for us. We played for a fortnight to poor but appreciative houses, then folded up. It's a fortnight with few bright memories. One is of the best and biggest house we had, though it was nearly all "paper". Foster went to Westminster, did some heroic canvassing, and brought nearly half the House of Commons to see the play. Another memory is of suddenly feeling a pair of hands on my shoulders as I sat making up for the show. I looked up in the mirror to see a long, Robespierre-like face above a collar almost hidden by a high and tight black cravat. The apparition announced himself as Hannen Swaffer and said, "There's only one thing wrong with your acting. It's too modest!" [89] Then he disappeared as swiftly as he'd come.

Five week's rehearsals without pay had strained my resources, although I'd drawn on my salary in advance. During the last week of the run it was difficult to squeeze even half-a-crown out of the Treasury for food. There was one day when I'd nothing between breakfast and tea. I found a café where I could get bread and butter and jam for eightpence. I plunged my last coppers on an unsatisfying apology for a meal and went to the theatre with exactly one half-penny left in my pocket. During the show I had to put two halfpennies in a collection-box. I rifled it of the score or more coppers I'd put in earlier.

At last, after seven weeks of hard work during which I'd drawn exactly ten pounds, I had to wire Dow for my fare home.

As soon as I got home I took the first steps to get free of my contract with Macdermott. Unduly touchy and sensitive, perhaps, I thought him too highhanded in his methods of dealing with me. Although I had given him sole control over my plays, I felt he might have taken the trouble to consult me on certain questions, if only as a matter of courtesy, instead of apparently regarding my enquiries as so much unnecessary fussing. No doubt my disappointment over the fiasco of *Young Imeson* had something to do with my decision, though I did not blame him for it. Macdermott, probably finding me too prickly a customer to work comfortably with, raised no strong objection, but pointed out, quite naturally, that he had lost money on the two productions. On my agreeing to let him have one-third of my future royalties until these losses were made good, the contract was annulled and I was my own master again.

---

[88] The new play at the Everyman Theatre is *Young Imeson*, a Yorkshire comedy by James R Gregson. It too is a muddle, but of a different kind. Mr. Rice is an intelligent man, trying a very difficult experiment, and naturally tying himself up in knots in his attempt. Mr. Gregson is a man with a good idea for a first act, and in difficulties because he does not know how to spin his play out longer. The first act is quite amusing in itself, and gains a quite legitimate amusement from its portrayal of Yorkshire character. It concerns a strike in a jam factory, with a hard old Yorkshireman as the owner, and his educated and illegitimate son as the strike leader. But after a meeting of these two in the first act the play begins to peter out sadly. For one thing the son becomes so impossible a prig. There is only one amusing moment after the first act, and that is when we discover the old engineer whom everybody had thought a blackleg, had only gone back to work to see that the owner's engines were smashed. This turns the defeat of the strikers into a success, yet the only thing we get from our hero is a surprising lecture on the necessity of being high-minded and fighting fair. But the morality of the whole play is extremely conventional, and, as always happens on these occasions, the only sympathy we have left at the end is for the villain of the piece. *The New Statesman*: March 22nd 1924.

[89] Hannen Swaffer (1879-1962) was a journalist and drama critic. He joined the *Daily Mail* in 1902. He was editor of *Weekly Dispatch* and helped develop the *Daily Mirror* into a popular paper.

*James Gregson – portrait (1927): painted by John R Gauld*        (BM)

Peter Brook: *Going Home – Birds Royd Lane, where James Gregson would have frequently walked, to the railway station or to the town centre* (Molly Brook)

# Heaton Park Congregational Band of Hope

### Established 1869

## THE NEXT

# 𝕸onthly 𝕸eeting

### will be held on

## Monday December 1st, 1913

Doors open at 7-0          Meeting to commence at 7-30 prompt.

Chairman        -        -        -        Mr. H. H. DOLPHIN
Speaker        -        -        -        -        Mr. WORTHINGTON
(of Eccles)
Accompanist        -        -        -        Miss E. GILLIBRAND

## PROGRAMME

Hymn                                        Prayer

Chairman's Remarks

| | |
|---|---|
| Song        ..        ..        .. | ..        Miss Wilcockson |
| Irish Reading        ..        " Biddy among the Yankey's " | Mrs. Howell |
| Duet        "The Spider and the Fly" | Mrs. Gregson and Mr. Howell |
| Song        ..        ..        .. | ..        Miss Wilcockson |

Hymn

Address        -        -        -        Mr. WORTHINGTON

### " ALE and ANARCHY "

### An Endbridge Comedy in 2 scenes.

—— Cast ——

| | | |
|---|---|---|
| Peter Pater, a customer        ..        .. | .. | Mr. H. Nobbs |
| Dicky Dill, the landlord        .. | .. | Mr. J. R. Gregson |
| Kate        ..        .. | .. | Miss L. Hardman |
| Mrs. Wigglesworth        .. | .. | Miss E. Maull |
| Sam Wigglesworth        ..        .. | .. | Mr. H. Nobbs |
| Richard Grey | | Mr. J. R. Gregson |
| Flora Hine | Members of | Mrs. Gregson |
| Elsie Deyne | the Endbridge | Miss E. Dennis |
| Arthur Ford | Dramatic | Mr. K. Howell |
| Edward Highgate | Society | Mr. E. Barlow |

Scene 1        Snuggery of the Ring-o-Bells.
    „   2        A room in Grey's home.

Doxology                                        Benediction

Come early and in good numbers and let us have an enjoyable and profitable evening

---

Admission : Members Free on showing their cards paid up to date.                Friends One Penny

Mr. S E Horrocks
    „   A Mayor        } Hon. Secs
    „   R Yates
Mr. J. R. Gregson, Treasurer

*Programme: Heaton Park (1913)*                                        (CA)

# Rowarth Sunday School.

### ANNUAL

# TEA MEETING

### AND

# Entertainment

### WILL BE HELD

## On Good Friday, April 6th, 1917.

### ARTISTES:

**MR. & MRS. JAMES R. GREGSON, Mellor.**

**MISS A. LYDDIARD, Birch Vale.**

**MR. H. MELLING, Birch Vale.**

**MR. CHAS. STAFFORD, Birch Vale.**

**MR. W. HALSTEAD, Birch Vale.**

**Accompanist - MR. TOM WATERHOUSE.**

Tea on the Tables at 4-30 p.m.

**Tickets for Tea & Entertainment 10d. each, Scholars 6d. each.**

G. H. BAILEY, PRINTER, NEW MILLS.

## PROGRAMME.

Opening Hymn ... ... ... ... ... ...Audience

PRAYER.

Recital ... "The Cremation of Sam McGee" Service ... James R. Gregson

Song ... ... ... ..."Love the Pedlar" ... Mrs. Gregson

Song... ... ... ... ... ... Mr. Chas. Stafford

### "CLEAR PROOF"

(A Trifle by James R. Gregson)

John Merton ... ... James R. Gregson
Kate, his wife ... ... Florence Gregson

Song... ... ... ... ... ... Miss A. Lyddiard

CHAIRMAN'S REMARKS.

Recitals ... { (a) " Little Orphant Annie " (Riley) } James R. Gregson
              { (b) " Cuddle Doon " }

Song... ... ... ..."Happy Summer Song" ... Mrs. Gregson

Song ... ... ... ... ... ... Mr. H. Melling

### "KING JOHN"—Act IV, Scene I.

(Shakespeare)

Hubert ... ... ... James R. Gregson
Arthur ... ... ... Lucy Walton

Song... ... ... ... ... Miss A. Lyddiard

Recitation ... ... ... ...Mr. W. Halstead

Song... ... ... ... ... ... Mr. Chas. Stafford

Selections from Sheridan's

### "THE SCHOOL FOR SCANDAL."

Sir Peter Teasle... ...James R. Gregson
Lady Teasle ... ... ...Florence Gregson

Song... ... ... ... ... Mr. H. Melling

DOXOLOGY.     BENEDICTION.

(CA)

*Programme: Rowarth Sunday School (1917)*

# PRIMITIVE METHODIST SCHOOL, COMPSTALL.

SATURDAY, MARCH 29th, 1919

## THE MARPLE DRAMATIC SOCIETY

WILL GIVE A PERFORMANCE OF

# "YOUNG IMESON"

*A Comedy in Three Acts, by JAMES R. GREGSON.*

*Characters in order of appearance.*

| | | |
|---|---|---|
| Kenneth Imeson | … … | Herbert M. Prentice |
| Laura Imeson | … … | Elsie Clarkson. |
| Harry Clough | … … | Herbert Williams. |
| Joan Morrill | … … | Marion Prentice |
| Andrew Weatheredge | … … | James R. Gregson. |
| Asenath Wagstaff | … … | Carrie Kenyon. |
| Nathan Wagstaff… | … … | Walter Fawley. |
| | | Ernest Capper. |
| Joe Smith… | … … | Millė Fernley. |
| Bella Buckley | … … | J. R. Kershaw. |
| Jackson Pinnefether | … … | Fred Winterbottom |
| Clifford | … … | |

The Action takes place in Railton, a village in the West Riding of Yorkshire, in the year 191—

**Scene : Living-place of Imeson's House.**

Eight weeks pass between Act I and Act II.

One week passes between Act II and Act III.

In Act II the Curtain will be lowered for one minute to indicate the passing of a few hours.

### THE PLAY PRODUCED BY THE AUTHOR.

A Programme of Instrumental Music will be rendered during the evening by a company of artistes under the direction of MRS. W. J. HENMAN.

Stage-Manager : J. R. KERSHAW.

Assistants : J. WATERS & C. BRADSHAW.

Doors open 6·30   -   The Performance will commence at 7 p.m. prompt.   -   Proceeds in aid of Trust Funds.

## Admission by this Programme. 1/6

J. Hambleton, Printer, Compstall.

*Programme: Primitive Methodist, Compstall (1919)*

(CA)

*Programme:*
*Huddersfield Theatre Royal (c1920)* (CA)

*Programme:*
*Albert Theatre,*
*Brighouse (1922)* (CA)

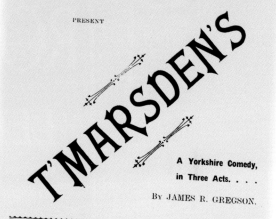

## ALBERT THEATRE,
### BRIGHOUSE.
**MONDAY, TUESDAY & WEDNESDAY, OCT. 2nd, 3rd & 4th.**

## The Huddersfield Thespians

PRESENT

# T'MARSDEN'S

A Yorkshire Comedy,
in Three Acts. . . . .

BY JAMES R. GREGSON.

### PRICES:

| CIRCLE | SIDE CIRCLE | BALCONY | AREA |
|--------|-------------|---------|------|
| 2/- | 1/3 | 1/- | 6d. |
| EARLY DOORS: | | | |
| 2/4 | 1/7 | 1/3 | 9d. |
| | (Including Tax). | | |

Early Doors at 6-45. Ordinary Doors at 7-0. Commence 7-30.

The Premier Printing Co. (Brighouse), Ltd.

*This invitation will admit one person only on*
**Saturday, November 1st, 1919**
*Not available on any other date*

### STOCKPORT GARRICK SOCIETY

|  |  |
|--|--|
| President | BURLEY COPLEY |
| Honorary Secretary | A. H. PAGE |
| Honorary Treasurer | ARTHUR W. SLATER |

## THE MARPLE DRAMATIC SOCIETY
IN

# "YOUNG IMESON"

A COMEDY IN THREE ACTS

By JAMES R. GREGSON

GARRICK CHAMBERS : WELLINGTON ST.
STOCKPORT

*Invitation: Stockport Garrick –*
*Young Imeson (1919)* (CA)

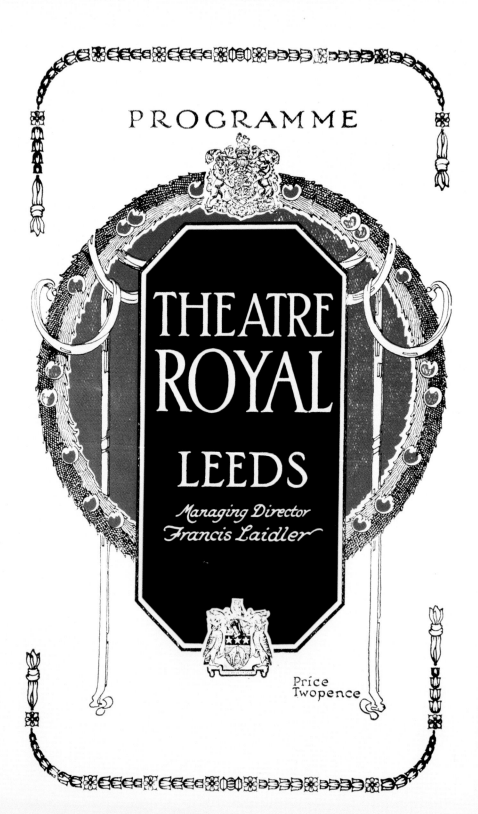

PROGRAMME

THEATRE
ROYAL
LEEDS

*Managing Director*
*Francis Laidler*

Price
Twopence

*Programme: Theatre Royal Leeds (c1924)* (CA)

# Chapter Fifteen

The question was then, what next? The answer came without my seeking it. I had had quite enough of London and the professional theatre for a while, my self-confidence had been sadly shaken, two expensive incursions upon London had left me, apparently, with little more than a bundle of interesting press cuttings and an uncertain future.[90]

My job as director of the Industrial Theatre had gone too. The third season had been interrupted and curtailed by my absence in London, and when I saw Dow on my return it was to hear that the firm could no longer afford to subsidise a venture which had exhausted its publicity value. The firm had lost eleven thousand pounds in the year just ended and ten thousand in the year before that. Luxuries were cut, and I was a luxury. He had decided therefore, that if I was willing, I must be found some work in the office.

I became his "Repairs Clerk" and, as a makeweight to what was a very minor job, took over the circularizing work as well. I put forward one or two ideas for improving our catalogues and leaflets which Dow thought might help. "Though", he said, "the only thing that will put the pram trade on its feet is an Act of Parliament imposing a tax on bachelors and imposing penal sentences for the use of prophylactics. Even then I doubt whether we would pull through unless they gave us a monopoly of the industry!"

I'd hardly settled into the routine when a vacancy occurred in the costing department. I asked Dow if I might have it.

"What do you know about costing?" he asked.

"Very little", I replied. "But perhaps a bit more than the chap who's going."

"Likely enough", he grinned. "All right. Cost clerk you are! And you get a pound a week more for your cheek!"

So, with four pounds a week and my railway fares, I joined the costing department to find myself the junior of the two laziest men in the factory. Even to my uninstructed mind the costing we did was a farce. We measured, for each model, some thirty-odd pieces of timber, weighed six to twelve bits of metal, squared the area of the leather-cloth and priced all these together with various quantities of buttons, tapes, nuts and bolts and paint. To these we added rough estimates of the labour cost supplied by the various foremen and some mysterious percentages for waste and supervision and overheads. The result was a figure which, as we found later, bore little relation to the

---

[90] The comedy did well. It pleased the critics and filled the theatre. Mr. St. John Ervine was so delighted that he told the London managers that they ought 'to make a corner in Mr. Gregson' as undoubtedly he understood how to write comedy. But none of the West End managers took his advice. The play was Yorkshire. And whilst Lancashire comedians may flourish in London, and Scottish and Devonshire plays succeed, there had been no precedent for a Yorkshire play. It was dialect and managers were afraid.
An article written by "Playfellow", possibly 1927 or 1928, after a revival of *T'Marsdens* at the Everyman Theatre in 1927, which Gregson never mentions.
Unattributed Newspaper cutting Gregson scrapbooks West Yorkshire Archives, Calderdale, GRE2

actual cost – a figure which, apparently, was never checked against the output of the factory.

I was, to put it mildly, scandalised at these slip-shod ways, and one morning, when Dow was rallying me about some "up-in-the-air" proposals of the Labour Party and criticising reformers and idealists for their lack of business acumen, I let him have a real broadside. I reminded him that the last man who'd made a song-and-dance about "a business man's government" was Horatio Bottomley.[91] And I pitied the state whose civil servants ran its affairs no better than he ran his factory.

A smaller man than Dow would have promptly put me in my place by sacking me on the spot. Instead he waited until I ran down – making a better show of being amused than I could have done – then challenged me with "All right. Down to brass tacks, MacGregson. What's wrong with my running of this place?"

I pointed to one of the percentages on a cost sheet, and asked, "Can you prove to me that that figure's right?"

He couldn't.

"And neither can anyone else here! – Why?"

"Rhetorical question – Go on!"

"Because you've a costing department that only estimates and never checks!"

"A Daniel come to judgement!" Then came a typical turning of the tables. "And what's my costing department doing to allow such a shocking state of affairs?"

We set up, gradually, a system of output checks on every department. At the end of three months we had proved that our estimates of the labour costs in the Saw Mill were 15% to 20% too high, and that the cost of supervision was nearer 20% than the 10% we had been adding.

The first result of this was that we cut our selling prices five to ten per cent. The second was that I was launched on a brief but glorious career as an efficiency expert.

It was a case of the blind leading the astigmatic! The truth was I was as lucky in this as I had been in that first demonstration rehearsal on my first morning with Dow. As he himself put it, "We've lived so long with prams that we can't see 'em any more. Your usefulness will last just as long as your ignorance!" He threatened that if he ever caught me looking at a real pram he'd sack me instanter.

The process grew like a snowball, one economy leading to another as naturally and inevitably as the opening of a flower.

A simple question one morning – a question asked in genuine ignorance – led to an investigation in which I discovered we were using $2^3/_4$d worth more leather-cloth than

---

[91]  Horatio Bottomley (1860-1933). His career veered wildly from failure to success, and from fame to disgrace, ending in the grotesque sight of the journalist who had proclaimed himself "the soldiers friend" being sent to prison for defrauding thousands of ex-soldiers of what little money they had.

ADVERTISERS' ANNOUNCEMENTS. 5

# STORIES OF BUSINESS PROGRESS.

## A FACTORY WITH THE PUBLIC SCHOOL SPIRIT.

*Our cricket and football teams win most of their matches, our tennis courts are crowded, and we take the City Town Hall for our thousand dancers.*

*We run the only Industrial Theatre in the world—and a jolly good one, too. See what the big newspapers say about it.*

*Our Boss calls his workpeople by their factory nicknames. . . . We are keen, intelligent workpeople, and we all believe we make better baby-cars than anybody else. The trade believe it; our output is five times the other man's.*

That is " The Song of Our People." It is the hymn and the hum of the Factory with the Public-school Spirit. And should you have the least doubt about it, you may see the original framed in a workroom at Hunslet, Leeds, signed in their own handwritings by a blacksmith, a joiner, a saw-miller, a painter, an engineer, an upholstress, and last—as one among them all—by the Boss.

*The principal " Simcett " factory at Hunslet, Leeds.*

These happy workpeople spend their days in an endeavour to make every baby in the country as happy as themselves. They sing as they plane the wood, fix the springs, adjust the hood, and arrange the waist belt, slung on two short straps, which will make baby perfectly safe while allowing him to coo and throw himself about in the sheer ecstasy of his young life.

As you will have guessed, they make baby carriages—beautiful baby carriages. They make them by the hundred thousand. For that they are paid.

But these men and women, boys and girls at heart, think they ought to do more than ensure the comfort and safety of Britain's babies. They had the idea that in their spare time they could do something to brighten the lives of grown-up people too.

### " REHEARSALS " AT WORK.

So they turned their attention to the drama, and studied Shakespeare with a view to performing him. Sir Frank Benson, who heard of their intention, gave them every encouragement, and they went ahead, committing to memory while at their work the lines of " The Merchant of Venice."

" *The quality of mercy is not strained*," murmured Portia, who by day is a typist, as she made out the pro forma invoices of baby carriages put on rail.

" *If every ducat in six thousand ducats Were in six parts, and every part of ducat . . . .*" hissed a clerk in the despatch de-

before it is passed to the workshops every bit of it is tested.

Simpson Fawcett are using a new varnish, the glossiest and most enduring that can be obtained They tested 87 samples to pick out the best. Each sample was applied to a panel corresponding to the side of a perambulator, and the 87 panels were exposed to the open air, in all weathers, for a sufficient period.

The varnish that came out best in this long, practical test is the varnish used on their baby carriages to-day.

The three-ply timber used is carefully chosen, and then properly seasoned in the firm's own yards and their special drying rooms.

The axles—a very important part of a perambulator—are made on war machines originally installed to manufacture the bolts of 3 per cent. nickel (an extraordinarily hard material) for the huge aeroplanes that were going to bomb Berlin. Simpson Fawcett never have a complaint about a broken axle!

Plating that never rusts, because it is done by the firm's own plant, formerly used to plate shells from munition factories in all parts of the country; special handle-bars designed and fixed in such a way as to give more hand-room, greater leverage, and an easier " tilt "; and adjustable hood-joints, so that the hood can be regulated to any height required, are other features of " Simcett " or " Star " prams.

### DETAILS OF PERFECTION.

You may have a soundly built, serviceable pram without the clever little details which give perfect ease of control. But it will not be a " Simcett " or a " Star " pram. The manufacturers of these baby carriages make the perambulator de luxe, which it is a joy to wheel—a joy to you and to baby. And their prices are moderate.

Simpson Fawcett believe they are the only firm in the world who obtained an Act of Parliament to protect a patent. It relates to a special kind of hammock spring—the character of the various springs, you know, is a most important consideration in baby carriage manufacture—and, owing to a technicality in procedure, it was discovered that the patent had lapsed. So a special Act was passed regranting the patent; the document is signed by Queen Victoria and bears £800 worth of wax stamps!

*The " Simcett " Underslung de Luxe, embodying the latest style of springwork and tubular handle.*

*Simpson Fawcett – advert (c1922)*

*(CA)*

we needed to. We turned out at least 1300 prams a week. When I reported to Dow he promptly doubled my salary, and I became the highest paid man on the staff, not excluding the factory manager.

Another query led to our using five-ply instead of timber for the loose seats – a better job at less cost – and this new departure led to a further saving in leather-cloth, and so on. An investigation into the cost of "repairs" to prams still in process of construction led to our changing the route which the bodies of the prams had to travel through the factory. This saved some ten pounds a week in repairing the damage they suffered in transit, and another five in the labour required to transport them.

We cut our prices again and our sales went up. Our people drew much better wages. Another simple idea that came like a revelation to the innocents that we were was that the percentage we put on each pram for overhead charges was not a law of the Medes and Persians. If 25% was right for a yearly output of £70,000, it was too high for an output of £100,000. This all too obvious conclusion led to our slashing our prices on our export lines and our capture of the Danish market.

Our rake's progress in reverse went on merrily. The first year our losses were down

FROM MILL BOY TO PLAYWRIGHT.—Mr. J. R. Gregson, here demonstrating a century-old perambulator at the British Industries Fair, is the successful Yorkshire dramatist who as a boy began work in a Brighouse mill. He is associated with a Leeds firm and writes plays in his leisure.

## MOTOR-CYCLE FOR CHILDREN

The latest invention for children. A miniature motor-cycle, to be seen at the British Industries Fair, which will open on Monday at the White City.

*British Industries Fair – James Gregson, with pram and bike (1927)* (CA)

to £2000, the second year we showed a modest profit of £100, the third found us between two and three thousand to the good. We were still gaily engaged in what Dow called "the general pursuit of the fraction" when, without the least warning, our collaboration came to a sudden end and once again I had to cast about for another job.

During the happy years of my reign as a profit-maker – a period I can never look back upon without smiling at the ironic comedy - our family circumstances improved out of all recognition. We cleared off all our debts, moved to a larger and better house, refurnished and replenished our scanty wardrobe, and began to take real holidays. The one fly in the ointment was Florence's sad state of health. She suffered from bouts of vertigo and sickness which grew steadily more severe, frequent and prolonged, until she became afraid to venture out of doors and life became a prolonged misery. A fortunate, chance encounter with an unknown young doctor revealed that she was suffering from Meniere's disease. The recovery was painfully slow.

For some time after my non-success in London I devoted all my time and thought to making money any way I could. I was fully occupied at the factory, away from home from eight in the morning until six-thirty at night, but in my spare time I wrote odd articles and short stories for my local papers and made no attempt at anything worth while. Nobody appeared to want it from me, anyway. I did draft the first act of a farce which I thought might be cheap enough for the multitude, but, losing faith in my ability to make anything even of that, I put it aside. I'd found easier ways of making money than the theatre, and I meant to make it. I'd done enough sweating and unpaid work for art. If I had to do "owt for nowt" henceforth I'd do it for mysen: No more "thank-you" jobs for me!

But I was not allowed to sulk for long. In the Autumn of 1924, Charles F Smith offered me a semi-professional engagement to play "Zero" in *The Adding Machine*.[92] One of the moving spirits of the Leeds Art Theatre, he had plenty of time to pursue his hobby – or rather his passion – for experimental drama. He was in charge of a family business in Leeds, a clothing factory specialising in women's coats and costumes. He ran it efficiently with surprising little personal attendance and supervision. A very moderate actor, an ambitious producer, he was at his best and happiest as an organiser and impresario. He had a special penchant for religious plays, excellent judgment, and a real flair for the theatre. Had he more money to burn he might have done bigger things – I doubt if they would have been more worth while. He did for Leeds what Barry Jackson did for Birmingham.[93] His contribution to the dramatic renaissance of the twenties was, to my mind, much more valuable.

Once again I had been fortunate in stumbling upon someone who could command my loyalty and full co-operation – someone, moreover, whose ideas were a challenge to

---

[92] Written by the American Elmer Rice (1892-1967). *The Adding Machine* satirised the growing regimentation of men in the machine age through the life and death of the arid book-keeper, Mr. Zero.

[93] The Birmingham Repertory Theatre was one of the most influential companies in the history of the English Stage. It was founded by Barry Jackson in 1913 and under Jackson quickly revolutionized English Theatre, promoting experimental production and pioneering innovations such as performing Shakespeare in modern dress.

mine, not only providing the opportunity to exercise my ability but daring me, even goading me, into making the best I could of it.

I was scared stiff of the part of "Zero" and would have turned it down but for the fee of £20 at the end of it. It was to prove one of my most successful parts and that production of Rice's essay in Expressionism the first of several. It was also to get me "the bird", for our audiences in York sat through the performances (thank goodness there were only two!) in a silence of disapproving horror that could be felt.[94]

It was not the most promising start to the venture that sprang from it, and whose details Smith and I discussed during our long journeys between Leeds and York – the Leeds Civic Playhouse.

*Edith*
*Ailsa*
*Geraldine*
*Craig, c1910*

National Portrait Gallery, London

The summer of 1925 saw me up to my eyes in work in a kind of "One foot in sea and one on shore" existence, for I was still shy of plunging completely into the theatre again. I stuck to my "efficiency expert" job with Dow, but all my spare time was taken up with preparations for the opening of the new venture, and appearance with the Leeds Art Theatre in the name part in *Androcles And The Lion* – the man, not the noble beast – and the writing of a new play.

"Androcles" was the occasion of my first meeting with Edith Craig who was, provided

---

[94] *The Adding Machine*

Among those who have merely read the play, *The Adding Machine*, there are many who regard it, on the score of a few phrases, as something tainted with indecency. After seeing it actually performed by the York Everyman Theatre Company last night, one can only say that the idea of indecency simply does not come to mind.

Let us, as Mr. Zero would say, get this thing right. This is a play in which, at times, an attempt is made to exhibit the minds of characters 'with the lids off'. To this end, the old-stage convention of the aside is revived and put to a new use. Instead of addressing the audience, the character speaks into vacancy the thoughts of his wandering mind. If he had two voices he could bear his part in dialogue at the same time; but as it is, you could get at any rate the thoughts of Mr. Zero while, for instance he carries on his mechanical clerking; and also the thoughts of the woman who works opposite. Some of them are thoughts of sex, and whatever some people may say, thoughts of sex do run through the processes of life, and in the circumstances of this play the exhibition of character by the method chosen would be false without them.

But this is only one aspect of *The Adding Machine*, with its bitter indictment of white collared slavery, and its savage lashing of the half-baked folk that are fit for nothing else. Whether one likes or dislikes it, this is a most remarkable play and last night's performance was far and away better than anything previously achieved by the York organisation.

Mr. James R Gregson's rendering of the plodding, petty-minded, horizonless Zero was fine work, whether in scenes where he had nothing at all to say, or where he had everything, as in the trial scene. He compelled dislike of the character, for there was nothing in it to like; but he compelled pity too.

*Yorkshire Evening Post* : February 25th 1925.

she approved of me, to be my producer.[95]  I was ushered into the presence of the formidable, unpredictable genius with suitable awe.  She sat upright in her armchair, a majestic, gracious figure in black and red, her white hair almost hidden by a red bandana sheathed like a turban.  She was eating peppermint creams – a habit she'd contracted as an antidote to smoking which her doctor had forbidden.

Her first question was, "Can you fall?"

I thought I could.

"Show me!"

I did a few falls, throwing in a somersault or two for good measure.

She eyed me keenly for a moment then offered me a peppermint.  I'd passed.

"Heaven help you!" murmured my sponsor.  "You're for it, all right!"

I was.  She was the most exasperating, exacting, fascinating and delightful of slave-drivers, cooing, storming, cajoling, flying into tantrums, with bewildering swiftness. If she cast you for a part, you had to be good in it.  It made no difference whether it was a part made for you, or a part for which you weren't really suited.  If it was your part, she drove you frantic by her insatiable demands for perfection.  If it wasn't your part she broke your heart proving she couldn't have been wrong in thinking it was.  I suffered under and revelled in her torture through many productions.  I had one terrific row with her, goaded into defying the Olympian storm.  I was sent to Coventry.  For two days she looked through me at rehearsals as though Part Four of *Back to Methusaleh* had no "Elderly Gentleman", but on the first night as I took my curtain call, I felt myself lifted off my feet, hugged and kissed whilst she whispered, "Thank God there's one artist in Yorkshire!"

"Edie" had all the Terry charm and a fair share of the family genius.  Like most of the slaves who hated and loved, laughed at and revered her, I would not have had her otherwise.  Her memory remains green - and grateful.

The play I was working on during that summer of 1925, which was to have its first production in the first season of the projected Leeds Civic Playhouse, was the stage version of a serial story which nearly wrecked a newspaper.  The incident is worth recalling not only because of its place in my story, but as a tribute to a good friend and a devoted journalist, Richard Hawkin.

I met Hawkin soon after my arrival in Huddersfield to work for Wareing.  He was the editor of his local Labour weekly newspaper, and almost its sole contributor.  Hawkin was a native of York, was and still is a Freeman of the city by birth, as a descendant of an earlier member of one of the City Guilds.  Like all Labour papers in those days, The Huddersfield Citizen – or was it called Worker?[96] – was having a hard struggle to exist, and it's a measure of Hawkin's devotion to Socialism that he stuck to what

---

[95]  Edith Craig (1869-1947).  An actress, producer, and designer in the early 20th century, she was the daughter of the legendary actress, Ellen Terry.  In a testimonial given when Gregson joined The Leeds College of Music, she said: "Leeds does not realise what a fine and true artist it possesses in Mr. Gregson."

[96]  It was *The Worker*.

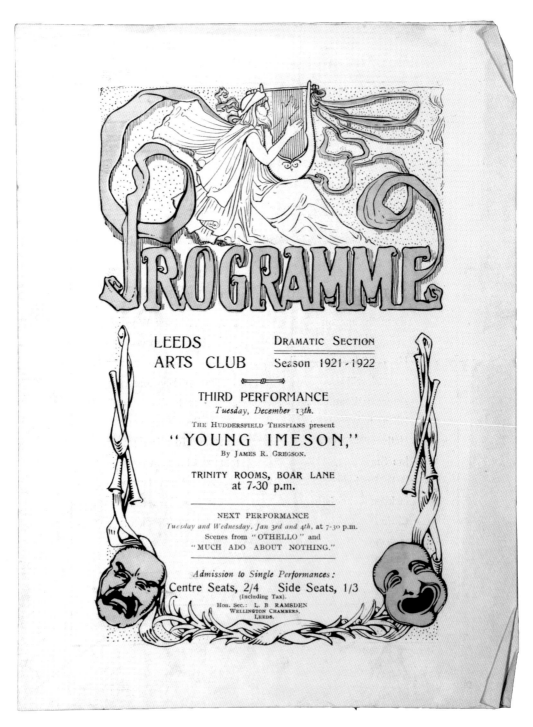

*Programme: Leeds Art Club (1921)* (CA)

PRESENT

## "The Adding Machine,"

### By ELMER L. RICE,

—— IN ——

CENTRAL HALL, EXHIBITION BUILDINGS,

YORK,

On TUESDAY & WEDNESDAY, 24th & 25th February, 1925.

AT 7-30 P.M.

# PROGRAMME.

*Programme: York Everyman Theatre (1925)*                    *(CA)*

## THE HUDDERSFIELD THESPIANS

### QUALITY STREET

BY

SIR JAMES M. BARRIE

PROGRAMME

THEATRE ROYAL, HUDDERSFIELD.   DEC. 15, 1920

**QUALITY STREET**

By Sir JAMES M. BARRIE.

Act I.                  The Blue and White Room
Act II.                          The School
Act III.                          The Ball
Act IV.          The Blue and White Room

Ten Years elapse between Acts I and II.

*The names of the players in the order of their appearance*

| | |
|---|---|
| Miss Fanny Willoughby | Constance Waller |
| Miss Willoughby | Kitty Montgomery |
| Miss Susan Throssel | Beatrice A. Beard |
| Miss Henrietta Turnbull | Kathleen Johnston |
| Miss Phoebe Throssel | Andrea Woolner |
| Patty | Judith Dawson |
| The Sergeant | George Geissler |
| Valentine Brown | James R. Gregson |
| Arthur | May Milnes |
| Isabella | Margaret Fuller |
| Charlotte | Mollie Lee |
| Ensign Blades | Harry Broadbent |
| Harriet | Edith Elmslie |
| Lieutenant Spicer | Stanley Charlesworth |
| Old Soldier | A. Morgan Lee |
| A Gallant | William Reeds |
| At the Ball | Isabel Moxon |

Children at the School—Ida Michaelbacher, Sylvia Fleming, Betty Cotton,
Muriel Hirst, Kathleen Cheetham, Winifred Black, Jessie Booth, Phyllis
Thornton, Nora Beaumont, Kathleen Fenton.

Producer                    Andrea Woolner
Stage Manager               G. H. Crossley
Musical Director            Laurance Turner

The Society desires to thank Mr. Alfred Wareing for his generosity in
giving the use of the Theatre, Mrs. Haines for arranging the dances,
Mr. Arthur W. Kaye and members of his orchestra for providing the music,
and Mr. John R. Gauld for the design of the programme.

*Programme, Huddersfield Thespians (1920)*

(CA)

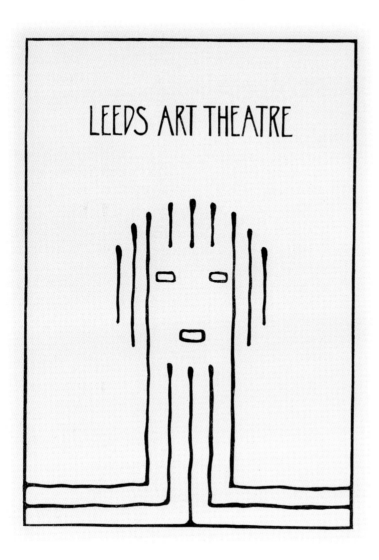

*Programme,*
*Leeds*
*Art*
*Theatre*
*(c1923)*        *(CA)*

was, undoubtedly, an underpaid job compared to one he could have easily obtained elsewhere. It wasn't long after our meeting before I was contributing a weekly column of magazine stuff.

I kept up my contributions during my out-of-work period, and finally launched on a serial story which I called *The Shining Steps.*[97] It concerned two rather sorry specimens, who, after a disastrous start to their marriage, were to climb, in rivalry of each other, hating each other at first, to great heights of selflessness and sacrifice. Naturally, in pointing the miracle of a lily growing on a dunghill, I had to make sure that my readers understood what a deplorable dunghill it was. It proved more than the readers and advertisers could stand. The serial had been running some weeks when I noticed that that one of the regular, larger adverts on the front page was missing. Hawkin confessed

---

[97] The concluding part (the eighth instalment ) was on Saturday April 29th 1922.

ruefully that it wasn't the only one he'd lost. Moreover a considerable number of readers had stopped taking the paper. When after much probing, he admitted that the reason for the boycott was my story, I offered to withdraw it. This he would not hear off, I was a free contributor, he said, in every sense of the word. If a man writing for nothing couldn't say what he wanted, who could? If the paper couldn't exist on such terms, so much the worse for the paper. He'd sooner be without the job than give in to such misguided pressure.[98]

Grateful as I was for his loyal backing, I was angry at the blind, foolish Puritanism behind the boycott. Why should I offer the best I had to give to such narrow-necked idiots? I wound up the serial summarily in the next instalment and wrote no more for the paper.

The play that came out of that unfinished story, *Sar' Alice* has never made the grade.[99] It is curiously uneven – the first two acts amongst the best work I've done, the last two, too loosely constructed and truer to the theatre than to life. Its major weakness is a scene in which the audience watch my leading character at the moment of his religious "conversion", - a scene better left to the imagination; which is why, I suppose, it has proved much more successful as a radio play.

---

[98] The future of the Worker

We beg to intimate to our readers that the WORKER will be reduced to one penny commencing with next week's issue ……….. We are slightly altering the size of the paper, but we are hoping to introduce new features, and to give a more national weekly review of the Labour Movement. We very cordially appeal to all our present readers to do all they can to help us increase the circulation of the paper. In view of an early General Election in the country it is of the highest importance that Labour must have its own organ in every constituency. We trust that the change which is taking place will result in increased support of the WORKER. *The Worker* : October 21st 1922.

Unfortunately, it was not to be, the paper ceased production five weeks later on November 25th 1922. The General Election took place on November 15th 1922, when the Liberal, Sir Arthur Harold Marshall was elected. Huddersfield had had a Liberal MP from 1857, apart from 1893-1895, when a Conservative was elected. Ironically, there was another election a year later, on December 6th 1923, when the Labour candidate was elected.

One can't help thinking that over the last few weeks of the paper's existence, that the scathing, almost virulent, attacks on the other parties must have limited its readership to the faithful hardcore. However, as this is based on the perusal of only a few weeks issues, and it was over 80 years ago, it is now difficult to appreciate the mood of the times or Huddersfield's then radical reputation.

[99] The Civic Playhouse

Mr. Gregson and title of his new play

Mr. J R Gregson of the Leeds Civic Playhouse, in an address to the 19 Club in Leeds yesterday on the "Civic Playhouse", describing the aims and origin of the organization, revealed some very interesting facts about his new play, which is due for production today, *The Shining Steps*.

The name he said, as a matter of fact, had been changed to *Sar' Alice*, the name of the chief character, at the suggestion of Miss Clemence Dane. Originally, he had called the play *A Bonny Pair*, but he had adopted *The Shining Steps* as a title because it was equally appropriate to the play in question and to another one which he had in mind, and which would have been substituted for it, had the present play been produced, as at one time was likely, in London. He had to admit that he had sold his soul over the play. He had changed the sad ending, which he was sure was the right one, for a happy ending, in deference to the universal demand of his friends. His wife had pestered him to death, his actors assured him that they should never get it over, his old schoolmaster sent him a telegram with the one word, "devil", and Miss Kathleen Boutall, who was playing the chief part, had said she should not play it if the ending was a sad one.

*The Yorkshire Post* : December 11th 1925.

# Chapter Sixteen

I have neither the space nor the knowledge necessary to tell the full story of the Leeds Civic Playhouse. The only man who can do full justice to the now historic venture is Charles F Smith, who was its mainspring and genius from its inception, through its years of growing success, until the end when it declined into professionalism and lost its experimental aims and character. But the years in which it was leading the amateur movement in the country, growing in achievement and influence, cover the happiest, most hard-working and perhaps the most truly successful period of my life.

The Leeds Civic Playhouse had never any official backing or support, much as it deserved it. It was a purely private venture designed to bring the drama within the reach of the poorest, to appeal to the widest possible audience and to present a catholic programme of worthwhile plays, mainly modern in age and outlook, employing amateurs from all over the county, and experimenting with the newest methods of staging and production.

Apart from these ambitious aims, the Playhouse had a somewhat unusual feature. It was a free theatre.[100] No charge was made for admission and although it was possible to reserve a seat at the cost of sixpence, the seat was forfeit unless occupied at least ten minutes before the rise of the curtain, and free to be occupied by anyone who cared to claim it. We depended mainly on the collections we took up at each performance. And as, during our first years, our receipts from both booking and gifts averaged 8½d per head, our financial circumstances, even with full houses of five hundred, which were soon the rule, left much to be desired. So did our accommodation.

We rented the Albert Hall, a smaller, inconvenient replica of its London namesake. The circular auditorium was too lofty. The platform was over thirty feet across, but only ten feet from back to front at its deepest, and was utterly devoid of any staging equipment. As we were not allowed to fix anything to the walls or damage the fabric in any way, we had to erect a temporary apron to enlarge the acting area and a wooden

---

[100] Letter to the editor
The Leeds Civic Theatre
Sir – The conclusion of your excellent leader in Thursday's issue on the new Leeds Civic Theatre, warning the promoters of this striking venture that people who most need dramatic education will not go, even for nothing, to listen to performances which do not promise entertainment that they can understand, rather begs the whole question I think. It takes what is merely a sketchy outline (as the announcements of the Leeds Civic Theatre had of necessity to be) as their complete and definite programme.
As one with whom Mr. J R Gregson has discussed the project, I am convinced that the promoters are fully alive to the dangers of being labelled 'high-brow'; there is no fear that they will repeat the errors of the more advanced 'Little Theatre' schemes.
The suggested plays are certainly of a high order, but this does not mean they are uninteresting. On the contrary, they are first and foremost fine dramatic material, of which Mr. Gregson, with his direct treatment and sound sense of humanity will make the fullest use; moreover they all lend themselves to striking and imaginative scenic treatment.
I hope the plays will, in Mr. Gregson's vivid phrasing, act like 'yeast in the sour dough of our mind'.
A J Spilsbury
The Grammar School, Wakefield
*Leeds Mercury*: March 28, 1925.

framework to carry our proscenium, staging drapes and lighting. Everything had to be carted in and out for every production, and, when not in use, stored in our modest headquarters, severely restricting our inadequate rehearsal space. None of us found these and other handicaps worthy of comment. We had all known worse.

We had a stage carpenter and an electrician who handled each production for a little pocket-money, and I was engaged as producer, to act as and when required in addition, for a fee of £20 per production. All the rest of our workers, stage hands, actors and front–of-the-house staff were amateur volunteers. Smith ransacked his factory and provided us with enough out-of-date material for a set of tabs and curtains. The press were most kind to us and before our first season was over, we had a most enthusiastic following who referred to the theatre affectionately as "T'Civic". We became the vogue and our performances took on the character of family gatherings – a large and growing family – and a most heterogenous one! I remember one instance of this which is well worth recalling.

One night as the audience were assembling I caught sight of one of my old Industrial Theatre players in lively conversation with Sir Berkeley Moynihan, soon to become Lord.[101] The following morning, at the pram factory, my joiner-actor greeted me with a grin. "What do yer think o' me hobnobbing with that Doctor chap?" he asked. When I asked in return why shouldn't he, he said, "Well, I mean to say, he's a "sir". Though yer wouldn't think it to hear some of the tales he told me! My word, but he's a caution, is yond. There's a good actor wasted in him. I'll bet he knows moor about acting nor thee!"

When I told Moynihan of this later, he said, "A doctor who can't act isn't much good to his patients. As often as not acting's half the treatment – and the secret of success". A pause, then, "I sometimes wonder if I shouldn't have been more use in the playhouse than the operating theatre. Drama, with its power of emotional release, is a great medicine!"

Medicine or not, our audiences took it gratefully. We played in a warm, friendly atmosphere, expectant and encouraging, lively and responsive. One had to give one's best.

I found myself the focal point of this happy family. Charles F. Smith, in spite of his devotion and his gifts, was too shy and diffident to claim the limelight, but he felt that the venture until, or if, it were established, must be built round a personality, the theatre must have its "star". As producer and leading man I was the obvious person, and he promptly set about grooming me for the position. Needless to say, in my then mood and boundless ambition, I was by no means averse to the publicity and the response it evoked.

---

[101] Rt. Hon. Lord Berkeley Moynihan (1865-1936) was born in Malta where his father was an ensign in the Army. He enrolled at Leeds School of Medicine in 1883. By 1910 he was nationally known. Between 1926 and 1931 he was President of the Royal College of Surgeons. Knighted in 1912, CB in 1918, Baronet in 1922 and first Baron of Leeds in 1929.

For our first season we planned five productions, each to have five performances. The Albert Hall was occupied each Wednesday evening in the season by the members of the Institute for their lectures. This meant a hectic Thursday erecting our equipment and scenery, followed by a dress rehearsal usually scrappy and incomplete, and sometimes an all night session by the stage staff to make good deficiencies in our settings and get it all right for the Friday first night. Tuesday was another all-night operation, clearing everything away after the last performance.

The five plays we planned became seven before the season was over. We opened, for no other reason than its appropriate title, with Sutton Vane's *Overture*.[102] As a fanfare it fell rather flat.

Our second production was *Oedipus Rex* in which I was to play the lead. I think we were all dreading the outcome of our ambitious choice – I certainly was – but it proved an arresting, challenging success from which we never looked back. I had decided to discard our proscenium and designed a set consisting mainly of flights of steps stretching across the width of the stage, rising from the auditorium floor and topped by huge pillars and doors that would dwarf the actors. But I dare not risk the same austerity of treatment throughout, and so I concocted a "modernist" lighting plot, spot-lighting the players in different colours, with some sixty-odd changes and cues.

The dress was the most farcical affair. The construction of the huge set, most of it prefabricated in the pram factory, although begun midnight on the Wednesday, was far from complete by the time my actors were assembling. I had a crowd of over a hundred supers who were in entire ignorance of what they were supposed to be or do. They were to begin the play down in the cellarage, two floors below, weeping and wailing, rush up stairs traversing the circular corridors of the intermediate floor, then dash up more stairs and burst into the auditorium through various doors and flood the lower levels of the stage. It worked well in the end but by the time I'd got this all set it was almost bedtime. I'd just time to show the part players their various positions, run through my lighting changes and tell everybody that everything was going to be all right, before dashing for my train hoping it was it was going to be all right, to spend my usual pre-production sleepless night, thinking how to make sure it would be. After an early start next morning and a long and arduous day we were barely ready to start at the usual time, but somehow managed it, and I went on to play one of the most exacting parts I know, keeping an eye on my unrehearsed electrician and snapping my fingers when he was late on his cues.

Our third production was that of my specially written play, *Sar' Alice* with Kathleen Boutall in the female lead, the first dyed-in-the-wool professional to be engaged by us for a special part. I played the male lead, "Ted", Florence found another wonderful opportunity in the motherly, gossipy part of "Ellen", and young Florence had her first speaking part as "Emma Jane". It was quite a promising debut. The play pleasing our audiences more than it did me, and I began almost immediately to re-construct and re-write the latter half.

---

[102] See Appendix 5 for a copy of the inaugural programme.

From *Sar'Alice* we turned to very different fare – the production of *Everyman* in Trinity Church, Boar Lane. This was not in our original schedule, but Charles F Smith was not to be denied his beloved religious drama for long. We produced the play and I had the difficult muse part – difficult to me at least, because of the archaic idiom and verse. It was tiresome to memorise and almost impossible to <u>think</u>. The run was almost over before I was speaking it as my own, living language.

Smith's production was wisely simple – almost austere, - designed to let the play speak for itself. The effect was surprising to me and, whatever the effect it had on the congregations who crowded to see it, it provided me with an unforgettable experience for which I have always been grateful.

We had to close down at the end of three weeks for the production of another startling contrast – *The Adding Machine*. Leeds loved it as much as York had detested it. (Incidentally, it had amusingly varied receptions in different towns. Our production of it in Huddersfield, for example, tore the town into two violently argumentative factions. Their wordy warfare brightened the pages of the *Huddersfield Examiner* for three weeks. Comments were often more pointed than polite. One defender of the play reminded the critics that "To the pure all things are pure". He was told to remember that the next time he had a bad egg for breakfast!).

The most amusing feature of the Leeds production of *The Adding Machine* was the impression created by the lighting. It was forced upon me to some extent by our limited equipment, and was essentially merely an elaboration of the old pantomime techniques of "spotting", hotted up by the use of bizarre combinations and contrasts of colours. The critic described the result as a "revelation of the possibilities of psychological lighting".

I have a sneaking belief that Elmer Rice began to write this Expressionist masterpiece with his tongue in his cheek – as a squib to be put under the tails of Greenwich Village starry-eyed highbrows, but that something got into him, or hold of him, with the result that Scene Six, in particular, is not only sincere writing of a very high order, but one of the finest pieces of high comedy written in this century. It is a sheer joy to play.

Our first season was to have ended with *The Mask And The Face* but cashing in on its success, Charles F Smith decided we should put on Masefield's *Good Friday* during Holy Week. He produced, and I was given the sympathetic part of the "Blind Beggar" with the most beautiful and moving verse in the play.

And on that note ended our first season. We had kept within our narrow but growing means, we had established a reputation for unusual experiments in plays and their presentation, for good and improving standards of production and acting and had found the formula for our future programmes.

I had two more seasons working at full stretch and at every possible moment for the Playhouse before events led to my withdrawal from complete immersion in the work, but before turning to those events I may as well round off this part of the story.

These two seasons saw our audiences growing and our runs becoming gradually longer until we were playing continuously from mid-September to mid-May with some special out-size production during the summer and it soon became impossible for me to produce every play and play in it as well. We found a gifted and loyal colleague for me in the person of an old friend, Arthur E Payne who, like myself, had been an amateur in his prentice days. Even then, the programme became so heavy, that we called from time to time on such well-known outsiders as Edith Craig, Norman Marshall and Kommisarjevsky for special productions.

Norman Marshall showed his quality as a producer not only in *Danton* – one of our typical non-proscenium plays in which Tom Denham scored a great success in the name part, and in which our audience actually shared in the last scene shouting and cheering and following our crowd leaders scattered amongst them, even to storming the stage and smashing the court furnishings in the finale – but also in Bruno Franck's *Twelve Thousand*, perhaps the finest historical play of the century which gave me a great opportunity as "Faderit", the little, pedantic secretary who rises to a moving moment of almost unemotional heroism.

Amongst Edith Craig's productions were *The Dybbuk, The Shining Sun, Back To Methusaleh* and a dramatized version of the oratorio, *St Paul* – another of our Church productions.

*Lewis Casson (MM)*

Productions of my own I specially remember are those of Strindberg's *The Father, Spread Eagle* and *Granite* in which I also played as "The Nameless Man" washed up by the sea. Arguing that I appeared on the scene almost as though in answer to Judith's prayer to the Devil and that, to her, I should have something of the fiend about me, I decided that in my scenes with her alone I should look like someone out of hell. By means of a complicated make-up, and an evermore complicated arrangement of red floods and green spots I was able to change my appearance at will. The effect was to surprise and mystify the audience to such an extent that the play itself suffered sadly. Lewis Casson who had just produced the play with himself and Sybil Thorndyke in the leading parts took me to task severely about this.[103] Somewhat nettled, I'm afraid, I retorted he was only jealous because he hadn't thought of the stunt himself. I knew he was right, though, and that I had overreached myself.

---

[103] Lewis Casson (1875-1969). Actor and theatre director, and husband of Dame Sybil Thorndike.

One of the happiest of our out-of-season ventures was the production of two of Houseman's "Little Plays" to celebrate the septcentenary of St Francis of Assissi. It was also a good means of raising the wind and publishing our forthcoming season. With a brewery lorry for our stage and some searchlights loaned by the military we

Mr. James R. Gregson is undoubtedly the most significant figure of the amateur movement in the West Riding of Yorkshire. He was born at Brighouse, near Huddersfield, forty years ago, and for a time worked as a railway clerk in Lancashire. At Heaton Park he founded a dramatic society for which he wrote four plays. At Marple he founded the Hollywood Players, for whom he wrote *T' Marsdens*, which, with his other well-known comedy, *Young Imeson*, was subsequently produced at the Everyman Theatre, Hampstead.

Mr. Gregson has done nearly everything in the business of the theatre from writing, producing and acting in plays, to selling programmes and scrubbing the pit floor. Once in his early days he was limelight man for Pavlova; he has been the assistant manager of a theatre (The Theatre Royal, Huddersfield); he has run a picture house. He was the chief mover of the Huddersfield Thespians; he founded the Leeds Industrial Theatre, an organisation run by factory workers; he is now the "star"—if such a term is permissible—of the Leeds Civic Playhouse.

His powerful one-act play, *Melchizedek*, has just won the first place for Yorkshire in the British Drama League Festival of Community Drama, and this month, Mr. Gregson will be coming to London for the finals in a play written, produced and acted by himself.

*James Gregson (1927)*          *(CA)*

*Personalities in the Kirkstall Abbey Play (1927)* (CA)

toured various pitches in the city, and whilst we were changing between the plays, various Ministers of the different denominations gave talks on the great man whose memory we were honouring. One evening it rained cats and dogs but the audience wouldn't hear of our calling it off and we played to a "house" of umbrellas. I was surprised to find what an amount of water a tonsured wig can hold! We finished on a Saturday night outside the Town Hall, our audience towering above us on the huge street of steps. The performance went on to the rumbling accompaniment of the busy traffic; it was interrupted twice by the loud bells of the fire-brigade; our speaker that night went on too long, and towards the end of the second play, the Town Hall clock start to chime nine o'clock. We had to pucker in our last lines between the strokes.

The most spectacular of our summer ventures was a production in the ruins of Kirkstall Abbey of a large-scale pageant-cum-play based on Longfellow's poem *Robert of Sicily*. It was written and directed by Nugent Monck of the Norwich Maddermarket Theatre.[104] As writing, it didn't command my respect, as a production it was superb. It ran for three weeks, but the most magical moments, to me, were before the show, when our two hundred players in their medieval costumes strolled about the ruined cloisters which were our open-air green room.

As the seasons went by our lengthening runs increased our casting difficulties. They became almost insoluble. It was never difficult to find amateurs of the right stature willing, even eager, to play leads and major parts, and we could, and did, call on players from all over the Riding. But no matter how keen a player may be, he doesn't take kindly to the idea of giving up six weeks of his evening and weekend leisure to rehearse and appear in a play when he has little more to do than announce that "the carriage awaits"! We eased this problem of "bit actors" at first by finding "apprentices" – young students who could afford to work for nothing more than the chance to learn their craft in our theatre. The next step was a small payment in addition, the next the engagement of young professionals to fill in as required for a modest salary. The increasing strains on the treasury which this entailed drove us, rightly or wrongly, into less adventurous paths with less emphasis on the novel and the experimental and more on the "safe" commercial play. There is a limit to what any amateur theatre can do. We had reached it, but instead of limiting our productions to our amateur acting resources, we went on until our success plunged us into out-and-out professionalism, and a brave, infinitely worth-while venture with a truly wonderful record of first–class work was at an end.

The three seasons during which I was most closely associated with the Leeds Civic Playhouse were as I have said not only supremely satisfying and happy, but busy to a degree. Besides holding down my factory job and running a theatre, I was writing at full pressure and always against the clock. In addition to turning out several newspaper serials each running to seventy or eighty thousand words, I had a weekly column in the *Leeds Mercury*, did some book reviewing, and articles for here and there, and on top of all that found time during 1926 to write my most successful play *The Devil A Saint*.

---

[104] Walter Nigel Monck (1877-1958). Theatre director and founder of the Maddermarket Theatre, Norwich, which was opened in 1921 and was the first permanent re-creation of an Elizabethan Theatre.

My weekdays fell into well-defined compartments. Up at seven a.m. in Huddersfield, in Leeds by nine. Nine to twelve-thirty costing. Twelve-thirty to one-thirty churning out my thousand word instalment of the current serial, lunching meanwhile on a pastie, a bar of chocolate and an orange or apple. One-thirty to five-thirty, costing again. Five-thirty to five-forty five a nap sitting in my office chair, my hand on the blotting pad. Five-forty five to ten-fifteen or later rehearsing or playing. Then home to Huddersfield for a brief snack and talk with Florence and an always too short a spell of bed. Weekends, often eaten into by rehearsals, were reserved for correspondences, the odd articles and family life. At this time I was drawing from various sources the almost incredible sum of £700 a year. I was on top of the world.

*William Armstrong* (MM)

During the comparative leisure of the summer of 1926 I wrote the evidence on which I was cross-examined a week or so later by His Majesty's Royal Commission on "Drama in Adult Education.[105] I also spent a first, delightful long week-end in Oxford and lectured on drama in an extra-mural course on that subject. Naturally I had to take my typewriter with me and in order to keep my serials going, had to type on the crowded train my machine perched on my knees.

We were enjoying a much-needed holiday in the Isle of Man when I received an urgent

---

[105] In his submission Gregson advanced the idea that the theatre was a repudiation of the "insane ideal of standardisation" imposed by his old Board school. He found a more human, discursive and conversational method of tuition, where they were encouraged to think for themselves and to follow their individual bent. He goes on to say :

"Only in drama did I find the fullest scope for this vital activity and in the service of the drama I have acquired, as a bye-product, what real knowledge I possess and what real mental ability I exercise.......I know what modern industry means in terms of monotonous routine tasks. I know what a working-class home life means, with few outlets for emotional 'release' save the 'pub' and the 'chapel'. I know the mental apathy and the crippled spirit they engender. I have spent my life fighting against this state of mind and temper, both in myself and in my fellows."

He also recounted his experiences with the Leeds Industrial Theatre. One wonders though, if anything tangible ever came out of the Royal Commission. The British Drama Festival was already on the go in 1926.

telegram from William Armstrong who was in holiday in Italy.[106]  He was at that time director of the Liverpool Playhouse and had produced there my two comedies, *T'Marsdens* and *Young Imeson*, with such success that I had promised him he should have something he could announce as for the first time on any stage.  At a loss for an idea, rummaging amongst my file of false starts and unfinished scripts, I came across the first act draft of a farce I'd thrown aside called *In the Midst of Death*, if I remember right.[107]  It struck me as promising but thin.  I introduced another character to prepare for extra complications later in the play, sent this revised first act off to Armstrong and went on with my other work. Armstrong replied quickly that he liked what he'd seen, and if he could have the play by the end of August he'd open his next season with it. I promised to comply and forgot all about it. The telegram was followed by letters, the production date was put back and back, I slowly ground out the farce in which I could see very little that was worth while, working mechanically at weekends with Joan hanging round my neck ready to supply the odd word when I halted.  I worked in every gag about death and funerals I could remember or invent, and Armstrong had the complete script by Christmas.  He wouldn't let me have it back for revision but put it on in February 1927.  It was not an overwhelming success; it has never had a London production; but in spite of that has proved by far the most profitable of all my work.  Thirty years old as I write this, it is still in constant demand by amateurs. It has made me more money than all my other work put together.

---

[106] William Armstrong, who had earlier acted at the Liverpool Playhouse, became its director in 1922.  He remained director until his retirement in 1944, at the age of 62.

"Another summons came to a successful actor called William Armstrong who served as a kind of dramatic coach-tutor to the family, though his real job was to keep an eye on Hugh's drinking and other failings. Armstrong ,who later turned from acting to directing and transformed the Liverpool Rep into the best regional theatre in the country, found it humiliating to have to sit at a separate table for dinner, like an upper servant." Paula Byrne, *Mad World : Evelyn Waugh and the Secrets of Brideshead* :  Harper Press, London 2009.

The "Hugh" mentioned was Hugh Lygon , second son of Lord Beauchamp of Madresfield, who was the inspiration for the character of Sebastion Flyte in Evelyn Waugh's novel *Brideshead Revisited*.

[107] In the *Midst of Death* became the *The Devil a Saint*.

# Chapter Seventeen

Between 1920 and 1925, besides *The Devil A Saint*, I wrote only the one-actors – *The Way Of An Angel* and *Saint Mary Ellen*.  We were to put this latter play on at the "Civic" but the Lord Chamberlain refused it a licence on the grounds that "it might give offence to the sentiment of religious reverence", which I interpreted to mean that he thought it blasphemous.  Actually it is the most "religious" of all my work, though it tilts at notions which were being questioned then and are held by very few today.

The immediate result of the ban was that I rushed the play into print and sold a thousand copies within a week in Leeds and Huddersfield alone.  We made the most of the publicity at the "Civic" and capacity audiences crowded to see *Melchisedek* which we put on as a substitute and to give me a heartening reception when I made my entrance as the old, half-crazed nightwatchman.

For six months afterwards I went about reading the play from the pulpits of chapels and at various religious and literary meetings.  The discussions that followed were marked by their thoughtful, reverent mood, and though my views were generally criticised and refuted there was never the slightest suggestion that my play was in bad taste or that the ban was justified.

This is not the place in which to argue the question of censorship, but I must say that my main objection to it is that it is inefficient.  I have had experience of many ridiculous rulings by the Lord Chamberlain, like most producers, but those rulings once made can and are evaded easily, very often by persons ignorant of their details, and there is no machinery to ensure that the script of a play as finally passed by the Censor is adhered to.  In the case of plays printed before being submitted for a licence to perform, there is no obligation on the part of the author or publisher to withdraw the play and reprint the licensed version, our stage censorship is something of a farce.[108]  By the middle of 1928

---

[108]  *Saint Mary Ellen* involves a discussion, largely in dialect, amongst Mary Ellen and others who have 'passed over' to the other side.  She airs her conceptions and desires which the conditions of the new atmosphere do not satisfy.  She speaks freely of her earthly vicissitudes, and passes judgement on the Creator for "Making nowt better nor me, for not making me better nor I am".  "And so", she says "we'll make things ready for another and a better than him."  *The Huddersfield Examiner* reported (no date)
The decision became all the more surprising when it was remembered that another of Gregson's plays, *Melchisadek*, whilst being licensed without question received a visit from the police when first performed in Leeds, as a result of objections raised by those who had seen it.  But the police could do nothing, as the producer had the Lord Chamberlain's licence.
Banned Play  1930
Mr. J R Gregson, the Yorkshire playwright, whose latest one-act play *St. Mary Ellen* has been banned by the Lord Chamberlain, refuses to be angry with Lord Cromer.
Speaking in Bradford on Saturday night to the Playgoer's Society of which he is president, he said "If I said what most of you think I ought to say against him, it would be ungrateful of me".  Four one act plays of his, he said, had only brought him in about £20 in three years, but when *St. Mary Ellen* was banned he got over £300 worth of advertising in a few days.  One result had been that the play had been rushed into print straight away.  The trouble about censorship, he said, was that it was illogical in its operations.  Things written with the purest of intentions were banned, but a comedian could indulge in suggestive business on the stage.  Lord Cromer could stop the performance of *St. Mary Ellen* for the public, but he could not prevent a private performance in a theatre.  The play could even be made into a 'talkie'.
As long as we had an official censor, and one censor whose powers were not too wide, and too drastic, we were all right, said the speaker.  There was a question of the abolishing of the censor and leaving the matter of entertainments to the local police or Watch Committee to see that nothing offended.  "As an author" said Mr. Gregson, "I would much rather be at the mercy of Lord Cromer than a semi-Nonconformist, semi-licensed victuallers' committee in any city."
Unattributed newspaper cutting ,'Gregson scrapbook',  West Yorkshire Archive, Calderdale,GRE2.

Florence was well on the way to full health again, and our circumstances were such as to warrant our buying a new house on the outskirts of Huddersfield. I had two days off from the factory to help with the removal and on my return was summoned for a conference with a very chastened and subdued employer. Holding his pipe between his rigid palms, his face a vast grin of rueful embarrassment, Dow told me that our latest idea of saving money had proved only too successful. We had suggested that one costing department should price the products for both the Leeds and the London factories seeing that both were producing identical models. Our suggestion had been accepted with one vital difference – the costing was to be done by London and not by us. The reason for this decision was, I suspected, some clash or other between Dow and his senior directors. Whatever the reason, the decision meant I should be out of a job and Dow was giving me the earliest warning he could. He assured me I should get at least three months formal notice and that probably meant I had five or six months in which to find a corner elsewhere.

I went out to lunch dashed and only faintly amused at the thought that I was the victim of my own efficiency. I suppose most men in my position and especially in view of my progress at the Civic Playhouse would have plunged completely into full professionalism. But I had grown chary of unemployment and shied at the uncertainty of the theatre. The last few years had allowed us to make good the wastage of the earlier, leaner ones, but had not wiped out the memory of them. I don't think I really considered for a moment any other course but getting another "safe" job. I walked into one that very day.

After lunch, I went to the office of the *Leeds Mercury* to pick up a few books for review and hand in some copy.

The editor, now Sir Linton Andrews, was in the office he shared with his leader-writer and secretary.[109] W.L.A., as he was, and still is, better known, is not only a brilliant and indefatigable journalist, but one of the kindest and most helpful of men, always on the look-out for talent and ready to foster it. I used to envy the speed and precision with which he digested a story or dictated an article. He'd always time to discuss an idea, throw out a hint or two on how to tackle it, and more often than not, from his prodigious memory, dig up some out-of-the-way bit of information to give it a fresh angle. But though always willing to help, he never pampered his staff, never excused slackness and never spared criticism. In the years to come I was to learn much from him – to admire and respect him.

That particular day, discussing my last article whilst opening and digesting his mail at a terrific rate, he said "I've an idea there's a good journalist lost in you".

---

[109] Sir William Linton Andrews (1886-1972) was born in Hull and educated at Hull Grammar School and Christ's Hospital. From school he entered journalism and worked on a number of provincial newspapers, including the *Sheffield Telegraph*, before the First World War. He served with the Black Watch during the war. Afterwards he was sub-editor on the *Daily Mail* and in 1923 was appointed editor of the *Leeds Mercury*. He remained with the Mercury until 1939, when it was decided, partly as an economy measure, to amalgamate with the *Yorkshire Post*. He took over the editorship of the *Yorkshire Post*, on amalgamation, and finally retired as editor in 1960. He was knighted in 1954.

"Why, would you give us a job?" I asked without thinking.

"Like a shot."

"Really?"

"Really. This minute if you wanted it."

"Well…." I hesitated the merest fraction of a second.

"Well, what about it?"

"What about what?" He picked up the telephone.

"Giving me a job."

He asked for a number. "You want one?"

"Of course."

"When can you start?"

"Any time you say."

"Do you know anything about the Denby Dale Pie?"[110] This was a local fete being planned, the main feature of which was a monster pie containing I don't know how many cows and sheep, rabbits and game. Some of my friends were on the planning committee and I was sent forthwith to Denby Dale with instructions to be back at eight that evening with a thousand words of "comedy stuff" about it.

I was back at his desk by seven. He was correcting galley proofs with his usual speed and precision. Without looking up he asked, "Got on all right?"

I thought I had.

"Got a story for tomorrow?"

I hadn't.

"Every journalist worth his salt always brings back his story and three others to chase!" He turned to my article. "You've got your opening paragraph in the middle. There's nothing like a good burst off. Start with a bang, shove the heavy stuff in the middle, and finish with a flourish – Now, what about tomorrow?"

I remembered that at Netherton, just outside Huddersfield, there were three cradles – one for triplets, one for twins and one for single babies. They'd been bought by public subscription when the village's first triplets had made their appearance. They were kept, one at each of the three pubs, for the use of anyone who needed them. The following day I was outside Netherton, chasing this "human story" with a photographer at my heels.

And this time I brought back a story to chase the following day. And the next. And the next. After about a week of it, it struck me I had better let Dow know what had

---

[110] The first recorded making of a pie in the village was in 1788 to celebrate the recovery of King George 111 from mental illness. Since that time nine other pies have been baked, usually to coincide with a special event or to raise money for a local cause. The seventh pie was baked in 1928 (Gregson's pie). Before the National Health Service, hospitals depended very much on voluntary contributions and Huddersfield Royal Infirmary urgently required funds to improve its services, which was a major factor in the decision to bake the seventh pie in August 1928. Because this was to be the biggest pie to date, a new tin was built measuring 16ft. long, 5ft. wide and 15 inches deep.

happened. Dow roared with laughter, dismissed me with his blessing and three months salary in lieu of notice.

My first week on the staff of the *Leeds Mercury* had marked me out as the man for the "lighter" stories. Murders, suicides and the grimmer side of life were not for me, and in the years that followed I had few assignments that were in the least unpleasant. I was regarded with amused tolerance by the staff as "the literary bloke", a stray being only half of their world to be protected from its pitfalls and to be helped with ideas for stories that would provide the "magazine page" with a touch of comedy whenever possible.

Lessons were again the order of the day. They came at odd moments. I ran into Andrews one day as I was dashing off to York. When I told him I was to interview a centenarian, he asked "And what are you going to get him to say?" I hadn't an idea. "Well, you think up a smashing story for him to tell you between here and York!"

Another instance of my innocence was when I was sent to the mining township of Castleford. The government had launched a scheme to assist the emigration of unemployed colliers. The Labour Exchanges were all set for an expected great rush of applicants.

"And don't forget the tremolo stop!" said Schofield, the chief reporter. "Get these men to tell you why they're leaving their beloved Motherland – heart throbs – thousands of men, broken, seeing no future for themselves or their families in the Old Country!"

I went to Castleford to find there hadn't been a single application. I went back to Leeds to tell Schofield there was no story.

"No story!" Schofield looked positively ill. "Good Lord, man! That is the story! Skip back like the devil. Root the men out and get 'em to talk. Why won't they leave the Old Country? Because they don't think she's down and out. Get me? Undying patriotism and faith – sob stuff!"[111]

I remember a poster on the wall of the reporter's room. It read, "Always remember the public is always interested in the following subjects", then followed a short list.

---

[111] Few Yorkshire recruits for Canada Scheme: less than 12 at Castleford with 13000 on unemployed books.
Yorkshire has not made a good response to the Government Scheme for helping our unemployed by assisting 10000 of them to go to Canada for the harvesting.
The Scheme in brief
Up to 10,000 men required. The Dominion Government has expressed a strong preference for men from the mining areas.
Special reduced rate to and from Winnipeg of £12 each way.
Men who satisfy the Employment Exchanges that they cannot pay their outward journey will, on passing the Dominion examination, receive a free grant of £5, credited to the shipping companies.
They will also receive, through the Employment Exchange an advance of £10.
Every effort will be made to place them when the harvest is over in winter work on farms.
*Leeds Mercury* : August 7th 1928.
In the end, the actual numbers reported as having gone from Yorkshire were, Barnsley, 25, Doncaster, 23, Pontefract, 20, Harrogate, 5. Liverpool and Newcastle contributed the largest numbers, approximately 1,000 men each.Two of the main reasons few men from Yorkshire went, were the uncertainty of the work after six months , and no concessions being made for married men

*Florence
Gregson
Jnr.
(1927)
(CA)*

I'm not certain now of their precise order, but the first three were Sex, Money and Food.

We had arranged to spend three weeks in the summer of 1928 in Germany with a band of teachers and senior pupils.[112] We were to be guests of their German counterparts and present a programme of plays and folk songs in their schools. My main part was that of "Shylock", and as, by this time, Hitler had the younger generation of Germany in his pocket, Shakespeare's Jew was not persona grata.[113] The following year, when we repeated the experiment, things were even worse. I was often spat at, sometimes jostled, as I made my entrances and exits through the auditorium.

For the 1928 tour Andrews asked me to supply a thousand words of daily coverage which I did, usually writing my stuff in the early hours of the morning after prolonged beer parties. The sub-editors did me proud. One headline ran "Gregson in the Workhouse" and another announced I was having trouble with the Lubeck police. In the first instalment of my story, dealing with our departure from Grimsby, I referred to the port's characteristic odour of fish. This evoked several indignant letters from Grimsbyites, and these I reported back to the office. I was shown the contents bill for this issue carrying their angry complaints.

---

[112] Mr. & Mrs. Gregson, and their daughter Miss Von Gregson, are by the way, joining a party of Castleford Secondary School students who are giving performances of Shakespeare in Germany. They were known as 'The Lord Halifax Players' and were led by Mr. T R Davies, the Headmaster.
Unattributed newspaper cutting 'Gregson scrapbook' West Yorkshire Archives, Calderdale, GRE2.
Von Gregson should have gone down well in Germany!.

[113] In August, following an invitation from The Central Institute for Development and Education in Berlin, the 'English Travelling Players' as they call themselves in German, paid another visit with Mr. Dawes, his wife, and others including Mr. Gregson, who played a special part as Director, Scriptwriter and Producer. On the way to Berlin they stopped in Hannover from Thursday to Saturday afternoon to perform to 1,300 scholars from upper schools in the area. On Thursday morning they performed scenes from *Midsummer's Night's Dream* and *The Merchant of Venice*, also a short comedy sketch by Mr. Gregson, sea shanties and an Irish dance. The performances were impressive, particularly Mr. Gregson's Shylock.
Unknown Hannover paper – kindly translated from the German by David Cant.

THE YORKSHIRE WEEKLY POST, SATURDAY, AUGUST 31, 1929.
19

# THE LORD HALIFAX PLAYERS TOURING GERMANY

SHAKESPEARE PRODUCTIONS.—The Lord Halifax Players, pupils of the Castleford Secondary School, who are touring Germany in Shakespeare productions under Mr. T. R. Dawes, the Headmaster, and Mrs. Dawes.

*Lord Halifax Players – German tour (1929)* (CA)

*James Gregson and his wife, Florence are seated on the end of the second row, on the right. Their daughter, I think, is stood behind Mrs. Gregson.*

It read, "GREGSON GRIEVES GRIMSBY".[114]

Naturally enough I quickly graduated as the Mercury's dramatic critic and through this became a contributor to the *Manchester Guardian*, an honour I rated highly indeed. My most exacting assignment on the *Leeds Mercury*, was an investigation into the Yorkshire Coal Industry which was then passing through a very bad period. Andrews told me I could deal faithfully with the present black position but to end on as hopeful a note as I could manage when summing up the future prospects of the industry.

The first half of my brief was easy enough, but it was almost impossible to visualize full employment at any future date for the man-power the pits then commanded, - at least half as many again as they have today. New methods of fuel saving and coal getting were reducing the demand for labour and were likely to continue to do so.

There was one hope, I saw, provided the owners could mend their stupid ways. That hope was our export trade which was feeling the competition of Poland and Germany. We were being undersold because we wouldn't learn to pool our resources. As an instance, I went down one pit, where the men had to travel three miles to the coal face, which was within a quarter of a mile of another pit shaft. The miners from this second pit did the same thing in the contrary direction. Both pits were producing coal for export when they could sell. Amalgamation and the use of each other's pit heads would have saved at least four shillings a ton in the cost of getting the coal. Either the owners were too stupid to see this or too foolish to come to terms about it. It was yet another instance to me of the incompetence I'd found too often in our so-called leaders of industry. I discovered, too, that bitter as feelings were between employers and employed, the masters and owners had their rivalries and jealousies which rendered them blind and incapable of making the most of their own assets in their own interest, not to mention the nation's.

This piece of investigation occupied four weeks, the result was eight articles, splashed

---

[114] Smells that mean romance: Mr. Gregson at a seaport: a Grimsby man replies

A seaport smells

Mr. Gregson has made the discovery.

"That port of disreputable appearance and smells" – so he describes Grimsby, from which he sailed on his visit with the boys of the Castleford Secondary School to North Germany.

Further, he says in a message to the 'Mercury' –

"Hamburg looks like a Grimsby with German signs – the sheds, ugly contraptions of brick and corrugated iron – the miscellaneous shipping – the foul and befouled water, looking like a slutty down-trodden relative of the sparkling expanse over which we have travelled – all so like Grimsby that it is almost a grievance to discover that the smell is missing".

I am not sure that the injury Mr. Gregson does to Germany's greatest seaport is not deeper than the insult he offers to the greatest fishing port in the world.

A glimpse from the train as he went down to the boat at Grimsby Docks Station probably was enough. 'Disreputable'. A sniff. 'Why it smells'. Fish, hemp, sea-lapped steel and wood of ships, timber, coal and merchandise. A seaport does smell.

…………..If the traveller leaves the dockside, he can see another town rich in history and legend which has no smells. It is bright and clear, and is not smutted and besmirched by the industrialisation that despoils so many of the towns of Yorkshire. Gad, how some of them smell and make you cough. There is no romance and colour there, only brass – and reputableness.

Seaports have their 'disreputable' sides and smells, just because people in these reputable inland towns must have fish and produce, and wood and wool and what not. And these folk sniff.

The sea-lover just smiles. B.E.E.

*Leeds Mercury* : August 25th 1928.

as by "Our Special Commissioner", and a warm note of commendation from Andrews which I still treasure.

Interesting as journalism was, it had one over-riding drawback. It kept me from the theatre except as a weekly critic, and even there I had not space to spread myself or take any pride in serious treatment. Besides being barred from acting or producing by the exigencies of my work, it played the very dickens with serious writing of any kind. The barren period was getting on my nerves, and I began to doubt whether I should ever write anything of more than ephemeral interest again.

At length, not without some soul-searching, I decided to turn free-lance. As early as 1924 I had made my first Broadcast and had appeared in various radio plays.[115] I decided to cultivate this new medium, although fees were very low – in those days actors seldom got more than two guineas for three or four rehearsals and the transmission, and an author's royalties for original work averaged six guineas for a half-hour play. I also took odd jobs with the Playhouse and other groups to make up my earnings from the newspapers. I still jibbed at turning completely professional in the theatre, but the time was coming when I was to jump in with both feet.[116]

---

[115] His first broadcast – a fifteen minute talk about theatre work – was in 1924. He received no payment.
James recalled: The studio was like a padded cell. The microphones were of the carbon type. When they became tired and faint, the engineer would kick them about the studio to shake them up. Producers had to 'twiddle their own knobs', technical work that has long been done by engineers.
*The Yorkshire Dalesman* : May 2009.

[116] It was around this time (1928) that Gregson was the subject of a 'Character Sketch' by 'Playfellow'.
Off the stage he is a curious mixture of the inconspicuous and the impish. His only hobby apart from his work is gardening or poultry, occasional chess, and a fondness for playing the family man, and to these observations one must add that he possesses an unusual inability to rest idle. All those who have acted under him or with him know that he is a glutton for work. He does not, it is true, rehearse long, but he does rehearse hard, and his capacity for combining half a dozen jobs at once is exceptional. He writes slowly, even when at white heat, and does a great deal of revision, and he is as much at home in the routine tasks of organisation as behind the curtain.
Unattributed newspaper cutting  Gregson scrapbook  West Yorkshire Archives, Calderdale, GRE2.

# Chapter Eighteen

Before the time came for that long-delayed plunge our younger daughter, Joan, died suddenly. It was a sickening blow to both Florence and me.

Joan had always been a lively, exacting child with a mind like quicksilver and a temper as mercurial as the weather. Combined with a bright, leaping intelligence, an uncannily acute sense of fun and a masterful nature, she had a highly individualistic streak. She was a born rebel, volatile but very lovable. A difficult child with very winning ways whom few could resist for long. At the age of seven she fell in love with the young doctor who had been responsible for diagnosing and curing Florence's complaint. The trouble was that young Florence was also in love with him. Joan won the battle with her usual unscrupulousness. She refused to allow the doctor to remove her tonsils until he promised to marry her.

After the operation she thrived wonderfully, lost her elfin looks and her tantrums. We had this new delightful member of the family little more than twelve months before she went down with scarlet fever. Pneumonia supervened and we were called hurriedly to take our turns besides her bed, to watch her struggle for life. Mercifully she was unconscious most of the time. When she was awake it was difficult to parry her questions as to when she was going home – we had promised her she would only be away three weeks – and had to watch her pulling off the loose scraps of skin from her wasted hands and arms in a desultory, lack-lustre fashion.

Sitting by the side of her cot one afternoon towards the end, swathed in an antiseptic overall, I had a long quiet watch. The tiny room was dreadfully still; the child's breathing seemed to heighten the quiet. From the distance came routine sounds from the other wards – the cries and laughter of children, the clatter of crockery, the clack of passing feet along the polished corridor.

The child's wasted hands began their fugitive activity. The dark eyes were watching me and the peeling face wavered into a smile of recognition.

"Only four days now, Father!" I could barely hear her.
Speech was as difficult for me.
"Are you stopping all the time with me?"
"Only till teatime, love."

Tears gathered and I explained I had to go to Halifax that evening to appear in a show. She fell into a doze until I rose to steal away. She awoke, there was desolation in her sunken eyes.

"Mother will be here soon, and I'll come back as soon as I can" I promised.
She tried to raise herself, failed, and held out her wasted arms.
"Love me, Father! Just for a minute. Love me!"

The room was empty, and disregarding the rigid rules, I leaned over the cot and held her a moment. For the last time I felt her arms about my neck. Felt them fall away as she sunk again into sleep. I settled her again and slipped away.

The play that night was *The Devil a Saint*, in the second act of which I was supposed to believe I was dying. I'm told it was as funny as ever, though I remember nothing about it, or of the performance at all.

The next day, or maybe the next but one – I can't remember, there was an urgent telephone call before breakfast.

We dashed to the Hospital to find the child in an oxygen tent. Just before the end she opened her eyes to ask, "What are you crying for?" and without waiting for an answer, closed them.[117]

---

[117] Joan Gregson died in 1928, aged eight.

# Chapter Nineteen

Life went on, of course. It had to be endured no matter how mechanically. Bread-and-butter work had to be got through and was, but without drive – no longer a pleasure but a task. The loss of the child deepened the depression into which I had been sinking for some time. It seemed to me I had reached a dead end. I had long since discarded my dreams of fame and wealth but had found consolation in the pioneer work of the Civic Playhouse. But the organisation was now well established, could and did carry on without me, and there seemed no adventure to pursue, no new service I could give to the theatre. I had no spur.

James Lansdale Hodson supplied it. [118]  I had known him from the early days of the Civic Playhouse. He stalked into the rehearsal room one evening, a gaunt fellow with a long nose, sunken cheeks, an actor's mouth and piercing eyes. He was a striking figure, in his large black hat and an overcoat that appeared too heavy for his slight frame. I likened him at once to the Pied Piper.

In his deep, flat, watery Lancashire voice, he told me he'd come for a story for the Northern Edition of the *Daily Mail*. He knew the story he wanted, and got it. The interview was a model of painless extraction. As soon as it was over he gathered together his slack frame, his hat and umbrella (carried, perhaps, to assure the timid that Pied Pipers <u>could</u> be respectable) and left as quietly and casually as he had come.

Our friendship developed just as casually – an affair of infrequent meetings and off-hand correspondence – and I was alternately amused and irritated by his calm self-confidence and value he put on himself. He cursed me for under-valuing myself. I envied him not only his sophisticated, analytical mind, but his quietly dynamic method of working. He had disciplined his innate ability until writing had become a habit – an addiction. Whatever demands his brilliant journalistic career made upon him, he found time, somehow, for a constant stream of novels, plays and diaries. He had schooled himself to write anywhere under any conditions. Years later, during the Second World War, his training was to serve him in good stead. He roamed the world on his assignments, his vivid, accurate reporting always distinguished by its fine writing and literary quality, but in the intervals of getting the story of the day, whether enjoying the flesh pots of a Cairo hotel, suffering the bugs of an Italian cabin, the mosquitoes of Malaya, the discomfort of an Atlantic crossing in a cargo boat, he could always find time to set down something of more permanent value. And all the time his shrewd eyes and ears were noting odd touches of character, his long sensitive fingers were catching the texture of a mast or a dead face, his long nose was alive to every scent and change of atmosphere, and his tenacious memory was storing everything for possible

---

[118] James Lansdale Hodson (1891-1956) was born at Hazelhurst, near Bury in 1891. He joined the northern staff of the *Daily Mail* at an early age and was eventually news editor for five years before leaving Manchester for Fleet Street in 1929. From then on he worked as a war correspondent for various newspapers. During the second world war he acted as a special correspondent, and became closely associated with the Ministry of Information. He wrote nearly a dozen novels in which journalism and Lancashire supplied much of the background. *Grey Dawn – Red Night*, based on the 1914-1918 war was perhaps his most successful novel.

future use. Everything was grist to his insatiable mill. And yet, in spite of his astonishingly large output, created, one might almost say manufactured, so methodically, his work varied very slightly and never fell below a consistently high standard. He had all J.B. Priestley's sense of character, the same keen eye for the comedy of life, the same genius for inspired reportage, but whereas Priestley's prose is sometimes prosy, Hodson's was often touched with poetry. Priestley's wit and humour have the deftness of a well-handled quarterstaff, Hodson's the flicker of a foil. Both of them supreme craftsmen, Hodson had less need of a foot-rule.

But Hodson had surprisingly little of the sense and feel for the theatre that Priestley has, and never really learned to trust an actor's inflections or an audience's perception to fill in the gaps of a broken line. His dialogue was always too explicit, and he was always irked by the scenery the stage imposes on an author.

*Diana Wynard (MM)*

This weakness was apparent in the first full-length play Hodson sent me for my comments. I'm afraid he didn't take much notice of my suggestions and I was surprised when he decided to give the play, *These Fathers*, a try-out in Blackpool with a scratch company largely recruited from the Liverpool Playhouse amongst whom were James Harcourt, Lloyd Pearson, and a young actress called Diana Wynyard who was on the point of leaving the Liverpool Nursery to try her wings in London.[119] I was engaged to play one of the old character parts. It was Hodson's first taste of theatrical management, and a rather expensive one.

It was during that week in the summer of 1928 that I confided to Hodson an idea I had for a touring company of genuinely Northern actors with a repertory of genuinely Northern plays with the aim, as I hoped, of doing for Yorkshire what the Irish players had done for Ireland.

---

[119] Diana Wynyard (1906-1964) was born Dorothy Isobel Cox. From 1927 to 1930 she was a member of William Armstrong's Liverpool Repertory Theatre. She then returned to London, becoming a star in *Sorry You've Been Troubled*. Briefly, she made her mark in Hollywood, but her career there never really took off, even though she had an Oscar nomination in Noel Coward's *Cavalcade*. This, however was an era dominated by gangster films and musicals, and after a handful of forgettable films she came back to London and continued her West End career, with a further string of hits.

Hodson was fired by the idea, but nothing could be done about it then, and the project fell into the background until, soon after Joan's death, Hodson became insistent that we should go ahead with it.[120]  It was the tonic I needed.  It was a venture with something of a crusade about it, another chance to do something worthwhile.  We formed a partnership, and turned ourselves into a limited company, began to recruit our actors and book dates.  Hodson wrote amusingly about it later in his book, *No Phantoms Here*.  Here is part of his account.

> N.P. Rubinstein, another dramatist, was our lawyer. I believe he secretly thought us daft; he was certainly frank on the point that he would never invest a penny of his own in any enterprise of the theatre….
>
> I asked him what right any man had to expect a manager to risk his money in a play that the author won't support to the extent of a penny.
>
> He replied that a manager's job is to be a manager and the author's job to be an author.
>
> I said , "At all events we've got a sporting chance.  If we win we shall have created a company that may become as well known and perhaps as distinguished as the Irish Players, and that will add something to the dramatic literature of the North.….This is worth doing even if failure is a foregone conclusion."
>
> I went on to assert that not only is Gregson the best dramatist the North Country has produced since the war, but is, furthermore a good actor and  producer and apart from his inability to write music and sing he is as much a theatrical genius as Noel Coward.
>
> "You need a backer," said Rubinstein.
>
> I demurred to that also.  "We've got enough to find out whether we can

---

[120]  For a year or two I had been saying to James Gregson " If ever I make a lot of money I'll finance to tour your own  plays and perhaps one of mine also."  When a novel of mine *Grey Dawn – Red Night*, ran through edition after edition it looked as though the hour had come.  But the book struck the United States market six months too late; and my finding all the money for a theatrical adventure, seemed to my fairly cautious eye, impossible after all, and  Gregson, anyway, finally said he thought he must find his share.

..........We called ourselves 'Lancastria Limited' and our company the 'Yorkshire Players'.  This was in some degree a compromise between Gregson and me for I am turbulently Lancashire and Gregson is Yorkshire, although I have always twitted him with having learned his playwriting in Lancashire, and having called himself a Yorkshire dramatist to escape the competition of Houghton, Brighouse, Monkhouse and others of the Manchester School.

..........Our company assembled in Huddersfield to rehearse, most of them undisputedly efficient in Yorkshire and Lancashire comedy and among them individuals who could paint you scenery or load a cart or make a dress or do a little wiring with the best.

..........Those preliminary weeks were exciting.  Printing, press publicity, the engagement of two or three London actors, accepting and rejecting dates, arguing about terms – these took every moment.  Gregson came to London and we turned my drawing room into an audition chamber wherein men and women did their lamentable best with a Yorkshire accent.  However, we treated them like men and women and not, as I have seen managers do, like cattle.  We gave them their travelling fares and entertained them to tea, and it embarrassed us more to find out how unsuitable most of them were than it did them.  More than one seemed about as cut out for the stage as I am for the Archbishop of Canterbury.

J L Hodson, *No Phantoms Here*, London,  Faber&Faber,  1932.

succeed", I said. "If we win through we want all the honour and glory. If we don't – we'd better lose our own money than somebody else's"....

I daresay he shook his head over us, and hoped for the best. He was a good friend before he became our lawyer, and he offered to allow us to use his office as our registered office also. We called ourselves "Lancastria Limited" and our company "The Yorkshire Players"....We had walked over the Moors near his house in Huddersfield whilst we built castles in the air....

## A FAREWELL PERFORMANCE.

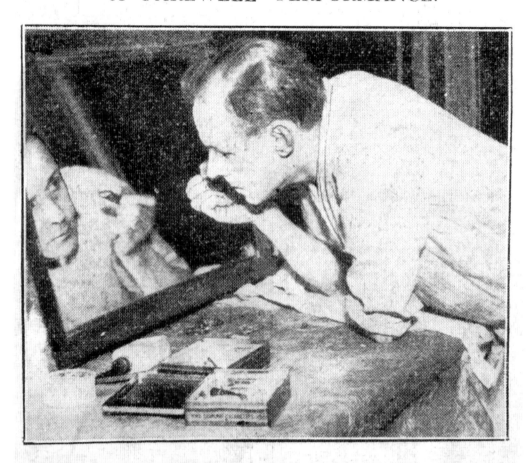

Mr. J. R. Gregson, the Yorkshire playwright and actor, who is severing his association with the Leeds and Bradford Civic Playhouses to take a repertory company on tour, is taking part in a farewell revival of his play, " Young Imeson," which opens at the Leeds Civic Playhouse to-night. This photograph shows Mr. Gregson making up for his part in the play.

*James Gregson – 'A Farewell Performance' (1931)*          *(CA)*

Gregson's wife Florence was with us. She is a true Lancashire woman and unsurpassed in her portrayal of working-class north-countrywomen. She is also unsurpassed in rebuking us.

"I'm having my own separate wage if I join your rotten company", she said. "No coupling me with Dick as a bit of a makeweight!"

"You'll do what you're told or you'll stop at home," I said, "and eat your heart out while the company makes pots o' brass and grows famous!"

Our notepaper was magnificent, bluish-grey, heavily embossed with a marginal list of the plays we controlled. My stature increased every time I looked at it….Our literature was not unduly modest. We had a slogan taken from a Yorkshire Post quotation, "Laughter All The Way"; and we asserted the Yorkshire Players were specialists in comedy. (We soon needed our sense of humour.) I observe we describe Mr. Gregson as something of a theatrical genius and that I was declared to have written both novels and plays of distinction. It was an easy matter to compile a series of genuine extracts from critics' notices of our three plays that Cochran or any other showman might not have despised….

The tour began at Selby Hippodrome, a theatre whose patrons had grown accustomed to seeing films on the stage instead of flesh and blood, and many of the audience on the first night or two paid for seats on the assumption that the Yorkshire Players were made of celluloid, and entered  half-way through the first house.  On learning of their predicament Gregson wisely allowed them to stay through the second performance….

We concluded in Truro, Cornwall, having in the intervening eight months learnt that not only is the provincial touring theatre dying out but, for the most part, is dead to such humour and acting as we were able to offer it.

Our fortune was poor in the sense that at Harrogate, where we succeeded, people tramped through eight inches of snow to see us, that we came to towns stricken with influenza or hit by strikes, that our seaside engagements enjoyed weather that was magnificent for holiday makers and disastrous for us, and that we played throughout in an economic blizzard which engulfed us as well as everybody else.

The company's experiences may be imagined from Gregson's letters to me. Writing from Scarborough, he said, "This place is a veritable death-trap. We are playing once-nightly at twice-nightly prices, and the town is dead. We opened on Monday to £1-11-0d. Our opposition at the other theatre are doing even worse. They had ten people in on Monday and not thirty last night, and I hear now that of those thirty only six had actually paid for admission. The leading lady – it's her own venture – had hysterics and had to be nursed through the night.

Our company had a meeting this morning and came to the decision to leave part of their salaries in suspense until things mend."

And again; Barrow was a nightmare, neither money nor much visible or audible appreciation. Here at Blackburn there is no money, but real appreciation. Other reasons for not doing better are the weather – it's bitterly cold with snow and biting winds; we have all got colds – a very cold theatre with the audience sitting with coat collars turned up to their ears, a religious week in progress in the town, flu, the slump and a liking for rough stuff and cruder acting than ours.

From Douglas: It'll be a blessed relief if ever I can write explaining why we've made money. Here is another ghastly week. Beautiful weather – hot days and heavenly nights. At rehearsal today in answer to my line. "Aren't you broke Raymond?" Phillip Robinson came back with the gag, "Not more than the rest of the Yorkshire Players!" "Ay well! All the best"

My part during all this time was small – I had simply to receive a weekly report from Gregson and send in reply cheques for more money to keep the company on the road. I shall not pretend that that I did not become a little restive under the drain and that I found it insupportable before Gregson decided on his last desperate throw in a Cornwall repertory season; but there was no bitterness, nor did his courage or spirit diminish. In Truro, after rehearsing most of the day, and playing two different plays each week, he sat down in his theatrical lodgings at night and wrote through the small hours, completing within a few days an entirely new full-length thriller which Truro liked better than *T'Marsdens*.

I found the company in Truro quite fortuitously. The general election was in progress and I was touring Cornwall. Driving from Truro station, I saw a poster of my own play on a hoarding…. I knew the company had suffered, but I was wretched and disturbed to find the redoubtable Florence so moved at seeing a friendly face that tears sprang to her eyes and she cried on my shoulder. I had gone round with some foolish thought of being hearty and cracking jokes about having come to the funeral, but I could only say, "another week, Florence, and you'll be home", and murmur something about them having put up a good fight.

Gregson was ironical about Truro. "You will observe", he said, "that all signposts read 'so many miles from Truro', never 'to Truro'. Many of the new houses they've built here have baths but no hot water laid to them. When the fishermen here consider going to sea they light a candle. If the wind blows it out they don't go – too stormy. If the wind doesn't blow it out they don't go either – no wind to sail the boat. Well here they use a candle to decide whether they shall go to the theatre."

We knew our adventure had failed, but we expressed no regrets. I still look upon it as an effort that had something of gallantry in it. Gregson was heavily in debt and had barely enough money in his pocket to live on for a week, but he refused any loan from me, and with his chin up went back North.[121]

If my chin was up, it was purely for effect. The truth was I went home with my tail between my legs, feeling not only beaten but humiliated. On the long, crawling Sunday journey back to base, I tried to strike a balance sheet. Nine months of hard work had left me with debts that I couldn't face with equanimity. I had thrown away every penny of my savings and all the money I'd earned by writing in the night hours had been flung into the venture. I had drawn no royalties from my plays whilst spoiling possible future markets for them. And having cleared off all the expenses I had exactly twenty-three shillings and three half-pence on which we had to exist until I could earn more.

Where had I failed? Not from extravagance. If we could have been certain of an average share of the receipts of sixty-four pounds a week, we could have covered our expenses, with the exception of my royalties, comfortably. Our company was a small one and the highest salary we paid was eight pounds. Florence, young Florence and I were on a joint salary of ten pounds a week. We lived on half that amount, the other went back into the treasury.

Where had I failed? Inexperience had helped. We had accepted some dates we ought to have avoided. The slump had hit us. Inefficient and uncomfortable theatres had not helped us to compete with the still novel "talkies" which could be watched in comfort in modern cinemas for much less than our prices. Perhaps we ourselves were at fault? Perhaps it was true that our shows were too clever to be a paying proposition, as one manager had told me. Another had said, "You're too near to life": another, "Folk like to see you're acting, they don't want you to be real!"

For nine months we'd been on a switchback railway with more downs than ups. Our highest, happiest peak had been a fortnight in Barry Jackson's Theatre in Birmingham whilst the resident company had a holiday. We were only the second non-Jackson company to appear there. Our predecessors had been the Irish Players. We had been selected because, as the manager, Bache Matthews, gravely informed us, "Your plays and your work matches theirs to quality and value": and Birmingham had proved one

---

[121] Gregson was about £150 in debt and had barely more money than was enough to live on for a week.
.........He spends his time now hammering a typewriter, turning out articles and stories. He is at work on a novel and a play, has undertaken production for Bradford Civic Playhouse, and occasionally hurries over to Leeds to broadcast his sketches. You may see him hurrying through the grey streets, walking as if he had twenty miles to go, the wind blowing his thinning brown hair, his brown eyes behind large metal rimmed goggle spectacles missing nothing. In the street there is something fragile and puckish about him, in command of a rehearsal he is dominant, in an armchair with a pipe and carpet slippers Rabelaisian and slovenly. He has the working man's fondness for his house, gets up and lights the fire, doesn't mind helping with the washing up, and can make a capital shot at cooking the Sunday dinner. Every Sunday night the livelier spirits of the Huddersfield Thespians gather at his house to eat Florence's parkin, tell racy stories and talk and talk and laugh and laugh. I laugh more myself in Huddersfield in one week than in London in six months. The place and people bristle with character.
J L Hodson, *No Phantoms Here*, London, Faber&Faber, 1932.
£150 in 1931 would approximate to £7500 at current prices.

of the few dates where we'd emerged with a profit.[122] Against that grateful memory was the black season in Truro which had broken us all. Six weeks playing two plays a week, most of them new to us; three rehearsals and four performances to each play; competing with the arrival of "Talkies" in the city; all the company on two-thirds salaries, the last two weeks playing to pitifully thin but friendly audiences. I remember we played one matinee to eight-and sixpence!

My women folk had risen to every demand I'd made on them, overworking themselves and living as cheaply as possible. In Truro, especially, young Florence had proved a real prop indeed.[123] When we arranged that she should join the company as assistant stage manager, "understudy and small parts", I had promised she should have the same thorough training in the theatre that Wareing had given me. By heaven, she got it! It was no joke for a girl of seventeen to play two different parts a week, find all the properties and furniture in a town of hostile tradesfolk and help to paint at least two sets a week.

*Edward Knoblock*
*(MM)*

But apart from the experience it had given her, there was no disguising the fact that the venture had been a real flop, either the public did not want good work, or I could not supply it. I went back, an utter failure to myself, to pick up what threads of work I could, cured forever of the fond dreams of fame and fortune I had dallied with too long.

What made my failure all the more galling was the thought that I might never have

---

[122] Yorkshire Players visit to Birmingham
One of these plays about Yorkshire folk – *Young Imeson*, by James R Gregson – was presented last night at the Birmingham Repertory Theatre by the Yorkshire Players, who are appearing in Birmingham for a short season. It is a very interesting drama in which Yorkshire individualism is exploited to the full against the familiar background of a strike.
Although it has an indeterminate and horribly sentimental conclusion, it is full of fine character drawing and – in the shrewd, businesslike Yorkshire sense – contains some humour.
The Yorkshire players act the drama excellently. Charles Lloyd-Pack is extremely facile as the hero; James R Gregson, the author, makes a most interesting study of the employer; Tom Denham is monumentally superb as the engineer and the whole company is highly competent.
*Birmingham Gazette* : July 7th 1931.

[123] Miss Florence Gregson
An interesting feature of the forthcoming production of *T'Marsdens*, which is to be presented at the Huddersfield Theatre Royal, during Bank Holiday week will be what might be termed the 'adult' debut of Miss Florence Gregson, the author's daughter. 'Von' as she is more familiarly known, has appeared on stage in several juvenile parts already, but on this occasion she is 'to put up her hair', an old term which in these days of bobs and shingles has lost its significance.
Newspaper cutting, circa 1929, source unknown – though probably the *Huddersfield Examiner*.

launched upon the tour at all, if only matters had gone a little more my way before we started out. With a bit of luck, I might have been starring in London instead of struggling in the provinces. We had started the tour, in fact, under the cloud of what was, perhaps, the bitterest disappointment of my life – my failure to secure the part of "Jess Oakroyd" in the stage version of Priestley's *The Good Companions*.[124]

Scores of people in the North told me they were certain it was my part. I was myself, but hesitated to apply for it, until Priestley's stepmother – a lovely woman, very like my own – asked me, "Have you written to our Jack about Jess?" and when I said I hadn't, she said, "Well, you'd better do it right away, because I've written to tell him you're the best man for the part!" [125]

I wrote and was invited by Priestley to meet Knoblock, who'd collaborated in the dramatisation, and Julian Wylie who was to put it on.[126] They were

*John Boynton Priestley, 1926*

*National Portrait Gallery, London*

---

[124]  J B Priestley (1894-1984), born in Bradford to a lower middle class family, his father a teacher put through teaching college by his father, a mill worker. Left Grammar School at sixteen (didn't want to try for University), went into the wool trade as a junior clerk, and not a very good one, by his own admission. He served in the First World War, from 1914 through to the finish, being wounded in 1916 by mortar fire. After the war he went to Trinity College, Cambridge, and thereafter settled in the South.
By the age of thirty he had established a reputation as a humorous writer and critic. His first major success came in 1929 with the novel *The Good Companions*, which made him a national figure. Other books followed and further established him as a successful novelist. However, some critics were less than complimentary about his work, and Priestley began legal action against Graham Greene for what he took to be a defamatory portrait in *Stamboul Train*.
He moved into new fields and became well-known as a dramatist. His best known play is perhaps *An Inspector Calls*, although *Dangerous Corner* and *Time and the Conways* were very popular, exploring J W Dunne's theory of time. Many of his works have a political aspect, containing references to socialism. During World War Two he was a regular broadcaster on the BBC, his Sunday night *Postscripts*, in 1940 and 1941 drew audiences of up to 16 million. But his talks were cancelled, apparently as a result of complaints that they were too left-wing. He was a founding member of the Campaign for Nuclear Disarmament in 1958, which didn't appear to stop him receiving the Order of Merit in 1977, although he had declined lesser honours before. He married three times, producing in total, four daughters and one son.

[125]  Two years after the death of Priestley's mother, his father married Amy Fletcher. As Priestley said of her, "I had a step-mother who defied tradition by always being kind, gentle, loving. Indeed, it was she who excused my teenage eccentricities, declaring, with that sardonic over-emphasis peculiar to women in the North, great flatterers of male pretensions, that I was a genius and therefore might be excused."

[126]  Edward Knoblock, born Edward Gustav Knoblauch (1874-1945) was a dramatist, a writer of scenarios, and novelist who wrote, among many other works, the much revived and re-made *Kismet*. He was born in New York of German parents but spent much of his professional life in England. *The Good Companions*, originally published in 1929 by J B Priestley, was dramatised jointly by Knoblock and the author in 1931. Julian Wylie (1878-1934). A large and enthusiastic North countryman from Southport, he was born Julian Ulrich Mettenberg Samuelson. His talent lay in management. He married a lady much older than himself who lent him the only capital he possessed – one pound! Wylie's rages were titanic. If the slightest hitch occurred he would hide his face in his hands and moan that he was ruined.

kindness itself but I soon realised that Priestley's idea of the part differed considerably from mine. I saw "Jess" as very like my father, a Yorkshire, homely, middle-aged Charlie Chaplin. Priestley saw him as a big bluff man. There was the further difficulty of the projected tour. Two local actor-friends, Phillip Robinson and George Beaumont, were turning professional, leaving their current jobs to go along with me, but Wylie assured me I need not worry. If I was all right there would be parts for the two boys as well as Florence and young Florence. We were all to appear two days later at the Theatre Royal, Leeds, for my audition.

We arrived to find Wylie at the theatre before me. He was walking round the stage examining the "Village Green" set – the opening set of the current pantomime. Chatting desultorily with us he went over every flat with an eagle eye and an expert thumbnail, trying the texture of the timber, scraping off little bits of paint, occasionally picking his nose! By the time the others arrived, I'm sure he could have told us the cost of that set to a penny!

*Julian Wylie (MM)*

We did two excerpts from my plays to an audience of three men and thousands of dust-covered seats. Then Priestley asked for something "more emotional" and young Florence and I did a scene from *Sar'Alice* – my daughter reading the woman's part and holding on to the script like grim death as I banged and flung her about the stage. Priestley said "Grand! I wish I could write for the theatre as surely as that!"

But when it came to the verdict, he said "You're too small, too intelligent, a bit light-weight. The "Jess" I saw when I wrote the story, is slow and solid – lumbering. And then, your dialect is more Lancashire than Yorkshire. Now your wife, she'd be perfect as "Mrs Oakroyd" – her dialect's the one I wrote the part in!"

Wylie patted Florence's arm and said, "You're a grand little actress, m'dear!" He told me they'd have to think it over and I "should be hearing". We knew what that meant. Five crestfallen actors went to the nearest café to console themselves with tea. No message came then or later, and that was that!

We should have been even more crestfallen had we known that I'd not only lost a good job for myself but been the unconscious cause of Florence missing her great opportunity, too. That blow was to come a few months after we'd returned from the tour, to be softened by an example of typical Priestley kindness, of which more in its proper place.

# Chapter Twenty

We arrived back from Truro on a dull morning in October 1931. Huddersfield was just stirring itself for work. We got our scenery into store, had a makeshift breakfast and the first real bath for seven weeks. By half-past ten I was in Leeds, talking to W.L.A. in the office of the *Yorkshire Post* and feeling none too cheerful. He had no vacancy for me on the staff and though he'd take as much as he could from me as a freelance, I should have to hunt my own stories; he couldn't feed me with assignments.

There was little doing for me at the Civic Playhouse either. It was now an affair of a small professional company, struggling to make ends meet. The prospect was bleak indeed. But there was only one thing to do. The first and anything that came to hand. For the next five weeks there was no time for inquests on the past, no time for introspection; no time for anything but the hunting of stories. At the end of that time I had earned exactly £12.5.0. It looked as though my creditors would have to wait a long time for their money!

It took us, in fact eight years to get properly on our feet again. It meant a lot of underpaid work, with an odd plus now and then to sweeten things. The most encouraging feature was the modest progress as a radio writer and producer, but though B.B.C. fees had improved a little, they were still far too low.

It was a chastening experience to find how little one's reputation and past work seemed to count when it came down to hard cash. I thought I had reached bottom when, during the tour, I churned out thousands of words for a cheap magazine at one guinea per thousand, but during the last months of 1931 I was gratefully hammering out an eighty-thousand-word serial for £50. I got this job through the kindness of John Hunt, then editor of the Yorkshire Weekly Post. He wanted, he said, something especially written as a change from the syndicated stories he'd been using.

"I want a Yorkshire *Hatter's Castle*!" he said.[127] "Plenty of rough stuff – heavy father, Puritan household, girl breaking away. Sexy, if you like, so long as you're discreet!" He was apologetic about the fee – "Chicken feed, I know" – but he explained that he could get a syndicated story, first release, for £40. "And just to sweeten things," he went on, "whilst you're getting it ready, you can do a series of real life stories for me – two thousand words, a guinea and a half each!"

Within a week I took him my first two articles and a scenario of the serial and we planned the first instalment in detail there and then. We kept up the process until the story was finished, putting into it every sensation we thought the readers would stand for. It had everything we could give it, from honest-to-goodness characterisation to something like a philosophy of life, with fires, strikes, strolling players, non-conformist missionaries, seductions and whippings and other rough stuff for good measure. It had a most unhappy ending – the last line, I remember was "Cold rain spattered the

---

[127] *Hatter's Castle*, a best selling melodramatic novel by A J Cronin, set in Scotland.

windows". We called it *Melody on Moorside*, and it raised nearly as much pother as the serial I'd tried to write for the Huddersfield Labour weekly, years before.[128] And like that earlier story, it later became a play which I renamed *Portrait of a Lady*.

I gave the play a more philosophical ending and I wrote what I think is the finest curtain line I have ever achieved – "Time is a great comedian!" I broke a long standing rule and sent the play out to take its chance. Basil Dean said it was a good play, but there was no money in it,[129] Herbert Lomas thought it "Most unpleasant. Not the fine, happy work we expect from you". Another manager kept it eleven months and I had to threaten an action before I got it back – unread. Diana Wynyard kept it for six months, then wrote a most charming letter of apology for neglecting such a "wonderfully fine and moving play". She took an option on it, but it lapsed during a severe illness she underwent. It has had exactly seven performances – by a struggling repertory company – and two broadcasts.

*Basil
Dean
(MM)*

For some years I was a regular contributor to the *Yorkshire Weekly Post*. My last job for Hunt was a five-instalment serial. I had finished the story a week before it was due to start. When I arrived with the script they were putting the last touches to the last edition. Hunt handed me a proof slip without a word. I thought it was the announcement that my story was to start next week. Instead, it was the announcement that the paper would cease publication with that very issue. The Directors, without a hint to anybody on the staff, had suddenly decided to close the paper down, only that morning. Hunt was still fuming at this cavalier treatment. "Why the devil didn't we print a trailer of your story last week and start it this" he asked of nobody, "pity you didn't" was all I could think of. "If I'd had the least notion this was in the wind," he declared, "I should have done! They wouldn't have shut us up until it was finished once it was started, and we should all have had four more weeks of life!"

That particular story, in its turn, became a radio serial called *Dead Reckoning* in which

---

[128] See Appendix 6 for a selection of letters both for and against the serial.

[129] Basil Dean (1888-1978) was an actor, writer, director and producer in both the cinema and the theatre. From a West End stage actor he progressed to become a theatrical producer, later moving into the film industry and in the early 1930s founded Associated Talking Pictures, which later became Ealing Studios. He publicised and worked alongside Gracie Fields and George Formby. His wives included Lady Mercy Greville, Esther Van Gruisen and the film actress, Victoria Hopper.

a young and struggling semi-professional known as Wilfred Pickles played the lead.[130] It proved the most popular and the most profitable, of all my radio writing, and was subsequently produced and revived in most of the major parts of the Commonwealth.

Another underpaid job for which I was most grateful at the time came from the Bradford Civic Playhouse. This organization had started as an offshoot and subsidiary outlet for the parent group in Leeds. Some of the keener members decided the time had come to claim their independence. They asked me if I would take charge, and a meeting was arranged at the home of Mrs. Priestley to hammer out details. J.B.Priestley, who had consented to act as President, was there, and it was finally agreed that I should act as producer and leading man for the first season of ten plays for the sum of £125. Allowing for travelling expenses it meant thirty weeks of evenings and weekend work for about three pounds a week, but it also meant that with my contributions to the *Yorkshire Weekly Post* and similar "magazine" articles in other papers, I should be free of the drudgery of hunting news stories on a haphazard three-halfpence-a line basis.

*Wilfred*
*Pickles*
*(MM)*

During that first season of 1932/3 I produced and acted in *Heartbreak House*, a revival of my *Sar' Alice*, *Granite*, *R.U.R.* and *The Knight of the Burning Pestle*. It was rounded off by a large-scale production of *Miracle at Verdun*. Other productions were of *Doctor Knock*, *The Balcony* and a new play of Priestley's – *The Roundabout*.

That meeting at Priestley's had more important consequences for Florence than for me. After the business part of it was over and we were sampling Mrs. Priestley's home-made scones and cakes, J.B. made his way to Florence. It was the first time they'd met since our unsuccessful audition at the Leeds Theatre Royal. J.B. told her how sorry he was that he "couldn't have had her for Mrs. Oakroyd"

"But you never asked for me" she replied.

---

[130] Wilfred Pickles (1904-1978) was an actor and radio presenter, born in Halifax. Pickles was a proud Yorkshireman, and having been selected by the BBC as an announcer for its North Region radio service, went on to be an occasional newsreader on the National service during World War 11. He was the first newsreader to speak in a regional accent rather than the "BBC English" of the period, and caused some comment with his farewell catchphrase "......and to all in the North, good neet". Pickles soon became a radio celebrity, and also pursued an acting career in West End Theatre. His most significant work was as host of the BBC Radio show *Have A Go*, which ran from 1946 to 1967. And who of my generation can forget those immortal catchphrases, "Are yer courting?" and "Give him the money, Mabel", or was it Barney?

"Because we didn't think you were free. You were going on tour with your husband."
"But he – he'd have been only too glad to let me go for a chance like that. He…."

Priestley's comforting hand on her shoulder almost broke her down. "Never mind," he said. They're going to make a film of it. I'll see you get the part in that!"

He kept his promise and the job, when it materialised, not only helped our straitened finances at the moment, but led to Florence getting other film work and ultimately blossoming out as a dialect expert.

I'd have given a great deal to have witnessed her first morning in the studio. In her first shot she had to iron some shirts. Another actress might merely have pretended. Not so Florence. She is a housewife off the set. She was a housewife on it. First of all, before she could really get going, she had to fold all the articles the way they should be folded, and show the property man where he'd gone wrong. Then, the iron in her hand, moving from the fireplace to the table, she had to try the heat of it in the normal way of Yorkshire housewives. Instinctively she spat on it. The studio roared with delight at the "business" and at Florence's look of disgust as she exclaimed, "It doesn't sizzle!" When she could be heard she let all and sundry have it. "There's nothing to laugh at! This iron should be hot, and t'spit should roll of it in little pellets. If this is how you produce films, you've something to learn! And that fireplace isn't Yorkshire – it's South Wales!" Before she'd finished pointing out their errors and shortcomings, the property man was at her side with a hot iron!

When Edmund Gwenn was asked to take over the part of "Jess" he insisted upon having someone to coach him in the dialect.[131] Florence was the obvious choice to the studio people, and so it came about that instead of three days work, she got nine weeks. The joke of it all to us was that she, a Lancashire woman teaching the Yorkshire dialect to a Welshman, earned the bigger half of the family's income that year! Gwenn showed his gratitude by giving her tickets for two appallingly expensive seats at the Charity premiere of the film, and Florence had the great pleasure of seeing Queen Mary, two rows in front of us, laugh heartily when the iron-spitting occurred.

Shortly after this, I had my first taste of film life. It was one of the unexpected plums which came along. It came in the shape of a letter from Associated Talking Pictures over the signature of Basil Dean. They were looking for a story for the next film they were planning for Miss Gracie Fields. On the attached sheet I should find their very rough outline of the main idea. Would I let them have a "story" of not more than 2000 words incorporating and built round this rough, main ground-plan? For this, whether accepted or not, they would pay £25. If accepted, they would offer me a further £400 for the full scenario. They remained, etc.

According to the "attached sheet", the suggested film was to be called *Grace Darling* and it was to include a flashback sequence in which Miss Fields was to play the part

---

[131]  Edmund Gwenn (1877-1959) was an Academy Award winning theatre and film actor. He appeared in more than eighty films during his career. He is best remembered for his role as Kris Kringle in *Miracle on 34th Street* for which he won an Oscar for Best Supporting Actor.

*Programme: Bradford Civic Playhouse* (CA)

of the Northumbrian heroine in a reconstruction of the rescue of the "Forfarshire". For the rest of the film, she was to be a modern descendent of the Darling family and the film was to end with this modern Grace pulling off a rescue even more thrilling and spectacular than that of her ancestress. In putting the flesh on to this skimpy skeleton I was asked to provide "scope" for comedy, and points at which Miss Fields can do her vocal numbers – comic, patter and sentimental.

Florence said, "Why it's money for muck! You get it written!"

I got it written – in one uninterrupted morning session. The midday meal was put back half an hour so that I could boast I once made twenty-five pounds before lunch. Florence, having read it, declared it was daft enough even for the films. I posted the script straight away. The cheque came by return. "You'd better get it into the bank before they read your stuff!" said Florence.

I fully expected that was the end of the matter, but about a fortnight later, I was surprised by another letter. My story wasn't entirely what they wanted, but could I spend some weeks in London working on it with their scenario editor? I was in Ealing Studios almost as soon as my acceptance. My first job was to wade through a score of other "outlines" submitted by other authors – some with names which told me that they'd been paid twice, thrice, ten times the money I had. It was obvious that all, like I had, had been only too pleased to jump at the chance of a bit of easy money.

In sending my own first outline in, I'd mentioned what I considered a major and irremediable flaw in their idea, which was that the flashback, if it were treated seriously as they intended, would make any succeeding rescue by the modern Gracie an anti-climax. And the more we worked on the script in the studio the more apparent this became. For five weeks, between innumerable, endless conferences, we worked over and over the script, switching the plot, changing the gags, and ad infinitum, and to my mind, the story got worse and worse. Sick of it at last, I said to Basil Dean, "You've wasted something like £2,000 already on a story that'll never wash; go to somebody who'll charge you five thousand to look at him and you'll have to take what he gives you, and you'll have a name that'll sell it!"

Within a few days, Priestley and Dean were flying to Capri with the rough idea of *Sing As We Go*, and I was in the train for home, having, as one of my temporary colleagues declared, "Bitched a beautiful job".[132] As an epilogue to this, Dean offered me a small part in the Priestley film and a fortnight's work as production assistant on location.

Both experiences left me with something approaching contempt for the "executives" of the film industry and a profound admiration for its technicians.

*James Gregson – with Jacob Kramer, well known Leeds artist (1892-1962)*      *(1929 CA)*

---

[132] *Sing As We Go* was a 1934 musical film starring Gracie Fields and Stanley Holloway. The script was written by Gordon Wellesley and J B Priestley and directed by Basil Dean. Considered by many to be Gracie Field's finest film. It was set in the industrial north and designed to boost morale in the days of the depression. Fields stars as a resourceful, spunky working class hero, laid off from her job in a cotton mill, who has to seek work in the seaside resort of Blackpool. The decision to film on location brings the film a life and immediacy all too often absent from most films of the period. The film provides us with a snapshot of life in a seaside resort in the 1930s. The final scene of the millworkers returning to the re-opened mill while Fields leads them in the rousing title song, has become an almost iconic film cliché.

Between the end of 1931 and the outbreak of the Second World War I wrote only one professional play. Alfred Wareing had discovered that it paid him, in the sense that he didn't lose as much, to employ me and my semi-professional friends instead of booking a touring company during certain "bad" weeks of the year, such as Holy Week, the week before the Pantomime, and the weeks before and after the local Operatic Society had occupied the theatre with their annual production.[133] For these special weeks he would pay us all our individual modest salaries, my royalties, and provide the necessary scenery. We rang the changes on my four most popular plays until I felt they were losing their appeal. I decided to try out a fresh play by another established Northern author, and was on the point, a fortnight before production, of starting rehearsals, when it occurred to me that the new play would mean no royalties for me. I sat down at once at my typewriter and began work on *Storm in Port*, a light and flashy farcical comedy which proved as successful as any other of my plays, always excepting *The Devil A Saint*. Rehearsals of the first two acts were well under way before the actors got the script of the last, and from start to finish the writing, including a complete revise of Act Three, took less than a fortnight.

In 1936 I began a five years spell as a Labour member of the Huddersfield Town Council. I

James Gregson

Zachariah Briggus

(1932)

(CA)

---

[133] Losses on recent plays

Mr. Alfred Wareing, the director of the Theatre Royal, Huddersfield, makes a striking statement regarding the insufficient support of the local public. He declares that he is, at present, "fed up" with the town, and he wishes he had never seen it. "I cannot go on" he adds. "I shall be driven to give up my ideals and run the theatre as a very second-rate provincial concern".

There is more in the same vein before he concluded:

"I utter this warning – unless the Huddersfield public supports the theatre better than they have done in the past they will wake up one fine morning to find it has passed to other uses."

*Yorkshire Evening Post*, May 17th 1922.

A decade or so later he was still running the Theatre Royal, presumably having settled his differences with the Huddersfield public.

won a bye-election by advocating a revision of the scales for public assistance. The scheme, sadly mutilated, when finally put into operation increased the rate by a penny in the pound. I failed in an attempt to enlist municipal support for the Theatre Royal. I almost failed to secure re-election for a second term. It was only after several recounts that I was declared elected by a majority of two in a poll of some four thousand.

I doubt whether my own earnings between the end of the tour and the outbreak of war would have enabled us to live and get straight with the world as well, but my women–folk came to the rescue. Young Florence worked two years as assistant stage manager for my old friend, Herbert M. Prentice, at Northampton's repertory theatre, then went on tour in Walter Greenwood's *Love On The Dole,* until after three solid years of having a baby twice nightly, she went off to London to try her luck there. But the great standby was Florence who had a series of film jobs and touring engagements whilst I kept the house going in between my journalism, broadcasting, productions and other hit-and-miss jobs.

By the Spring of 1939 we were out of debt, had a small car – our very first, bought by Florence out of her earnings in *South Riding* – and enough money to see us through till the following Autumn when I should begin to draw fees for the scripts to be worked on during the summer.

# Chapter Twenty One

At the end of August 1939 I was looking forward to the best season I had had since the early Civic Playhouse days. I was booked solid with Little Theatre Productions for the whole winter and was to act in eleven broadcasts, nine of them based on my own scripts, fixed for transmission before Christmas. By the second week in September, I hadn't one engagement left uncancelled, and all my markets for articles – I was a purely regional writer – had gone too. I achieved the distinction of an overdraft, had to ask to be allowed grace in repaying the mortgage on the house and, in short, was at the very bottom, on my beam ends once more. Two things I specially remember about that black month. The first was a request from some amateur entertainers to let them have my *Devil A Saint* free of royalties for performances they had been engaged to give to the troops. I wasn't surprised at all. As an author I'd become hardened to such requests for all manner of objects – new chapel organs, church restorations, this cause and that – objects in which I'd no interest whatever.

The second memory is of a call from the B.B.C. in Manchester, urgently asking me to go across on an important matter. I thought it meant a war-time job for me, but it was only to ask me, supposing the Manchester headquarters were to be bombed, should I be prepared to leave whatever I might be doing at the moment, dash over to Leeds and take charge of the regional news department. All prospective details agreed, I was dismissed with thanks and no mention of the expenses I'd been put to, and which I couldn't really afford. It was two years before the B.B.C. again remembered my existence.

For the first year of the war I earned about three pounds a week as a collector of industrial insurance premiums – work known locally as "sneck lifting" – going from one door to another, knocking and then walking in without waiting to be invited and picking up amounts varying from two pence to four or five shillings a week. My round was on the hilly outskirts of Huddersfield and during that first hard winter it meant trudging miles through snowdrifts and occasionally burying myself in an unexpected one. During this period, I picked up a few odd pounds playing small parts in infrequent weeks with the local repertory company.

I really couldn't face another winter like the first had been and the Labour Exchange sent me to a local chemical factory.[134] Here I acted as clerk attached to a group of maintenance fitters. The work was simple and straightforward. The wage was $1/3\frac{3}{4}$d per hour. The office was warm and stuffy, my workmates were kindly and genial, I was allowed time off for my Town Council duties on condition I made it up by working weekends, and, apart from feeling forgotten and once again in a blind alley, I was happy enough.

The factory was a fascinating place, always exciting, occasionally dangerous. At least three men lost their lives during my time there. It was no unusual sight to see a man,

---

[134] This would appear to be ICI Ltd, Leeds Road, Huddersfield.

supported by two mates, rolling and staggering like a drunk in a farcical file, tears of joy and laughter rolling down his cheeks, being taken to the clinic to be treated for a dose of some gas or other. The commonest sights of all were the workers in the sheds where the colours were made. The powder flew everywhere, penetrating clothes and skins, and the workers took on the current shade – yellow, puce, red, blue and what-have you. The one I liked least was a livid, vivid green, known as "malachite", and one picture that still remains with me from the bitter second winter of the war is of a woman labourer, green from hand to foot, crossing a patch of purple snow, carrying a canary in a cage – the birds were used to test for trace of gas in the vats and retorts.

I never understood the processes that went on there but I remember with amusement that from one "shed" – called I think, an "intermediate shed" – the material produced was, in succeeding and differing processes, converted into a covering for aeroplane wings, a substance for delaying the explosive action of naval mines, a green powder to stain the sea and mark the whereabouts of a plane that had "gone into the drink", and colours used in the preparation of food powders and medicines and in the curing of kippers.

A great deal of the unskilled labour in the factory was provided by women – the majority of them with menfolk serving in the forces. One of them in our gang suffered what might have proved a dreadful, if not fatal, accident. She and the fitter she was working with were engaged in replacing a valve on a vat containing double vitriol. The pipe to which the valve was fitted was corroded by the acid to a dangerous extent. In spite of all the care the fitter was taking over the job, the pipe broke and a stream of viscous, vicious liquid spurted all over the woman's face. Quick as thought, the fitter picked her up, dashed to a standpipe nearby, held her under the spout and stunned her with the heavy jet of water. His prompt action saved her face from being scarred for life, but she had slight burns on her body where her clothing had prevented the escape of the diluted acid.

When I saw her a few days after the incident her face was still covered by some kind of greasy ointment and she herself looked a little wan and shaken. I commented on her lucky escape and she agreed it "might have been worse".

"What does your husband think about it?" I asked.
"Oh, he hasn't written yet!" she replied. "He's away at Aldershot, yer know".
"But didn't you feel upset or anything?" I went on.
"Well, I… I mean it were a bit vexing, like!"
"Vexing?"

Then, with simple, naive gravity; "Ay. Yer see, they had to send my husband backward. He were coming home for a day or two on what they call this here "passionate leave".

Towards the end of 1941 the B.B.C. suddenly remembered me – or rather, as I learned later, Philip Robinson, who'd shared our ill-dogged tour with us, reminded them I was still alive. He was, by then, an announcer in the expanding Overseas Service of the Corporation. Hearing that still more Northern voices were required by the American section – Southern accents and intonations were regarded as "cissy" by North American listeners – he mentioned me.

By the time I was called for an audition, John Chalmers, the head of Overseas

Presentation, had heard that *Radio News Reel* wanted another scriptwriter. Realising that my writing and journalistic experience would be much more useful in a news programme, he surrendered me to Norman Collins, who passed me on to Peter Pooley.[135] I was asked to report for duty at Evesham where the news and newsreel units were operating, and at the age of fifty-two I became a "new boy" again. In the News Department, to which I was first drafted so that I could refresh my ideas of what made a story, the staff consisted of three teams who worked in changing shifts all round the clock. As the junior member of my team I was given the "hits" – stories worth only a line or two which came at the end of the bulletin, or more often than not were left out on account of time. It sounds a simple job but I didn't find it at all easy to gut a pile of tape to its barest bones. As a playwright I thought I knew all about economy in the use of words, but I learned I'd still a lot to learn. It was a whole fortnight before anything I had sweated over was heard on the air – a miserable couple of lines at that. I'd begun to wonder how soon I should be found to be no good and given the sack when, one Sunday night, expecting to sit as usual biting my nails and waiting for the odd crumbs from the editor's file for nine hours, I found I was the only one there besides the great man himself. Something had gone wrong with our transport. It meant we had to bring out the bulletins between us. He took all the big war stories and I the lesser stuff, as usual, but my contributions filled the last three minutes at least. I felt I was getting on!

Three months later I was still working on the bulletins, apparently forgotten by Peter Pooley of the News Reel, when Frank Singleton, the editor of my shift, came to the table where I was writing the Russian section – the "Number Two" story of the day. "Do you know anything about *Radio News Reel*?" he asked.

"Only in theory."

"Well, now's your chance to get a little practice. Reggie Pound who should be doing the African edition should have been on the job two hours ago. He must be ill, and you've no time to waste. You go on the air at seven."

Quaking in my shoes, and only partially re-assured by my producer, Rosemary Sellis, a grand, quietly competent slip of a girl who was to prove a most helpful and loyal colleague during the years to come, I sat down to digest a pile of scripts and tried to think of those which would wind six or seven different topics into something like a homogeneous programme. With Rosemary's tactful guidance and help, I sweated out a script and somehow we scrambled on the air.

I deputised for Reginald Pound until he was well again, became general deputy and relief scriptwriter and ultimately found myself in charge of the North American and Pacific editions.

The *Radio News Reel* set-up was the happiest and most hard-working of all the news

---

[135] Peter Pooley (1912-1996), devised *Radio News Reel* as an outlet for the BBC's staff who had become war correspondents. The first edition (July 1940), broadcast to North America, included a talk by a bomber pilot about the fortnight he had spent drifting in an open boat. Editions of *Radio News Reel* for Africa and the Pacific were added in 1941 and the programme rapidly became a popular success.

sections. Peter Pooley, with his quiet friendliness and deceptive unassertiveness, had created something of a tradition for the programme and welded a motley crew of writers, researchers and producers from the press, the stage, and the teaching professions into a real team. Our principal readers or "narrators" were those fine actors Robert Harris[136] and Robert Beatty;[137] our producers included George Inns and Jan Bussell, who spent all his spare time with the puppets which were later to become the stars of Children's Television; amongst our scriptwriters were genial Reggie Pound, now television critic for *The Listener*, and the novelist Woosnam Mills.

*Robert Beatty, (MM)*

The work was hard, often onerous; the hours were long but always interesting, often exciting and occasionally hectic. A sudden news flash would call for the scrapping of an almost completed programme and a scrambled re-arrangement and revision. My worst night was that when Allied troops made the first landing in North Africa. We were caught quite unprepared for it, with not a single talk recorded in readiness for use on any topic remotely touching on the new area of war. By the time we had been briefed and had collected what books and press cuttings we could, I had less than an hour and a half in which to dictate to my secretary a script for seven narrators to fill the necessary thirty minutes. The unrehearsed programme had been on the air nearly five minutes when I ran down to the censors with the last few pages. Another, though not quite so hectic a night, was when, halfway through my nightly dictation, I learned that a relief force had got through to Leningrad. Again we had little recorded material that was of use to us, but I chanced upon a cutting from the *Daily Express* – a story of an old woman at a tram stop in Leningrad, asking the conductor, "Tell us, comrade, do you go to the Park or to the Front?" I built an eight-minute dramatic sketch out of the story, Jan Bussell roped in some of the canteen staff to play the parts and recorded it, and it took its place in the script I had largely re-written in the meantime. There was one unforgettable occasion when the whole prepared reel was scrapped five minutes before we went on air. But this time no re-writing was necessary. It was the night when Stanley Maxted, dirty and dishevelled and looking like a man tired to the point of death, walked into

---

[136] Robert Harris (1900-1995). Shakespearean actor, made his first professional appearance in 1923 in *The Will* by J M Barrie at the Westminster Theatre. His last appearance was in William Templeton's *Make no Mistake*, in 1971 in Guildford.

[137] Robert Beatty (1909-1992), born in Canada, was an actor who worked in radio, film and television for most of his career and was especially known in the UK. The highlight of his career must surely have been when he appeared in an episode of *Dr. Who* (The Tenth Planet, as General Cutler)!

the studio from Arnhem, to go straight on the air to America with the first impromptu story of the gallant venture he'd shared from the first touch down of the planes to the last bitter moment of the evacuation – a broadcast that was a masterpiece of tense, dramatic reporting, destined to become one of the classics of radio.[138]

Of the brilliant team of war correspondents who served the B.B.C. I think Stanley Maxted was easily the most radiogenic. Technically he was a supreme master of the medium, but in addition he had a direct, friendly, homely style and a simple sincerity which came through to the listener and transformed him from a distant personality into a kindly neighbour at one's own fireside. He was more than an observer of events, he lived through them and made his listeners live through them, too.

*Robert Harris*
*(MM)*

Others I remember particularly are Richard Dimbleby who was even then the slick well-oiled recording machine he is today; efficient and apparently effortless, with a camera eye that nothing escaped; cool, detached, a master of objective reporting, the fine bloom just marred by a faint tinge of his magisterial attitude towards people and events.[139]

The most brilliant, dynamic, far-seeing and incisive of them all, to my mind, was Chester Wilmot.[140] He could grasp and convey the true inwardness of what he was reporting – dissecting and interpreting the most complicated of situations and anticipating their consequences. He had a dry, forceful style, a stark honesty and utter

---

[138] Stanley Maxted (1897-1963), born in Canada, was a producer, commentator, compere and actor. He appeared as himself, in the film *Theirs is the Glory* (1946), shown in the USA as *Men of Arnhem*.

[139] Richard Dimbleby (1913-1965), was a journalist and broadcaster widely acknowledged as one of the greatest figures in British broadcasting history. During the war, he flew some twenty raids as an observer with Bomber command, including one to Berlin, recording commentary for broadcast the following day. After the war Dimbleby switched to television, eventually becoming the BBC's leading news commentator and is perhaps best remembered as the commentator on the Coronation of Queen Elizabeth 11 in 1953, and the funerals of George V1, John F Kennedy and Winston Churchill.

[140] Chester Wilmot (1911-1954), was an Australian war correspondent who reported for the BBC and Australian Broadcasting Corporation (ABC). After the war he continued to work as a broadcast reporter, and wrote a well regarded book about the liberation of Europe, *The Struggle for Europe*, in 1952. During the war whilst reporting for the ABC, Wilmot regarded the Australian General Thomas Blamey as incompetent and protested at his sacking of Lieutenant-General Sidney Rowell. In retaliation, Blamey cancelled Wilmot's accreditation, and he had to return to Sydney.
In 1953 Wilmot was sent by the BBC to Australia to participate in a round-the-world broadcast on Christmas day, where he narrated *The Queen's Journey*, telling the story of recent Royal visits. Wilmot was returning to Britain by air on BOAC Flight 781, a de Havilland Comet airliner, when it broke up in mid-air over the Mediterranean.

lack of humbug which made him something of a trial to the brass-hats he had to deal with and about whom he had no illusions whatever. Even more valuable than the recorded dispatches he sent us and which we used avidly, were his talks to us, off the record, in our morning editorial conferences.

He turned up at one conference unexpectedly, dismissed from the Normandy front by Montgomery for an alleged breach of faith, ignorantly or carelessly committed by a colleague. We felt the injustice so much that we began to consider strike action to get him re-instated. I was one of the deputation to put the matter formally to Peter Pooley and ask him to make our intentions clear to the higher-ups, but before events had developed much further, within a couple of days Wilmot walked into our conference room, his face one broad grin, to tell us that he was flying back to France immediately, in the Commander-in-Chief's own plane. "Monty" had found out the true facts and characteristically was making a prompt and full amends for his error of judgement.

*Reginald William Winchester Wilmot*

*National Library of Australia*

Life was far from easy on *Radio News Reel*. The long hours, very often in periods of strain and sudden emergencies, played the very dickens with one's nerves. On what was known as the "American" shift we went on duty at nine p.m. to find a typed brief and a list of recorded talks available for our use. After digesting the brief and the scripts, we spent two or more hours listening to the recordings themselves, discussing, cutting or discarding them with our producers. The line and shape of the night's programme agreed, the scriptwriter proceeded to his dictation and the producer to mark and occasionally re-record the discs. Sometimes at three, sometimes at four in the morning, the first programme, censored and rehearsed, would go on the air. A cup of tea (I soon found it wasn't wise to eat during the night hours) and one turned to the Pacific edition, sometimes writing an entirely new programme, which in its turn went out at eight in the morning. This was the routine eight nights on and two off.

The day shift, when one did the African edition for transmission at seven-thirty p.m. was not so long, but not so satisfying to me. There were too many distractions by the day staff and, even with Peter Pooley's gentle guidance, much less freedom and responsibility.

Every edition had its own style and set of don'ts. The stiffest format was that of the "American" reel, every talk included having to be introduced and dismissed with over-elaborate emphasis on its theme and the name and status of its contributor. The most colloquial and fluid of all, when in due course it was launched, was the "Forces Reel" which went out in the early afternoon. It was the only reel in which slang and humorous under-statement could be used in a free, sometimes off-hand style. One hadn't to remember Americanisms such as "truck" for lorry, or "sidewalk" for pavement; one hadn't to steer clear of words such as "concentration camp" which were taboo in the African reel because of the memories they evoked. Above all, one could introduce talks and speakers in a casual, allusive fashion.

These introductions were to me a constant, irritating difficulty. Every reel contained six, sometimes up to a dozen of them. Finding alternative, and when possible, new variations of one essential formula was a nightmare, and the recurring, niggling problem was further complicated by the fact that, without saying so in so many words, one had to imply that the talks were "live" not recorded. I spent plenty of my spare time trying to find or invent fresh substitutes for "here is".

*Richard Dimbleby*

Another amusing and irritating little difficulty was caused by the vagaries of the censorship. Apart from the fact that those who vetted our written scripts never seemed to realise what an actor could make of it when spoken, some of the bans were really stupid. Dispatches from Paul Winterton in Russia, or Gillard in Cairo, for example, would contain odd words and sometimes whole paragraphs which we were banned from broadcasting on the ground that the information might be useful to the enemy, although the dispatches had come to us over the air and had been "monitored" by the Germans during their transmission to us.

Our biggest problem was the nature or quality of the talks we had to handle – talks by "diplomatic correspondents" which contained half a grain of wheat hid in three minutes of woolly, ambiguous phrases; talks by "experts" who seemed unable to speak anything but their professional jargon; talks by politicians who had nothing to say and didn't know how to say it and addressed the "mike" as though it were a public meeting. The politicians were naturally long winded, and one had to listen to half-an hour of "guff" to pick out a couple of sentences worth half-a-minute on the air. Anthony Eden, with his endless clichés and pasteboard phrases, was a terrible trial. Occasionally we would reverse the entire order of the paragraphs in a piece of "expertise", or turn a fifteen minute's contribution, pedestrian and stumbling in delivery, into a brief, telling "interview", by giving the narrator a few questions, answered by odd sentences from the recording. Apart from the dispatches from the fronts, our most reliable and competent contributor was Lewis Hastings, our "military expert". His direct, idiomatic, salty style was a joy.

Our industrial correspondent was George Darling, now Labour M.P. for one of the Sheffield constituencies.[141] As a rest from the incessant grind of scripting news reels, I was made a sort of understudy to him, attending, under his wing, various conferences such as the World T.U.C. and the first meeting during the war of the International Labour Organisation. I remember the latter, mainly because of the windy verbiage of the American delegates. My job was to augment Darling's factual, informed reporting with little "colour" descriptions and character sketches.

The international gatherings were tedious affairs, a great deal of the time being taken up by translations of each speech into at least two other languages, but these intervals were livened by contacts with world figures in trade union and trade association circles with whom George Darling was on intimate, and often jocular terms. This departure from routine news reel work led to my becoming our team's parliamentary reporter, especially when the debate had an international interest. Again, my main brief was to supply the colour and character touches in order to make the proceedings in the House more "visible". A typical big debate meant two or three days almost without sleep. On the first day I would be in the office by nine-thirty a.m., writing a short talk for inclusion in the Forces' reel for that afternoon – a sort of trailer for our boys overseas. This talk recorded, I would set off for the House, whose sittings began much earlier in the day at that period. Whilst I was there, the news tape would be studied and marked by my producer, so that when I returned about six p.m. most of the portions I wanted to quote were ready to hand. My story written and recorded, the narrative in my voice, the "quotes" spoken by others, it would go out in the African reel at 7.30 p.m., very often occupying half to two-thirds of the programme. After a hasty meal in the canteen, I should be back in the House until it rose for the night, and then dash back to the office, to extend, condense and re-write my report for American consumption. This, to ensure the best possible reception over there would go out "live" but would be recorded for use in the Pacific edition at eight in the morning, at the time when, after an all-too-brief spell in bed, I should be getting ready for the second spell. This would be the drill as long as the debate lasted, the only difference being that on the second and succeeding days I should be re-writing for troops the previous day's story before getting away to the House for that day's instalment. It was a fascinating job, making one feel one was at the centre of things and bringing one into intimate contact with personalities in both parties – heroes one had worshipped, enemies one had detested, from afar. Few, on this closer acquaintance, measured up to either the virtues or the villainy one had ascribed to them. I had not only reached – I was an inhabitant of – the great world at last, only to find it wasn't so big nor its denizens so majestic, after all. Even the great man who had led and heartened Britain in our darkest, finest hour was

---

[141] George Darling, Baron Darling of Hillsborough (1905-1985), was Labour Co-operative Member of Parliament for Sheffield Hillsborough from 1950 to 1974. Darling was educated at elementary school and started work at fourteen in the railway sheds of Crewe. When he was made redundant in 1926 he went to Leeds University, where he was chair of the Labour Club having joined the Labour Party in 1923. Later he graduated in Economics at Cambridge. From 1942 to 1949 he was the industrial correspondent for the BBC reporting team.

still boy enough to distort his face in temper and stick out his tongue at the men whom the country had put on the Treasury bench in his stead.

A few months before I left *Radio News Reel* I had the supreme pleasure of reporting the opening of parliament. Hearing the Speech from the Throne – the first to be composed by a Labour Government in full power – I looked back over the long years which had brought us to this moment, thought of the many, many friends, harder-working and more devoted in their service than I had been, to whom this was perhaps the crowning moment of their lives. I thought, especially, of those Yorkshire friends with whom, in the disastrous election after the betrayal of 1931, I had stood, heartbroken and ashamed. This great moment paid even for that bitterest of memories.[142]

My days with *Radio News Reel* were coming to a close. For four years I had been one of a hardworking band whose loyalty and pride in their work had, in spite of all the difficulties and obstacles put in their way, made News Reel something of a miracle of war-time broadcasting. But the long knives were being sharpened in Broadcasting House. There were signs that our wings were to be clipped. It was a prospect I couldn't face. I got ready to leave, foreseeing these present days when it has become the mere, spiritless skeleton shadow of itself.

But I cannot leave this very sketchy account of those wonderful days without two little stories which illustrate the spirit which animated the set-up, and some of the minor snags which beset us.

One night, Pooley left instructions that I had to reserve a five minutes' space for Robin Duff who was covering a baseball match between two teams of American troops stationed near London. Five minutes before we went on the air Robin had not turned up. We were making hasty re-adjustments when he rushed into the studio breathless and dishevelled. I let fly at him for being late, but when he confessed he'd brought no story, I went up in smoke. He hadn't been near the match, but explained, apologetically, that on his way there, he'd called at his flat for something, only to find it "wasn't there". It had been totally destroyed by a flying bomb just a few minutes before he got there, and naturally he'd had to help in rescue operations. "I'm very sorry", he concluded, "but there's no story for you!" I remembered the day when Schofield, of the *Leeds Mercury*, had sent me after those non-existent emigrants from Castleford and its collieries. Duff went on the air to apologise to America for not bringing them the story he'd promised the night before and to tell them why – a much better story than the one he'd planned.

Another night, as I was settling in my bunk during one of the periods when the flying bombs drove the whole set-up below ground, I noticed that our night secretary, Rowena Killick, was perched precariously on her typing chair. I watched her for a

---

[142] Ramsey McDonald's second minority government in 1929 encountered economic crises, including the doubling of unemployment levels. This persuaded him to include the opposition leaders in a cross-party National Government. Unfortunately, this step lost him the support of his own party and the coalition was considered by many party members (including Gregson) to be a cynical betrayal of their hopes.

while, expecting every minute that she'd lose her infinitesimal purchase and land on the floor.

Finally, I asked, "What's the matter with you, Rowena?  Have you got piles?"

She was naturally affronted.

"Then why the devil don't you use your bottom properly?"

"Because, if you want to know, it's full of glass.  I've had eight splinters taken out today before I came here, and have to go to hospital again tomorrow!

The previous night, it transpired – one of her nights "off", she'd been fire-watching. The dropping of a flying bomb had sent her grovelling in the gutter, her tin hat between her and the anticipated explosion.  What she'd overlooked was that her rear was facing some plate-glass shop windows, and that windows that survived the blast were often shattered by the suction that followed.  She'd got thoroughly peppered. Unfit as she was, she'd turned up as usual for duty and, but for my curiosity, wouldn't have said a word to anyone.  I can think of no more typical instance of the spirit that enabled *Radio News Reel* to carry on – the spirit against which principalities and powers cannot prevail.

# Chapter Twenty Two

The end of the war saw us once more on the crest of a wave. In addition to my salary from the B.B.C. and the modest royalties from my plays, there were odd pickings from radio programmes outside News Reel and occasional jobs as a Drama Adjudicator and lecturer. Florence, too, in between defying the flying bombs in order to queue for food and the very occasional delicacies – such as the sole, solitary basket of strawberries we enjoyed during our four years in London – that came our way, found time for what broadcasting jobs turned up. We had actually begun to save for our old age.

By this time too, I had learned to accept my limitations – I'd always been conscious of them, even when gnawed and nagged by personal ambition – and was no longer fretted by them. My origins, my upbringing and experience had all tended to make the quality of the work more important to me than what I made out of it. It was apparent to me that *Radio News Reel* wasn't going to be a satisfying job much longer and so, although I was firmly established and marked out for further advancement, I began to cast about for a fresh and, if possible, even more rewarding niche in the B.B.C. Naturally I turned to the North and to Drama.

But the North, I found, were also looking to me. Before V.E. Day, John Coatman, the Controller of the North Region, had come along and offered me any job I wanted. My choice was no surprise either to him, or to the Programme Director, John Salt, with whom I was to work happily for two years before his untimely death.[143] I made only one condition. The Drama Department of the North was to be stationed in Leeds. Apart from the fact that I'd never felt comfortable when working previously in the overcrowded Manchester studios, I wanted to raise the status of the sub-station in which I'd done my best pre-war radio work with the help of old friends such as Philip Fox and "Bill" Page. Moreover, I was determined to live on my own side of the Pennines, if at all possible, in one of our delectable Dales. My terms were accepted and I warned Peter Pooley of my impending departure.

Then the fun began. It appeared that the position I was to take up in the North was two grades lower than the one I now occupied. It meant a decrease of £200 a year in salary. This was against all the rules and traditions of the Corporation. It could not be. We were in for a series of interviews and a torrent of inter-departmental memos. It seemed to me that every ex-naval and ex-military tom-noddy in the over-swollen administrative machinery had to put in his particular spoke. John Salt and I decided that there was only one thing to do. He undertook to give me a "freelance" contract to take effect the moment I left the Corporation. Fortified by this, I threatened to put in my notice. The tom-noddies capitulated.

Early in 1946 I was in the saddle in Leeds amongst friends I'd known from the pioneer

---

[143] John S.A.Salt was the great-grandson of Sir Titus Salt, one of the great textile paternalists who founded Salts Mill and the model village of Saltaire on the outskirts of Bradford. In June 1939, John Salt and Olive Shapley announced their engagement and were married on the following Bastille Day. The couple spent two years in London before moving to New York, where they rented Alistair Cooke's spacious Fifth Avenue apartment at a "decidedly uncommercial rent", while John took up a post as deputy North American director of the BBC. On returning to the UK, and shortly after the birth of his third child, John Salt died in 1947, aged 42.

*John Salt (1945) at The Commonwealth Conference on Broadcasting, held in London in February 1945. From Left to Right: A E Powley, Head of Canadian Broadcasting Corporation in London. Ernest Davies, BBC North American Service Organiser. Warren McAlpine, BBC North American Service Director. John Salt, BBC North American Director. Maurice Gorham, Director of the Allied Expeditionary Forces Programme of the BBC. S J Lotbiniere, Representative of the BBC in Canada. Howard Chase, Chairman of the Board of Governors of the CBC. E L Bushnell, Director General of Programme, CBC.* (BBC)

days of a one-room studio in an attic - a studio padded and draped until its atmosphere was that of a morgue, furnished with carbon microphones into which one played at lip distance, and so poorly equipped that all effects noises had to be faked and made on the spot by the actors. I also found myself faced with some hundreds of scripts – the accumulation of the war years during which regional broadcasting had been moribund.

Once again I was fortunate in my colleagues, from Philip Fox, who was in charge of the Leeds Station, to the players I gathered around me. Whilst I tackled the debris of wartime scripts and conducted auditions, "Bill" Page, the engineer-in-charge threw himself into the task of re-arranging and equipping our inadequate studios.

I was more fortunate in the secretary whom Philip Fox assigned to me, Lucy Hetherington. She was more than competent, utterly devoted to the job, quiet and unassuming - the perfect secretary. Very quickly she relieved me of all the routine administrative drudgery, "nursing" me in her self-effacing way, and handling my actors with consummate, kindly tact. By the time I arrived in the morning she would have sifted the heavy correspondence and typed the day's schedules of appointments, even to providing full details of buses or trains I had to use and of the people I was to meet. Without her unstinted, efficient help half the creative work of the next three years would have been impossible.

I had come back to my native heath convinced that what was wrong with the B.B.C. was the supremacy of London; that the Regions should no longer be regarded as mere local branches and subsidiaries contributing mainly sub-standard programmes with a local interest usually confined to their own wavelengths, that they should be treated as equal partners, given autonomy and a bigger share of the finance to use independently of headquarters; and that, to make good their claim to equal status and more freedom and prestige, the regions would have to prove that they could contribute to the national pool of programmes material equal in quality and general interest to the best put out by London.

John Salt, my programme director, had the same ideas. He was determined to preserve the Regional outlook and character of our programmes but to challenge London standards of presentation. He was always ready with support and encouragement, sometimes even with the spur. I was given a free hand, and as much money as he could in justice allow me, to raise the standard of our drama output, and, as a consequence, encourage regional drama in our Little Theatres and provide regional playwrights with an additional market.[144]

John and I had another thing in common. We were both Regional men with no ambitions Londonwards. He was a devotee, not a careerist. Already a stricken man, though neither he nor any of us guessed it, he bent all his energies to the task of raising the North Region to the status of London. Supported by a loyal and gallant wife, still known to listeners and viewers as Olive Shapley, he built up and inspired his staff, launching new projects and improving old programmes, with a total disregard of self, shouldering the responsibility for failure, claiming no credit for success.[145] His memory remains with me as that of a great, truly selfless man. I am proud to have been one of his lieutenants.

He faced death with the same quiet, equanimity he had lived, his one regret that his

---

[144] Yorkshire Folk and the Microphone
At the BBC's studios in Leeds is J R Gregson who, since his return from London (where he's had the responsible job of projecting Britain to America in *Radio Newsreel*), has been producing and writing Yorkshire plays and gathering around him a team of Yorkshire actors and actresses, a number of whom are broadcasting for the first time. Gregson produced Asa Briggs' play about the Corn Laws – *Repeal, Repeal!*
*Yorkshire Life*, Autumn 1946.

[145] Olive Shapley (1910-1999). Olive Shapley's socialism developed when she went up to Oxford in 1929 (she was great friends with Barbara Bells, later to become Barbara Castle). She indulged in a brief flirtation with Communism. The Establishment, however, did not forget, and even in her sixties she received regular visits from MI5. She looked forward to the officer's visit and "always made him a pot of tea". In 1934 she began her career with the BBC as Children's Hour organiser, with the responsibility of producing five hour-long programmes every week. Manchester, in those days, was a creative environment entirely suited to the skills and personality of their new Oxford graduate. With Joan Littlewood, Shapley produced *The Classic Soil*, which purported to show that little had changed since Friedrich Engels described Manchester as "the classic soil.... where capitalism flourished". Her other documentaries, including *Homeless People* and *Miner's Wives*, further reflected Shapley's concern for the disadvantaged to whom she increasingly offered the freedom of the air.

usefulness was at an end. He withdrew without fuss from his office to devote his very few remaining days to setting his personal affairs in order and making what provision he could for his young family. All other worldly distractions he put aside to live again the full tenderness of family life, to enjoy for the last time, favourite books, poems and music. He crowded that last fortnight with courage, beauty and peace. I mourned his loss as I had mourned no one's since I said farewell to Joe Harrison on that long ago first Armistice Day. They share an honoured place in my memory.

John Salt lived long enough to see the first fruits of his labours for the North Region and to rejoice unselfishly in the progress we were making in Leeds. During the war, I had conceived a new method of adapting novels too long for one-part treatment on the air. Instead of making a serial of thirteen instalments – a method I thought of as mere paste-and-scissors treatment – my idea was to pull the novel to pieces, if necessary, and re-assemble as much of it as possible and desirable into three long acts. As each act would last at least an hour, it allowed more scope for the building of climaxes and the development of character without sacrificing any of the quality and atmosphere of the story. This "three-decker" treatment also made it easier for our listeners to keep their appointment with us. To miss one instalment out of thirteen in the serialisation of a well-known classic might not matter a great deal. With lesser-known, more modern novels, it might have been fatal.[146]

We began this series of three-part adaptations with James Lansdale Hodson's *Jonathon North* in which Robert Donat played the name part at a fee hitherto undreamed of in North Regional history. I remember John Salt squeezed the Music Department's quarterly allowance to pay it. Listener Research reports showed a record Appreciation Index figure of eighty per cent. Going round the different quarters of the North Region we followed this with adaptations of *South Riding, Rogue Herries, The Stars Look Down, Wuthering Heights,* and so on.[147] The lending libraries began to ask for details of our future subjects so they could prepare for the greatly increased demand for copies of the novel which followed each production. One or two live publishers began to submit page-proofs of new stories with suggestions that we might consider producing a radio version to synchronise with the publication date.

For the first part of *South Riding* we had to break with our usual custom and play with a small audience in the studio. H.R.H. the Princess Royal, with the keen interest she takes in all developments in the county, had signified her desire to see what we were doing in Leeds. We were still rehearsing – a frantic last-minute run-over of a scene

---

[146] This treatment appears to have been successful . *Robert Owen* was a big Radio Success
Wireless plays are improving......The best are written specially for the microphone. Seldom do boiled-down stage dramas sound convincing without visible actors. The story of Robert Owen, written episodically by James R Gregson and broadcast last night, was dramatically moving and histrionically admirable.
Hannan Swaffer, Unattributed newspaper cutting, Gregson scrapbook West Yorkshire Archives, Calderdale, GRE2.

[147] *South Riding* by Winifred Holtby, first published 1936
*Rogue Herries* by Hugh Walpole, first published 1930
*The Stars Look Down* by A J Cronin, first published 1935
*Wuthering Heights* by Emily Bronte, first published 1847

I'd had to prune – when she arrived. Fortunately, all the scenes but one were to be played on microphone in the same large studio, so H.R.H. could watch the whole transmission. We had been warned that she might not stay the whole period, but to our relief she did, and Florence who managed her curtseys fairly well for a novice, told me afterwards that our visitor took her cue from the players and added her quota to the chatter and laughter of the crowd scenes.

John Salt was as anxious as I to find and encourage new Northern playwrights and besides allotting space and money for what we called our "workroom" matinee, in which both new writers and new players could try their first steps, he fell in readily with my idea of weekend schools in which our budding dramatists could get practical experience of the working of the medium. Wisely, I think, we relied more on demonstrations than lectures, and besides allowing our pupils to handle the equipment and "control" snippets of productions, we let them see and hear our players in excerpts from their own works, first as they'd submitted it to us and then as edited and revised, for purely technical reasons, by Rex Tucker, my second-in-command, and myself. We were out, not merely to match London, but to prove our right to a free, untrammelled existence – to cut our leading strings.

We didn't find, immediately, as much new, first-class talent as we'd hoped, but I am sure that had John Salt lived to back us the experiment would have had gratifying results. One discovery however pleased us all very much. We were offered a fifteen-minute script in verse – really a dramatic poem, which could be shared between a narrator and three speaking parts. The author's name was new to us, W.C.Scriven. He was a freelance journalist in Leeds, almost blind; a jolly, philosophic fellow, nevertheless, with something of the lovable enthusiasm of a puppy. Nursed by Rex Tucker, he came along with a half-hour play in verse, entitled *A Single Taper*, in which he recalled his own thought and emotions during an eye operation he had undergone without an anaesthetic. I think it's the purest bit of radio writing I know. It's more than a picture in words – it doesn't call for a single sound effect other than speech – one not only sees, hears, smells and feels what is going on; one is on the table in his place living through a vital, painful, rewarding experience. *A Single Taper*, most unusually, met with the success it so well deserved.[148]

Three years of auditions, script-writing on my own account, script-reading and

---

[148] Ronald Charles Scriven (not W.C.) (1907-1985)

.............R.C.Scriven has been one of the most distinguished genuine radio writers during the period 1960-1980. I would like to say something about this exceptional figure in the history of radio drama, particularly as he is now an old man who may be nearing the end of his creative life.

The astonishing thing about Scriven is that he has ever had a creative life at all. From the age of eight, when he contracted an ear infection, he has been almost totally deaf, and the same illness seems to have laid the foundations for the glaucoma which left him blind in the 1940s. Yet in 1947 he wrote his first radio play and the year later *A Single Taper*, which was an account in verse of the operations to try to prevent his blindness. Following this, much of his radio writing has been autobiographical and in verse. It has a powerful melodiousness and an intense visual quality, which would do credit to a man in full possession of his hearing and his sight.

The above article is a précis of a short extract from the book *British Radio Drama* edited by John Drakakis, Cambridge University Press (1981) entitled *British radio drama since 1960* – the passage in question is by David Wade.

"doctoring" for our up-and-coming and would-be playwrights, productions and multivarious outside lectures and public engagements went by swiftly and happily, leaving no time for stage work of any kind. Radio was my whole life. Although I had reached the normal age of retirement from the B.B.C., I had promised John Salt I would stay with him as long as he wished.[149] Apart from my great admiration for him, I could hardly afford to do otherwise, for our savings would not have sufficed to keep us long, and I had no pension other than the State allowance to look forward to.

A short time after John's death, my old friend James Lansdale Hodson asked me if I would consider joining him on the staff of *This Modern Age*[150]. My first instinct was to refuse. My one experience of writing for the films hadn't left me exactly enamoured of the industry. On the other hand, the salary he suggested was tempting indeed – a figure I had never envisaged, even in my most optimistic dreams. I fell for it, ultimately, but instead of the two-year contract they offered, I suggested a compromise of a trial twelve months. In March, 1949, I was back in London.

*James Gregson (1946) Publicity Photo (BBC)*

The documentary series of films known as *This Modern Age* was two years old when I joined Hodson and its originator and director, Sergei Nolbandov.[151] It had by then

---

[149] It is interesting to note the official BBC retirement age at this time was 60.

[150] One of the prides of British films today is a unique experiment in screen journalism called *This Modern Age* (TMA). It has won great prestige for Britain abroad, and is a popular success with audiences at home. It is therefore, in accordance with the peculiar logic of British film finance, likely to be closed down this autumn........
TMA is not only screen reporting, but screen leader-writing too, surveying everything from civil aviation to gambling, from Jamaica to Jerusalem. A remarkable amount of material is packed into the two reels, or twenty minutes of each film. Perhaps TMA's greatest weakness is that sometimes, anxious to include everything and to be fair to everyone, it produces a bewildering array of detail instead of telling a story in a single sweep.
As head of *This Modern Age*, which has made a brilliant success of the British point of view, Mr. Rank selected a Russian refugee. This is not as paradoxical as it may sound: after all nothing is more typical of the British way of life than its traditional and continual enrichment by technicians from the continent.
*Leader Magazine*: May 27th 1950

[151] Sergai Nolbandov (1895-1971). He was born in Russia, and came to Britain in 1921, as a penniless lawyer, where he found work as a film editor. He became associated with the famous producer Michael Balcon, first at Gaumont-British Studios and then at Ealing Studios, where he worked primarily as a writer and producer. Nolbandov worked on the screenplay of the 1937 Laurence Olivier and Vivien Leigh film *Fire over England*. During World War II he also directed a couple of films in drama documentary style (something of an Ealing trademark). He left Ealing in 1943 to produce short films for the government. After the war he produced the documentary series *This Modern Age* for Rank, which lasted from 1946 to 1949. This was Rank's attempt to adapt the highly successful American cine-magazine style of *March of Time* series to post-war Britain. It was less successful here. Nolbandov went back to producing feature films.
Sergei Nolbandov ….........is burly, bespectacled, and sometimes bad tempered: he can work 10 to 12 hours at a stretch without ever stopping for a meal. "If all the Russians are like him", says J L Hodson, his Associate Producer, "No wonder they are a world menace".
J. L. Hodson collection, Box 20, Manchester Archives.

*James Gregson (1951) on air – The Good Companions: James R Gregson (producer), Nolly Rankin (Miss Trant), Harry C Rycroft (Jess Oakroyd), Richard Hurndell (Inigo Jollifant), in a three part play James R Gregson adapted from J B Priestley's novel and broadcast in the North of England Home Service in June 1951.* (BBC)

achieved world-wide recognition and was regarded as the best thing ever to be sponsored by J. Arthur Rank. It remains so still, I think. A typically British version of *The March Of Time*, it avoided all the over-dramatisation of its American counterpart, was strictly factual and unbiased in its presentation of its topics, and although it was often described as "The Times of the pictorial world", it was even less partial than our august national daily.

One reason for this, I found, was that each programme was the result of long, arduous and sometimes acrimonious debates between men of widely divergent views and temperaments. Almost the first day I became the junior member of the editorial triumvirate I realised that I was there mainly in order that there might always be a majority vote in any dispute that arose between the principals. Hodson called himself a Liberal, and during the post-war election of 1945 had actually spoken on Labour platforms, but in truth all his deeper instincts were Conservative – at times what I can only describe as Tory – and the most stubborn of Tories at that – the "middle-class" variety.

Nolbandov, on the contrary, was truly Liberal in the finest sense of the term. His family were Tolstoyan in outlook and sympathies, and in the early days of the Russian Revolution, Sergei, then a young officer, fought on the side of Kerensky. After many vicissitudes, carrying two passes, but never quite sure which to present when challenged first by one side then by the other, he managed to reach Constantinople, as it was then known, where for twelve months he and many others subsisted on the charity of the Turks. Amongst his innumerable and fascinating stories there is one I specially like about his first day in London when finally he reached haven. Friends took him on his first afternoon to see a performance of *Hiawatha* in the Albert Hall, then in the evening to see a noted English actress, who shall be nameless, in a Shakespearean tragedy. Still shaken by these two samples of our native culture, whose quality fell considerably below his expectations, the final shock was delivered by some fanatical woman in Leicester Square, who seized him by the lapels, and cried "Repent! For the kingdom of heaven is at hand!" He says he felt like bolting for some other asylum.

If I could have written shorthand, I should have made copious notes of his talk round the conference and the dining table.[152] He was, still is, in fact, a brilliant

*James
Gregson
with
Frank
Morgan
(c1950)*
*(CA)*

*Probably
taken at
BBC studios,
Leeds.*

---

[152] In his application for a job at Simpson, Fawcett & Co. Ltd. He stated "I told him that I was a thoroughly competent clerk and bookkeeper, could take shorthand and could type". He had either forgotten his shorthand or overstated his accomplishments on his job application.

*Olive Shapley (1953): Children's Television – All Your Own: Rosemary Broad from Northern Ireland showing Olive Shapley, the compare, some of her puppets which she makes from papiere mache.*
(BBC)

*Olive Shapley (1951): Interview with Mrs Eleanor Roosevelt for the special Festival edition of Woman's Hour.*
(BBC)

conversationalist, extraordinarily well-informed on every possible subject, with a copious and almost infallible memory for anything and everything once read. His stories, told with amusing mimicry, were a sheer delight to us. A man of tremendous energy and insatiable interest in his work, he was at once the most fascinating and exhausting of colleagues. In many ways he was more English than either Hodson or I, but had retained the gift of standing aside and looking at our race objectively, and whatever British virtues of tolerance and fairness he had absorbed, he certainly hadn't lost a fraction of his Russian vitality or generosity. If I'd only had the sense and ability to take down his conversations, I could have been the Boswell to a more dynamic, modern and entertaining Johnson. As it was, I'd my work cut out learning my new, exacting job and, with my Left Wing sympathies, completing the political gamut, if not always contributing to the harmony of the trio.

Nolbandov is that very rare creature, a genuine democrat, and *This Modern Age* took its tone from him. The humblest member of the set-up was allowed to criticise commentary and visuals with the same freedom as the experts. Every production at every stage was analysed and subjected to the scrutiny of all concerned within the unit and many outsiders. Crucial points when they could not be agreed were decided by the majority vote. Only once in my memory was any issue decided by Nolbandov exercising his right to the casting vote. It was a hard, but to my mind the only, way in which to achieve the objectivity and impartiality which was our pride; every film we produced was finally approved by "the commonsense of most".

And to his credit let it be said that J. Arthur Rank never once interfered with us, never once mentioned, much less pressed upon us any views he might hold on any of our subjects. He let us go our way absolutely unfettered, no matter what effect the result might have, financially or politically. Indeed there were times when, at our monthly Board Meetings, he would quietly but firmly remind others that the prestige of the series depended on the freedom we enjoyed.

The days were long, but never long enough for the endless cycle of conferences, interviews, drafting of commentaries, digesting of film rushes, discussions as to the pictorial sequences, briefings by the research staff, etc.[153] We had always the camera teams out of the country on location with whom we kept in touch by cable, sending comments on the latest batch of film received, suggesting fresh lines and angles. With at least four or five films in various stages of preparation one had to be prepared to switch from one to the other at any moment. Any spare time we had was devoted to reading up current or future projects or meeting experts in the various subjects – as many experts on each topic as possible, so as to get every possible point of view on debatable matters.

Writing for films is a hard discipline. I found it painful, coming, as I did, fresh from a medium where everything depended on words to a medium where words must only be used in the last resort, to convey facts and ideas impossible to get across by pictorial

---

[153] The term 'film rushes' is used to describe the raw unedited footage shot during the making of a film, referring to the speed at which the prints are developed.

*This Modern Age: Editorial cutters in 'This Modern Age' laboratories are shown selecting the joining story sequences.*

(*Courtesy of Greater Manchester County Record, with Manchester Archives: ref.GB127 Hodson*)

means. Hodson never took kindly to the grind of clipping a phrase or remodelling a sentence in order to save a couple of syllables and make the "line fit the visual". Sometimes a radical, necessary change in the order of the pictorial sequences would mean the scrapping and re-writing of the necessary commentary, and always it seemed one was unearthing fresh facts, or hearing a fresh view from an outside expert, which called for re-wording or toning up or down. Hodson, much more a born, instinctive writer than I, and with some higher prestige in literature than I, was always in a state of smouldering rebellion at being expected to tolerate such journeyman conditions.

But no matter how long or full the day, its end always found Nolbandov as fresh and volatile as its beginning had. Sometimes our discussions went on after we'd closed up shop and adjourned to a nearby pub for a pre-supper slice of wallop, before going our separate ways. Occasionally, these counter conferences would be so protracted that we would take our evening meal of sandwiches and beer there. But the work was so absorbing and so rewarding, and Sergei's company, withal, so enlivening, that one had to stick it out. It's a significant fact – final proof that the work was its own reward – that neither of my seniors, both men of prestige in their individual fields, bothered about their work being anonymous. *This Modern Age* bore no credits in its title sequences – its prestige was at once our pride and our anxiety, sufficient in itself. But I must make it clear that it owed its high reputation in the first place, and mainly, to the brilliant ability and tremendous devotion of Sergei Nolbandov.

When I decided to join *This Modern Age*, I felt that a year of it would be quite as much as I could stand, and I made up my mind it should be a year of real work. There were to be no flesh-pots for me. Leaving Florence behind in Wharfedale, I embarked on a year of solitary hard labour. I made as few personal contacts, saw as few of my old colleagues, as I could. My only relaxation was an odd night at the theatre now and then, and Sunday Morning Service at the West London Mission in Kingsway, where Donald Soper, whom we'd learned to admire during the war years, was in charge. For exercise I walked daily from Lancaster Gate to the office in Saville Row and back again after work.

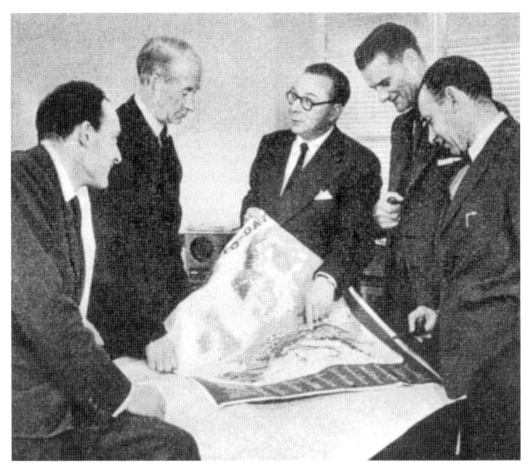

*This Modern Age: James Hodson (centre left) and Sergei Nolbandov (with glasses) discus an overseas location trip with the unit.*

(*Courtesy of Greater Manchester County Record Office, with Manchester Archives: ref. GB127 Hobson*)

I meant to earn enough in that twelve months to enable me to retire, except for the occasional odd job that appealed to me, paid if possible, unpaid if necessary. So every night practically, when the long day at *This Modern Age* was at last over, I went back to my little room and typed into the early hours of the morning. I went home about three weekends, Florence came down once or twice for a few days. For the rest, Saturdays and Sundays from lunch to bedtime were filled with freelance work for the B.B.C. During that year I turned out at least three three-decker adaptations, including *Fame is the Spur* and *Ivanhoe*, innumerable stories for radio and the large-scale pageant-play to celebrate the jubilee of the Labour Party. Necessary research into the history of the movement took nine weeks of leisure, the actual writing took three. I had planned it as a series of episodes linked by a chorus of four narrators speaking in the declamatory prose I had used so often in my B.B.C. "Feature programmes", but by the time I had drafted the first quarter of the script I had grown tired of the stale, outmoded technique. I started afresh with three "characterised" narrators, casting the story into free-running verse with irregular rhythms and rhymes. To my surprise this proved no more difficult than the prose narration and, when the play was produced, turned out to be much more "speakable" to the untried, amateur players who had to tackle it.

Before my twelve months contract expired, the Cinema industry went into one of its periodical slumps, and the Rank Organisation had to jettison quite a number of its "luxury" programmes. Among those thrown to the wolves – it's a mixed metaphor, I'm afraid, but not entirely inappropriate – was *This Modern Age*. So in March 1950, I was at home again.[154] In addition to the princely salary Rank had paid me, I had earned more as a free-lance for the B.B.C. than I should have done had I remained on the staff. For the first and only time in my life I had the dizzy, daunting honour of being called upon to pay super-tax.[155]

I settled down to enjoy what I purposed was to be semi-retirement, - only to find that leisure is not for the likes of me. The days are as full as ever but, thank goodness, I now have some little say in how they shall be filled.

It is a still, clear day. The Wharfe is hushed as it glides slowly past my window, a reflection of the unclouded blue above it. The limestone walls, patterning the lower pastures have a sheen of sunlit gold to warm their austere grey. Beyond and above, the Pennine fells are folded in quiet sleep, aloof and serene. The first leaves are falling, and soon the russet glory of the landscape will fade and dwindle to the spare poverty of Winter. The peace of the old, friendly house in which I write is a mantle of comfort.

---

[154] Extract from a letter to Lord Archibald, managing director of J Arthur Rank, dated January 25th 1950.
.........I needn't say I shall do my best not to allow TMA (*This Modern Age*) to get into difficulties over my departure, if it should happen I leave before it winds up. James Gregson has already told me he would be willing to come back on a short-term arrangement as that would considerably fill any gap there might be. I should of course be very sorry to go. I came in originally to fill a gap myself for four months and I've stayed 3 years! I think we've built up something that matters and quite apart from our noble selves, it will be a bad thing for Britain if it doesn't go on. So I'll continue to hope the miracle of going-on happens.
J L Hodson collection, Box 20 (Manchester Archives).
Hodson's hopes were unfulfilled. This Modern Age closed in Autumn 1950.

[155] Surtax for the tax year beginning 6th April 1949 started at an income of £2000, income tax was 9s in the pound.

I end my story in a mood to match the day.  Against the background of two world wars and many even more important events – the coming of the motor and the aeroplane, of the cinema, radio and television, the discovery of penicillin and the development of the hydrogen bomb, to name but a few – my history may seem like a chronicle of small beer; the story of an unremarkable individual whose happy life encompassed neither stark, tragic defeat nor delirious success – a man who blundered compassless, from point to point, seeking the bubble reputation, the blue-bird of happiness and the Kingdom of God, neither understanding nor able to recognize what he was looking for.

But the humblest life has point and significance for those with eyes to see; and the poorest life, in the telling, can be the occasion for grateful tributes to the kindly souls who helped one to make something of it.  For no man liveth to himself.  There is no such thing as a self made man – a fact for which, considering the botch that the best of us make of our lives, we should thank God fasting.

My story, therefore, must not be construed as my apology or justification for my existence, nor as a claim for any credit, either.  Let it be taken for what it is meant to be – a belated, incomplete tribute to the many, many friends who have made me rich with their comradeship; not merely those whose names I have recalled, but an uncountable host, known and unknown, who have a share, whether they are aware of the fact or not, in what reputation I have achieved, or what service I have been able to render.  I am merely the fortunate, happy man whose achievement, but for their help and their sacrifices, would have been little if not nil.

It is an overdue – long overdue – tribute, for I have been unconscionably tardy in arriving at the state of mind necessary and proper for the paying of it.  It has taken me far too long to learn what a paltry thing is personal ambition, how fragile and transitory is the reputation gained in its pursuit, how shallow a mockery is the success that comes from merely selfish climbing.  It has taken me far too long to recognize my limitations and to accept them – to find myself and reconcile myself to the discovery; to accept the truth that a man is never rich in goods but only in goodwill; to learn to walk humbly and gratefully, if not before God, amongst my fellow men.

It is with that lesson at last learned, with grateful humility that I dedicate this story to those who have made it possible – to

*MY INNUMERABLE COLLABORATORS*

*James Gregson (centre) with friends at Grassington (c1960-1965)* (CA)

*James and Florence Gregson.*
*(Ross Parry Agency)*

*James and Florence Gregson*
*– at home.* *(Ross Parry Agency)*

# Epilogue

Gregson's *Autobiography* only takes us up to 1949, when he was sixty. He would appear to have compiled it in the mid 1950s; it was never published and perhaps never intended to be published. In 1962, James and Florence Gregson held their Golden Wedding celebration in Brighouse, at the Black Bull. It is interesting to see that all his siblings were there, his brother, John G 'Sonny' Gregson, Mrs. Cora Crabtree, Mrs. Jane Wolfenden and Mrs. Anne Bentley. It is nice to see that they didn't lose touch with their sister who was 'given away'. Unhappily Florence Gregson died later in 1962, aged 77.

During his long life Gregson lived in a variety of houses. Apart from the ones mentioned in his *Autobiography*, Mill Lane, Providence Place, Birds Royd Lane (all in Brighouse), Heaton Park, Manchester and Marple Bridge, Derbyshire, he also lived at Marsh and Sheepridge (Huddersfield), where his younger daughter, Joan died, aged 8. After the second world war the Gregsons' lived at Linton in the Yorkshire Dales, before moving to Endicot, 14 Chapel Street, Town End, Grassington. Finally, with his eyesight failing, at his daughter's insistence he moved down to London to be near her.

Whilst in Grassington he acted as producer for the Grassington Players, who won several regional prizes under his leadership. He also directed the Skipton Players and for some years was the president of the Skipton Constituency Labour Party.

On Gregson's departure from Grassington to London in 1967 several newspaper articles were written. Two quotations give the respect and affection in which he was held.

Firstly :

> If we were asked to compile a list of real Yorkshiremen, there is one name that demands to be included, that of Brighouse born playwright and broadcaster, Mr. J R Gregson.
>
> Now we read that Mr. Gregson is leaving his West Riding home – for 20 years past in the Grassington area – to live in London with his daughter Jane, a T.V and stage actress, and his son-in-law Mr. Patrick Dowling, a BBC T.V. producer.
>
> At seventy-eight, Mr. Gregson says he's really a townsman, though it was in 1946 that he and his wife, Florence, who died five years ago, moved into Upper Wharfedale and settled into the country as comfortably as if they had been there all their lives.
>
> It is a far cry from the Brighouse days of the 1920s when as memory pleasantly recalls, Mr. & Mrs. Gregson held open house every Sunday evening, for any of their amateur theatre friends and journalists who cared to call in. Since then Dick Gregson has gone places in more ways than one, but his lively mind has never settled into inactivity and he says that when he gets to London he will still be doing some work for the BBC, with which he has had a continuous association since his wartime experience as a full-time broadcaster with *Radio Newsreel*.

And secondly :

> Who would have thought that Mr. James R Gregson, Yorkshire's grand old man of the theatre, would join the brain drain to the South?
>
> Well it is true that Mr. Gregson, the 78 year old broadcaster, dialect writer, playwright and one-time actor has sold his Grassington cottage and will be leaving shortly to live with his daughter Jane and her husband, BBC producer Mr. Patrick Dowling, in London. But it is not fame or fortune he is seeking.
>
> "With my living so far away, my daughter is anxious about me, especially after the death of my wife, and she persuaded me to live with them as soon as they found a house" he tells me.
>
> "I will miss the Dales, especially the countryside, and the Yorkshire dialect. But I think the change could be a good thing. It will give me a little bit more to do.
>
> I hope my daughter doesn't choose to live in too posh a neighbourhood. I enjoy going to the street markets and making contact with the Cockneys – they have their own form of humour.
>
> I am looking forward to renewing my friendship with Lord Soper. During the war my wife and I helped with his shelters for the homeless."

James Richard Gregson died in London in 1981, aged ninety two.

Unattributable Newspaper Cuttings, though probably, *Craven Herald* and *Yorkshire Post*.

# Appendix

# Appendix One

The following material on the Ramsden, Gregson and Hine families is extracted from the Census Enumerators, Returns.

## RAMSDEN
### 1871
### 15 Park Street

| | | | | |
|---|---|---|---|---|
| Samuel | Brighouse | | 50 | Boot & Shoe maker |
| Richard | Ramsden | Nephew | 38 | Boatman |
| Jane | Ramsden | | 35 | |
| Smith | Ramsden | | 6 | |
| Richard | Ramsden | | 8 | |
| Ann | Ramsden | | 3 | |
| Susannah | Ramsden | | 8 months | |

### 1881
### 23 Wakefield Road

| | | | | |
|---|---|---|---|---|
| Richard | Ramsden | Head | 48 | Corn Porter |
| Jane | Ramsden | Wife | 45 | |
| Dick | Ramsden | Son | 18 | Blacksmith |
| Smith | Ramsden | Son | 16 | Silk dresser |
| Ann | Ramsden | Daughter | 13 | Silk spinner |
| John | Ramsden | Son | 9 | Scholar |
| Sarah Alice | Ramsden | Daughter | 6 | Scholar |
| Adeline | Ramsden | Daughter | 8 months | |

### 1891
### 23 Wakefield Road

| | | | | |
|---|---|---|---|---|
| Richard | Ramsden | Head | 58 | Labourer Corn Millers |
| Jane | Ramsden | Wife | 54 | |
| Smith | Ramsden | Son | 27 | Labourer General |
| John R | Ramsden | Son | 18 | Cotton double |
| Adeline | Ramsden | Daughter | 10 | -do- |
| Sarah Alice | Ramsden | Daughter | 16 | -do- |

23 Wakefield Road was the third house down from the Robin Hood Inn (away from Brighouse).

The Robin Hood is still going strong but the houses down from it are long gone.

## GREGSON
### 1881
### 23 Mill Lane

| | | | | |
|---|---|---|---|---|
| Mary Ann | Gregson | Head | 45 | |
| William | Gregson | Son | 22 | Finisher |
| J E | Gregson | Son | 20 | Moulder |
| Charlie | Gregson | Son | 18 | Silk Dresser |
| James | Gregson | Son | 16 | Silk Dresser |
| M E | Gregson | Daughter | 9 | Scholar |
| Fred | Gregson | Son | 5 | Scholar |
| Alf | Gregson | Son | 1 month | |

### 1891
### 38 Mill Lane

| | | | | |
|---|---|---|---|---|
| Charles | Gregson | Head | 28 | Wire galvaniser |
| Ann | Gregson | Wife | 23 | |
| James Richard | Gregson | Son | 2 | |

### 1901
### 23 Foundry Street

| | | | | |
|---|---|---|---|---|
| Charles | Gregson | Head | 38 | Wire galvaniser |
| Lavinia | Gregson | Wife | 36 | |
| James R | Gregson | Son | 11 | |
| Cora | Gregson | Daughter | 9 | |
| John G | Gregson | Son | 5 | |
| Jane | Gregson | Daughter | 3 | |

Mill Lane runs parallel to Wakefield Road, about 100 yards to the south.

The mother, Mary Ann Gregson was born in Horwich, near Bolton, Lancashire, whilst all the children were born in Brighouse

## HINE
### 1901
### Royal Eye Hospital, Manchester

| | | | | |
|---|---|---|---|---|
| William | Hine | Head | 49 | Porter |
| Elizabeth | Hine | Wife | 51 | |
| John | Hine | Son | 24 | Malter ? |
| Charles | Hine | Son | 21 | Musician |
| Florence | Hine | Daughter | 15 | |
| Frederick | Hine | Son | 14 | |

William was born in Macclesfield, Elizabeth in Leeds, John & Charles in Oldham and Florence & Frederick in Manchester.

# Appendix Two

## Anti-Irish Riots

## RIOTOUS PROCEEDINGS AT BRIGHOUSE

The thrill of indignation which spread through the country when news of the brutal murder of Lord Frederick Cavendish and Mr. Burke was made known, has probably not shown the depth of its intensity more forcibly than in Brighouse, and it was certainly not expected that it would have given rise to such a state of things as has transpired in the district during the week. The proceedings of the past few days will no doubt go a long way towards creating a very bad impression upon the minds of strangers that its inhabitants are not the peace-loving and law-abiding citizens they ought to be, but on the contrary are those who have no respect for law and order. It cannot but be admitted that the disorderly proceedings which took place in the town some time ago have given a thirst to the more ignorant portion of the community for lawlessness and disorder, which in the event of not being curbed and checked has given rise and culminated in disorderly and disgraceful proceedings.

The news of the murder of the deceased lord naturally caused some excitement when published in the town on Sunday evening, and even then it was evident that the feeling against the Irish ran high. In the town and district there has been for many years an Irish element, perhaps in some respects small, yet in comparison to the number of inhabitants in the town not so small as has been imagined. In

*Lord Frederick Cavendish*
*National Portrait Gallery, London*
*Published 1883*

the past years frequent collisions between the two parties have taken place, but none of them have ever reached the dimensions which the proceedings this week have attained. For the last few years comparative quiet has been maintained between the two parties and no serious affrays have taken place. The proceedings of the last few days have without a doubt resuscitated the old feeling, which after such a lapse of time would have been expected to have died out. Like a spark thrown amongst dry tinder-wood a flame of disorder was ignited which led to far more serious consequences than could have been at first imagined.

The exact origin of the disturbance cannot be distinctly traced. It is known that a man, who rejoices in the cognomen of Jim Crow, whilst under the influence of drink began a quarrel with an Irishman in a public-house, which it was determined should be settled by a fight outside. On the street being reached a crowd speedily collected, and, as a natural consequence much sympathy was expressed with the Englishman: the representative of the Emerald Isle, after being a good deal knocked about, beat a hasty retreat. The feeling which had been rising began to find vent in threats and murmurs of dissatisfaction, which were expressed by the crowd.

After some little delay a spontaneous attack was made upon Taylor's Yard, Commercial Street, which has for years past been the locality where the bulk of the Irish population in this district has resided. The yard was soon filled by an excited mob, yelling and making the most hideous noises, but beyond a few windows being broken no further spoilation was done. A great number of the mob then contrived to possess themselves of large sticks, and, with these – after a raid on a house in Park Street, from which some of the furniture was taken and broken with the crockery in the street – they made their way to the Sun Inn, Elland Road, kept by an Irishman named Lawler, and which it was stated was the place where the members of the Brighouse branch of the Land League held their meetings. In passing along Commercial Street the mob presented such an excited and lawless an appearance that many of the shopkeepers took the precaution to close their places of business. On Elland Road being reached the mob immediately commenced a deliberate attack on the public-house. Several windows were broken, the door, which had been closed, was mutilated and broken open, and the mob then swarmed into the house. The landlord having had no warning of the approach of the mob was unable to make any preparations for defending himself, and had to flee for his own safety. The mob proceeded to pillage the house of its contents, tearing down the wood partitions, injuring the piano, and doing other acts of violence. The till was taken from its place and the contents scattered about the house, cigars were handed round, and beer taps interfered with; the bottles containing beer were smashed, as also were nearly all the glasses and crockery. No Irishmen were, however, discovered on the ground floor by the mob, who at once went up-stairs and commenced a search, with the result that one found concealed under the bed was dragged out and subjected to much ill-usage before he could effect his escape from the house; on doing this, however, several Irishmen were pursued down the street by the mob and had to take refuge wherever they could.

One of the unfortunate men, who was bleeding in consequence of injuries inflicted on his head, took advantage of the Gazette office, at the top of Briggate, being open and rushed in; the mob gathered in front of the premises and demanded his release, threatening to break the windows and commit other damage, but after a long hubbub cleared off without getting the man, not however without expressing their intentions of reprisal. The crowd then made its way down Commercial Street and along Bradford Road, Shillitoe's lodging house at Thornhill Briggs being its destination. They created no small commotion as they went along the streets shouting and yelling, the din being perfectly audible inside the Liberal Club, where a meeting was in progress. In a short time nearly all the windows of the house were broken, and the door likewise injured, the bottom panels being broken away. Shillito was struck by several stones and severely injured about the head and face, whilst his wife managed to escape by means of getting out at a back window, Shillito securing himself in one of the rooms of the house. A lodger named Peter Ryan, however, was not so fortunate, He got out by a back way and gained the wall, but was stopped by the mob and severely beaten, being found helpless by the police at the bottom of Hey Street. Ryan had only been in the town a short time, having come from Huddersfield. Another lodger named William Spennymoor was also severely handled by the mob and on Tuesday had to be placed under medical treatment.

After doing what damage they could at the house, the mob returned into Brighouse, but did not entirely disperse, as some time afterwards a house occupied by some Irish in Back Bethel Street was entered by the roughs and the furniture roughly handled. Inspector Hey and Sergeant Adams, however, arrived on the scene and put an end to the disorderly proceedings, which so far as Monday evening was concerned terminated. A number of Irishmen were during the evening assaulted by the mob. One of the first to feel the vengeance of the crowd was a young man named Michael Clark, a delver, aged 23 years, who lives near the Albion Inn, Lane Head. He had only just left his home and was proceeding towards the centre of Brighouse when he was stopped by the mob who commenced to beat him. Inspector Hey luckily came upon the scene at the commencement of the assault, but even then Clark lay on the ground helpless from the blows, and several youths were kicking him. The Inspector forced his way to the man, whom he rescued, and had him conveyed to the police station, where he lay insensible for two hours, but eventually came round.

On Tuesday the riotous proceedings were continued. In the early part of the day a number of young men from some of the stone quarries in the district met and went about where Irish workmen were engaged, saying if they did not stop or leave their work the mob would use force to send them away. In many cases the Irishmen employed voluntarily ceased working, whilst in others they had to be driven out, and it is reported that some violent treatment took place, some of the Irishmen being pursued as far as Hipperholme Railway Station, where they took trains for Halifax, Bradford, and other places. In some cases, however, the Irish were kept to their work by the masters, and told they would be defended in case of any attempt upon them; in others the Irish were found numerous enough to defend themselves and would not allow the approach of the persuaders.

The police authorities were actively engaged during the day making enquiries and preparations in the event of the previous night's attempts being renewed. Acting on the advice of Colonel Ormsby and Inspector Hey forty additional constables were drafted into the place from the adjoining towns, and were stationed at various points where it seemed their services would be most required. The mob began to collect between six and seven o'clock in the evening in the vicinity of the George Hotel, adjoining streets appearing to be literally alive with pedestrians. Between seven and eight o'clock the crowd was considerably augmented by numerous residents from the out districts, the greater part of whom however, seemed to be mostly children who kept up a constant yelling and shouting and caused no small part of the uproar. St Joseph's Catholic School, which is situated at the back of Upper Oxford Street and the main roadway to which is from Bradford Road, seemed to be the chief centre of attraction, the crowd congregating in the road and completely blocking the entrance to the Liberal Club.

Fortunately the precaution had been taken to station several policemen near the chapel and whilst the daylight continued the officers were successful in resisting the efforts of the mob to damage the building which would undoubtedly have been attacked had the officers not been present. About eight o'clock an alarm was raised that something unusual was taking place near Taylor's Yard, Commercial Street, and thither the crowd wended their way, but finding two policemen stationed there no outbreak took place. The Sun Inn, Elland Road, which had been attacked the previous evening, was next visited, but the officers were also again in charge there and no spoilation took place. The mob then proceeded up John King Lane and by way of Lane Head to Thornhill Briggs, where some windows at Shillito's lodging house, which had been left undamaged on Monday evening were smashed, after which the mob returned in a body down Bradford Road coming to a stop at the bottom of the road leading to the

Catholic Chapel. At dusk a number of the mob went into a field adjoining the chapel and being armed with stones commenced an assault on the building; fifteen constables were, however, present and successfully beat back the mob, not until a large number of missiles had been thrown and most of the panes in the east end of the windows smashed. These attacks were renewed at every convenient opportunity, the mob only waiting to secure a fresh supply of missiles before another assault was made. Such was the eagerness of the mob that not only were the only available missiles taken possession of, even the fence wall of the field was stripped of its top wall-stones which were broken up and utilised for the purpose of throwing at the building.

About ten o'clock a rumour got afloat amongst the crowd that a number of arrests had been made and that the officers were conveying the offenders to the Police Station. At the receipt of this information, which went with startling rapidity throughout the whole of the crowd, a yell of derision was raised by the mob and a terrific rush was made to the Police Station. At this juncture of the proceeding the scene was of a disgraceful character, many of the mob being knocked down and trodden underfoot, whilst yells and cries were heard on every hand. Brickbats were also freely thrown at the officers, who appeared to sustain very severe injuries, blood in many cases issuing from the wounds; one of the missiles thrown missed its mark but caught a young woman who was near, on the head and inflicting a severe injury; it was ascertained that the young woman was a domestic servant and resided in Elland Road. Arriving at the Police Station the mob gathered round the door expecting to see the prisoners brought in, none were, however, taken in to the office, and without any warning whatever, a volley of brickbats was thrown at the front windows completely destroying all but one pane; several officers were inside, but as it would have been exceedingly indiscreet to get outside and attempt to stop the lawless proceedings, this was not done.

The frenzy of the mob soon spent itself, and evidently satisfied with what had been done they retraced their steps to the old battleground and again commenced to storm St. Joseph's Chapel. It was at this point of the proceedings that the real character of the whole affair was revealed in its true light, for now the crowd had considerably lessened, and the line between mere idle spectators and the perpetrators of the outrage could be more easily discerned. A number of young men of rough and uncultivated appearance, apparently the ring-leaders of the whole affair, assembled at the bottom of the lane leading to the chapel and began to hold a sort of council as to what would be the best means of putting the officers to flight and practically destroying, as far as they could, the building. Several of the ringleaders were dispatched to gather up as large a force as possible, and this having been accomplished they all got well supplied with ammunition and proceeded to the attack. They had, however, not gone far, and at some distance from the building, when they were met by the constables, and after disposing of some of their ammunition they were compelled to beat a hasty and precipitate retreat. Nothing daunted, however, they made a second though feebler attempt, and failing to get near the building, through the watchfulness and vigilance of the constables they gave up the attempt. Prior to this taking place a man had got up a lamp post and turned out the light so that the police could not see the movements of the mob in the road; about the time of the last attack being made, half-past ten, the lamps at the Liberal Club were turned out, and the mob speedily dispersed, some appearing to go home, whilst others loitered about the streets discussing with apparent interest the events in which they had taken a part.

A large number of the extra constables remained on duty the whole of the night, whilst they all left the town shortly after six o'clock in the morning; great praise was due to them for the energetic manner in which they discharged their responsible duties, many of them sustaining very severe injuries thereby. Colonel Ormsby and Inspector Hey also came in for a share of the brickbats, and were hit several times, without fortunately sustaining any serious injury. Many stories are afloat of outrages committed in other parts of the town other than where the principal scenes occurred. One was to the effect that a number of young men set on an Irish labourer in Bethel Street, and brutally kicked him after knocking him on the ground; on getting up he asked what they had done it for, and for an answer he was similarly ill-treated. No policemen happened to be present at the time, but the man made the best of his way to the police office and remained there till a safe course had been cleared. The majority of the Irish residents in the town appear to have either taken themselves away or prudently kept out of sight for if the mob had been able to seize them it would undoubtedly have gone hard with them.

On Wednesday morning a large number of persons gathered in front of the Police office which presented a strange contrast to its usual neat and clean appearance. Mr Manley took a photograph of this building and also of the Roman Catholic chapel as the rioters had left them the previous evening, for inspection by the magistrates at Halifax. The Roman Catholic chapel has certainly come in for a large share of attention and has quite a woe-begone appearance. All the windows, with the exception of two panes of glass, were smashed in the east end of the building, whilst several of the side windows were mutilated. The building also bore traces of the assaults which it had withstood. Inside, the floor was strewed with broken glass, stones, etc., and on first appearance was anything but inviting. The scholars of the day school assembled as usual, but the children were given a holiday. The school examination by the Government inspector ought to have been held on Thursday, and it may be some cause of rejoicing to the rioters to know that this could not be held on account of the damage sustained by the school. It may also be a question whether the sum, resulting from pupils usually passed, can be recovered with other damages that may be claimed.

Between twelve and one o'clock Captain Stewart Russell, chief constable, Wakefield, Superintendent Hall, deputy chief constable, and Colonel Ormsby, Halifax, arrived in Brighouse and visited several parts of the town. Arrangements were made for a large number of constables from all parts of the district to move in, and they began arriving at both Brighouse and Clifton Road stations in the latter part of the afternoon. During the course of the day Mr William Camm waited upon the various employers of labour in the district, and the following placard was issued in the afternoon:-

> *Notice – We the employers of labour in Brighouse most earnestly advise people to remain quietly at home during the present excitement and thus prevent a renewal of the uproarious proceedings of the last two nights which tend to destroy the good name of the town – J C Bottomley, chairman of the Local Board – W & A Camm, A Goodall & Sons, R Kershaw & Co, Ormerod Brothers, Thomas Ormerod & Co, Ramsden, Cam & Co, Rhodes Sowden, Henry Stott & Sons, A Waller & Sons, Jonathan Stott, Thomas Sugden & Sons, H & J Sugden, Woodhouse & Mitchell.*

This notice although issued with the best of intentions does not seem to have any effect whatever as the evening's proceedings proved. About six o'clock a large crowd assembled in front of the Town Hall which had been taken for the use of the additional constables, and the arrival of every fresh detachment of officers was the signal for a derisive cheer, whilst in several instances hooting took place. By eight o'clock all the additional constables had arrived and the scene in front of the Town Hall was becoming lively. Nearly all the constables were provided with cutlasses which showed that at any rate the police authorities were determined to cope with the mob. There was no diminution in the number of persons congregating, if anything the crowd was rather increased, a large number of persons having come from the out districts and even some by trains from the adjoining towns. The large bulk of the crowd were, however, to be found opposite the Liberal Club and in front of St. Joseph's Catholic Chapel, which was well guarded by a good staff of constables. Another very practical precaution taken was to place policemen at the bottom of the road leading to the chapel, so as to confine the people to Bradford Road, and had the number of constables at the disposal of the officers in charge the previous evening allowed of this being done, the damage which the building sustained would have been prevented.

The officers stationed at this point had no easy task as they were subject to the continual jeers and hoots of the mob which had assembled in the road. Great commotion was caused by the movements of the younger portion of the crowd, at one time a large number of them galloping at a breakneck pace round the town raising the most derisive yells and cries; when they reached Bradford Road they secured a number of old worn out articles of tinware and forming a large ring threw them into the centre of the ring, whilst the most daring of them ventured to rescue them and then either threw them back again or pitched them amongst the crowd; in several instances they were thrown at the constables nearest at hand. As the evening wore on it was evident the officers were not going to have it all their own way as the mob began to assume a more determined attitude, large numbers congregating at one place, opposite the lane leading to the chapel. Shortly after nine o'clock the force in charge of the chapel sent a messenger to the authorities at the Town Hall that they must be reinforced or they feared the mob would be too much for them. The officers in charge of the constables also stated to the reporters that about the same time as they received the message from the men in charge of the chapel they also heard that the mob had commenced breaking the windows of the Liberal Club, and their services were required. The men were instantly told to fall in and Inspector Hey, accompanied by Chief Constable Russell, Deputy Constable Hall and Colonel Ormsby, took charge of No. 1 division, comprising forty men, and left the hall for the scene of the occurrence. The men were so divided that each inspector present had charge of a division. Inspector Hey promptly led his division without delay on Bradford Road, whilst several other divisions came out of the hall and took up positions at various points of the road, all of them, however, being received with hisses and hooting. When No 1 division had reached the corner of Hangram Street they were received by a volley of missiles, several of the officers and a large number of the men being hit. The mob separated to allow the division to pass along the centre of the road, but nevertheless hooting was heard, whilst nearly opposite and above the Liberal Club they were treated to fresh volleys of stones. The mob still stood their ground not appearing to be the least dismayed, and were certainly not expecting in the least what followed.

When the division had arrived opposite Claremont Villas, on the outskirts of the mob, they were commanded to halt which was instantly followed by the word charge delivered in a stentorian voice which was perfectly audible above the din and noise of the rabble. Then followed one of the most exciting and indescribable scenes that has ever occurred in Brighouse in connection with disorderly proceedings. No sooner had the command been given than the policemen with staff in hand instantly charged the crowd, driving it before them like a flock of sheep. Screams and cries of the most piercing nature rent the air, whilst the mob tumbled in heaps in their endeavours to get away, the constables using their staves with a powerful and telling effect. So rapid was this unseemly onslaught that in less than three minutes the whole road, which had been literally alive with an excited mob comprising several thousand persons, was cleared. People rushed in all directions to save themselves from the fury of the policemen's staves. Every available nook and corner was occupied by persons hiding, whilst the Liberal Club was literally besieged, the mob forcing an entrance and getting into several rooms; nearly opposite the Club steps a number of people fell, one of whom, a young man named Paul Airey, was frightfully injured on the back of the head and had to be carried into the Club, where he was taken to the kitchen and his wounds attended to by Mr. Walker, veterinary surgeon, who happened to be in the club at the time.

It would be impossible to collect a complete list of all who were wounded here by the staves of the police force, and of those who in the tumultuous panic endeavouring to save themselves, being trampled upon. The constables pursued the mob in every direction, along Hangram Street, Water Street, Dale Street, and Bradford Road, and were afterwards drawn up in a line opposite the Odd-fellows Hall. Chief Constable Russell and Colonel Ormsby then went to the Liberal Club and in answer to enquiries from Mr. Thomas Ormerod and Mr. Henry Sugden said that they would see that all the persons who had taken refuge in the club were conveyed safe past the police, the officers seeing the people into the streets which appeared to be quiet. Shortly afterwards two divisions charged the mob in King Street and Commercial Street and dispersed them, after which they returned to the Town Hall. It was rather surprising where all the people had got to, for the principal streets were now deserted, which but a few minutes before had been occupied by the excited multitude. The mob were also charged in Bethel Street, Mill Lane and Huddersfield Road, and were speedily dispersed.

At the end of Clifton Road two constables were assaulted with missiles, and this coming to the knowledge of Inspector Hey he took a detachment of men by way of Mill Lane down Phoenix Street, where he divided them, taking one half into Clifton Road. On arriving at the end of the road the mob imagining there were only the Inspector and another constable threw at them and the order was given to charge, the mob being driven down Wakefield Road, where they were met at the corner of Phoenix Street by the remaining half of the detachment and were belaboured by the officer's staves. This took place shortly after ten o'clock, and was the last charge of the evening. About this time Captain Edwards, a magistrate from Halifax, arrived on horseback, and several divisions of men were marched into the Town Hall, comparative quiet having been restored. Loud complaints were made at no warning being given the crowd before they were charged by the police, and numerous stories are afloat of persons who were present as spectators or passing on business having been seriously injured.

The following morning a strong feeling was prevalent in the town and expressed in language more forcible than elegant, that sufficient discrimination had not been used by the police in making their attacks, and whilst in many cases the ringleaders of the movement escaped uninjured, many who were mere idle spectators were injured. A number of constables were on duty in the streets all night, whilst some left by the first trains in the morning for their several destinations.

At noon on Thursday, a large crowd again appeared in the vicinity of the Town Hall, and the only topic safe to be indulged in by any passer by was denunciation of the police and abhorrence of the Irish. Almost the only Irishman seen on this day made an appearance near the Royal, and he had to flee for safety. There must be an exception of one of the letter carriers, who up to Thursday continued in his round, though frequently threatened and constantly abused. He is, or ought to be well known as a steady trustworthy servant, long resident and respected in Brighouse, and it is just as well known that he has had nothing to do with either the Land League or any other Irish Society. His case, however, is only an example of the blind unfeeling and unreasoning prejudice manifested against them bearing an Irish name.

During Wednesday the Manley Estate was visited by numbers of observers who wished to verify the reports they had heard in the afternoon, numbers of boys and girls undertook to complete the smashing already begun with the childish love of destruction which had actuated the mob in its onset. In the absence of the police, these children were busy trying to reduce the number of whole panes to nil, and carrying on any other petty work of destruction. Some of them being scholars felt a desire of revenge perhaps, on the home of discipline and instruction, and treated the clock to an open demonstration of their wish to destroy authority.

From the talks of the numerous groups it is impossible to conclude otherwise than that many of the evening mob come from places as distant as Mirfield, Elland, and towns which would be quite welcome to keep their roughs at home, so far as Brighouse is concerned. These considerations ought to have induced very many, in fact all, respectable householders to keep their families at home, as the authorities would then know with what they had to deal, and whatever harm had come the thoughtful stayers at home would have been unable to complain of hurts and bruises. It will be a great pity if one lesson of enforced quietness is not enough to teach what are the effects of having to put down a riot.

During the whole of the day rumours of reprisals for the action of the authorities the previous evening were rife. That the step was pernicious was argued by many urging that if given further warning the crowd might have dispersed. Many stories were related of innocent people being assaulted on their own property, one old gentleman residing near the Liberal Club being attacked in his own private street, and only a few yards from his own residence; a tradesman whilst in a laudable attempt to assist a poor aged woman into his workshop was surrounded by three constables one of whom freely used his truncheon. A member of the Loyal Peace Lodge on returning from Thornhill Briggs, where he had been visiting a sick member, was belaboured by an officer near St James' Church. Several women in Dale Street were injured, some of the police appearing to have been very indiscriminate in dispersing the mob, it being stated throughout the district that they attacked both women and children unmercifully.

The results of the attack were consequently exaggerated. A feeling of strong indignation was manifest, and whenever a policeman appeared it was a signal for expressions of strong disapprobation. Many were heard vowing vengeance should an opportunity occur. With a view to avoid any disastrous consequences Mr Francis Smith busied himself during the day upon a requisition, signed by a number of the leading tradesmen, for presentation to the police officials asking them not to send any constables into the streets so that the scenes of the previous evening might be avoided. On being presented to Colonel Ormsby at the Town Hall that gentleman promised that so long as the mob did not break the Town Hall windows or do any serious damage the police should be kept within the precincts of the hall, a promise which, when communicated to Chief Constable Russell, he wished to be carried out.

After the factories and workshops in the district had closed for the night large crowds began to collect in the streets adjacent to the Town Hall. Nothing was, however, done with the exception of shouting and hooting, until between eight and nine o'clock, when a large number of the roughest part of the crowd went up Huddersfield Road and armed themselves with sticks and cudgels, returning down the same road singing "We'll roll the old chariot along". They proceeded to the Roman Catholic chapel and drove the police away but did no further harm to the building. They then proceeded up Commercial Street towards the Sun Inn, Elland Road, and meeting six policemen who were patrolling Bank Street, they commenced an assault upon two of them named Dales and Lonsdale, both from Barnsley, who were severely wounded, and would have fared still worse had they not retreated into the houses of Messrs, Crossley and Gooder, Spring Street. Several windows were broken by the stones that were thrown about. Dr Brown had to be called in to the former when the constables reached the Town Hall which they did with some difficulty. The mob then returned, and at the top of Briggate sighted PC's Barber and Simpson, who by a hasty retreat into the Wellington Inn escaped unhurt, the mob throwing sticks and stones at the doors and windows, and then proceeding in a body to the front of the Town Hall. Shortly afterwards they commenced smashing the Hall windows and soon made short work of a large number of them; the doors of the principle entrance were also violently assaulted, but on being opened by the police the mob took to their heels; a division of about 35 constables were marched along the street but returned after proceeding a short distance up Bradford Road. Later on Captain Edwards and Mr Baxter, magistrates' clerk, Halifax, arrived, and after a consultation with the officials present had been held, it was decided to call the people together and read the Riot Act. After a number had been called together in front of the Town Hall some discussion took place between officials and the crowd, the result being that the Act was not read, the people quietly dispersing to their homes. During the evening one arrest was made, Inspector Hey securing a collier from Bailiffe Bridge, named Robert Stubbs, whilst in the act of throwing a stone, in front of the Town Hall. By half-past eleven o'clock the streets were comparatively clear, the police having been called into the Hall.

This morning (Friday) a large crowd collected in front of the Town Hall discussing the events of the previous evening, and some conversation took place with respect to a public meeting being called on the question.

*Brighouse and Rastrick Gazette* : May 13th 1882

# Appendix Three

## Altenbach Ltd.

ESTIMATED COST OF LABOUR FOR PRODUCTION OF 10 TONS

| | | | | |
|---|---|---|---|---|
| 1 | Works manager | | £ 4.0.0 | per week |
| 1 | Foreman moulder | | £ 3.0.0 | per week |
| 1 | Melter | | £ 3.0.0 | per week |
| 10 | Steel moulders | @ 36/- | £ 18.0.0 | per week |
| 10 | Malleable moulders | @ 36/- | £ 18.0.0 | per week |
| 10 | Fettlers | @ 30/- | £ 15.0.0 | per week |
| 10 | Labourers | @ 20/- | £ 10.0.0 | per week |
| 6 | Sundries | | £ 9.0.0 | per week |
| | | | £ 80.0.0 | |

Capital £ 5000

> £ 2000 to pay off existing loans
> £ 2000 for credit on this production
> £ 1000 working balance

Statement showing approximate net cost & estimated net profit on a production of a minimum of ten tons of various castings per week.

ESTIMATED NET COST OF PRODUCING 10 TONS PER WEEK

| | |
|---|---|
| 10 tons of scrap @ 60/- per ton | £ 30.0.0 |
| 20 tons of scrap @ 22/- per ton | £ 22.0.0 |
| 160 pots (clay)  @  1-2 each | £ 9.6.8 |
| Power | £ 3.0.0 |
| Wages (as above) | £ 80.0.0 |
| Office staff including management and directors' fees | £ 30.0.0 |
| Agents' remuneration under this production, per week | £ 20.0.0 |
| Sundries such as Gannister, Tools, Gas, depreciation, say | £ 10.0.0 |
| | £ 208.6.8 |

The minimum average selling price is calculated at £27 per ton, which is in no way excessive when it is found that a price of 4d to 5d per lb. is the general price obtained, and even a higher figure.  On 10 tons this shows a return of £ 270.0.0 per week

Leaving the calculated profit per week at £ 61.13.4

or say £3500 per annum, excluding what could be obtained from the profits to be derived from the manufacture of Tool Steel.

This profit on a capital of £ 5000 Debentures and £ 5000 shares would be amply sufficient to pay at least 50% dividend on such ordinary shares.

Besides producing castings the firm practically demonstrated the process at the works and was successful in selling the rights to manufacture for France at the very moderate sum of £ 2000 to Monsieur L A Wilczek of Paris as per contracts dated 20th March and 19th May 1906 respectively.  A works licence (for own use only) has been granted to Messrs. Werner Pfleinderer & Perkins Ltd. of Peterborough, and negotiations are in operation with the Daimler Motor Co. Coventry and the Britannia Engineering Co. Colchester.  As stated above the production of steel castings has been increased considerably from day to day and there is every prospect of attaining a considerable weekly out-put.

Castings under this process can be produced at the gross cost of 2½d per lb. for the finished article.  They are sold at 5d to 6d per lb.

The cost of producing castings under this process is slightly higher than that of the ordinary method, but as stated above the delivery is quicker and the quality superior and from the number of orders received it can be easily gathered that customers are prepared to pay the increased price provided they require good quality and quick delivery.

It happens, however, in general trade that Engineers require an inferior steel casting and also can wait for two to three weeks but wish to pay a less price, sometimes they require castings of very small size and which are not suitable for the above process. In order to cope with these inquiries Mr. Altenbach installed at these works a plant for the making of the following :-

Annealed Crucible Steel castings at prices ranging from 15/- to 30/- per cwt. With delivery in two to three weeks. Malleable Iron castings (small articles) from the Cupola furnace at prices ranging from 20/- to 30/- per cwt.

These three plants represent from a steel founder's point of view the complete manufacturing chain. Mr. Altenbach is able to meet his customers as regards price, delivery, good quality, and inferior quality, and is happy to say that he is fully stocked with orders although somewhat handicapped in not having enough furnaces at present.

In addition to the above named three kinds of Steel and Iron, Mr. Altenbach can, is able, and intends to produce Tool Steel of the finest quality, and Manganese Steel for Crusher Jaws etc. specially suitable for export purposes and which tasks he can readily undertake knowing the countries and their languages in general.

This is briefly an outline of the technical possibilities of this business and will readily be appreciated by a professional man.

The approximate profits which can be realised by the above named manufactures in normal circumstances and judging from the present experiences and figures are as follows :

| | |
|---|---|
| Manufacture at present one and a half tons special steel castings representing approximate value of | £ 60.0.0 |
| Secondly, ordinary steel castings annealed one and a half tons representing approximate value of | £ 45.0.0 |
| Thirdly, two tons malleable iron castings representing approximate value of | £ 50.0.0 |
| Fourthly, tool steel | none |
| | £155.0.0 |

| for these are used at present : | | |
|---|---|---|
| Wages | £ 50.0.0 | |
| Scrap | £ 20.0.0 | |
| Coke | £ 14.0.0 | |
| Crucibles | £ 12.0.0 | |
| Sundries, sand, coal, annealing ore | £ 5.0.0 | £101.0.0 |
| there remains an approximate profit weekly of | | £ 54.0.0 |

Mr. Altenbach invites a technical expert versed in steel matters to inspect these figures on the actual results.

The output can be doubled with the present installation with practically very little extra expense for the following reason, namely that the items for the office expenses, establishment charges, general foundry labour, annealing expenses, steam power would remain the same, with a very little extra cost for melting. The actual increase would be for the raw material, coke and pots.

Tool steel which has not been included in the above would realise a much larger profit than the castings namely £ 10 to £ 15 per ton clear profit.

# Appendix Four

## Liddy

*The Worker*, Saturday, December 25th 1920
The Art of James R Gregson
By Richard Hawkin

……..In my own belief, the finest of Gregson's plays is *Liddy,* a short one-act play.  It is a gem which sparkles as well in the daylight as in the limelight.  In the room of an ordinary workman's cottage there rests a coffin – a pauper coffin.  It is round this coffin that the various characters move, and by James Gregson's art, we look upon their naked souls.

An outcast woman and her baby have been taken into Ben Webster's house by Liddy, his wife.  The woman has died and is to be buried 'by the parish'.  And the incidence of the play begins just at that point where the coffin is to be carried to its final resting place.  Liddy is helping to fasten Ben's collar, and her bandaged finger is observed by her husband.  Liddy explains that she 'hurt it a day or two sin'.

To them enters Robert Frowse, the Relieving officer.  He is representative of the 'Rates'. The following fragment of the dialogue may here be quoted:-

> FROWSE :  It's queer that there's no valuables. One looks for them – a locket or some such trifle – in a case like this.
> LIDDY :  A case like this?  What d'yer mean?
> FROWSE :  You can guess surely.  Look at her face, refined, well-bred. Then there's the  child –
> LIDDY :  Yer don't believe she's – she's that sort of lass?
> FROWSE :  Of course.  How else can you explain the facts?  Then the absence of the wedding ring –
> LIDDY :  What's that on her left hand?
> FROWSE :  Why there is a wedding ring after all.  Queer I didn't see it before.  That's something towards the expenses, anyhow.  I'd better have it off before I forget.

Liddy, by her protests prevents the taking of the wedding ring until just before the coffin is screwed down, and then to the astonishment of Ben and the Relieving officer and the Minister – who has come in – the ring is seen to be missing.  Liddy has removed it from the dead woman's finger, and is accused of theft – of attempting to rob the Guardians.  Even her husband joins in the assault on her.

> LIDDY : She were a mother……t'best thing that's worth owt……T'one thing I've never been…….I envy her…..I hid mi bare finger so that tha wouldn't notice that mi ring weren't theer.  I couldn't bear to think o' that poor lass comin' among strangers an' being looked askance at, for want of a bit of a ring.  Think of t'things he (pointing to Frowse) were going to say till he saw

t'ring. Even t'minister thowt shame on her........I lent the lass mi ring, to save her from t'tongues o' careless an' foolish men, an' if it hadn't been for that rogue theer (pointing again at Frowse) wi his shoddy funeral an' his talk about Guardians an' rates an' all that; an' if it hadn't been for Master Cummins (the minister) being so respectable, an' thee (her husband) being so stupid; if t'three on yer hadn't been determined to rob t'lass of her good name, she'd ha' been buried as a honest woman. I hope yer satisfied wi yer work?

This is the thrilling stuff of great drama. It answers to every test may be imposed upon it. It is human and passionate, yet the author has it always under his control. The homely speech has a beauty all its own, and there shines like a beacon the soul of Liddy. By its brightness the souls of the other three characters are partially transfigured.

Whether drama such as this will become popular in these days remains yet to be seen. One wonders if in Brighouse – or Huddersfield – there is a rich man disinterested enough, to pay for the printing of *Liddy* and *T'Marsdens*, which two plays are the best of what Gregson has yet achieved. Not only are they works of art, they are historical documents also. Posterity may cultivate finer tastes than we possess, and I can perceive with what delight it will enter into the contemplation of these dramas produced in a period which I profoundly hope 'sets the children's teeth on edge'.

James R Gregson is a young man as yet. He is going to express the whole gamut of human emotion, I hope in plays he will write hereafter. His insight and his philosophy are alike humanistic; the 'humanities' have ever been in importance and in range, the first of studies. His characters are familiar to us – we jostle with them in every street – but Gregson has the art of presenting them just at the right angle, and just from the right standpoint, and we look at them as they ride on the air of Heaven. His vision may not be seen by the present generation of men. But if he can only bring us the understanding that there is a vision to be seen – ah, there's the question.

## MARPLE DRAMATIC AND LITERARY SOCIETY

The outstanding feature of the performance by the Marple Society on December 10th, 12th and 13th was the production of Mr. James R Gregson's new play *Liddy*. The author strikes a congenial theme in the exaltation of motherhood and the exposure of the hollowness of organised charity – both material and spiritual. It's not a new one but its treatment is unique and artistic. The development of the plot is ingenious but not obscure. The play's chief merit lies in its appealing simplicity and idealistic realism (if one may be permitted a seeming paradox) which compels a sympathetic responsiveness, without arousing great tension or stress.

*Garrick Magazine*: January 1920.

# Appendix Five

## Leeds Civic Playhouse

### A facsimile of the inaugural Leeds Civic Theatre programme for Gregson's production of *Overture* in 1925.

### Courtesy of Leeds Library & Information Services

LEEDS REFERENCE LIBRARY

HON. DIRECTOR—
CHAS. F. SMITH,
22, NEW YORK STREET,
TEL. 25356. LEEDS.

HON. SECRETARY—
GLADYS SWANNACK.

HON. TREASURER—
T. WRAY-MILNES.

PLAY DIRECTOR—
JAMES R. GREGSON.

The

## LEEDS CIVIC PLAYHOUSE

(AFFILIATED TO THE BRITISH DRAMA LEAGUE).

# A FREE THEATRE.

*Patron:* THE LORD MAYOR OF LEEDS
(Councillor Charles Granville Gibson, J.P.).

*Chairman:* Alderman PERCIVAL LEIGH.

*Vice-Chairman:* Councillor BLANCHE LEIGH.

*Patrons:*

Sir Gervase Beckett, M.P.
Major Birchall, M.P.
Alderman Sir Charles Wilson, M.P., LL.D.
Right Hon. Edward Wood, M.P.
The Vicar of Leeds
    (The Rev. B. O. F. Heywood).
Mrs. E. G. Arnold.
Lady Marjorie Beckett.
Rev. M. L. Cotter, B.A.
J. R. Cross, Esq., D.L., J.P.
W. B. Dow, Esq.
Henry C. Embleton, Esq.
Sir Berkeley Moynihan, K.C.M.G., C.B., etc.
Lady Kathleen Pilkington.
W. H. Maxwell Telling, Esq., M.D., F.R.C.P.
Mrs. Maxwell Telling.
H. Ard Watson, Esq., J.P.
Mrs. John Marshall.

Alderman Leslie Owen, J.P.
Alderman Ratcliffe, J.P.
Councillor Bentley.
Councillor Davies.
Councillor Dennison.
Councillor Dr. Friend.
Councillor Beryl Gott, J.P.
Councillor Horrell.
Councillor Morris.
Councillor C. V. Walker.
The Chairman, Leeds Board of Guardians
    (C. Nowland, Esq.).
Guardian Mrs Ives.
Guardian Mrs. Skelton.
Guardian Mrs. Hoyland Smith.
Guardian Mrs. Exley, and other Members
    of the City Council and Board of
    Guardians.

*The Theatre is the most potent cultural influence of modern life.
Its appeal is immediate and direct and no community can allow it to
be debased or disregarded without permanent injury to its development.*

W. S. Maney, Printer, Russell Street, Leeds.

THE LEEDS CIVIC PLAYHOUSE is founded in the belief that it is as essential for a healthy civic life that the dramatic masterpieces of our own and other lands should be placed within the reach of all, as that the city should provide libraries and art galleries.

## THE TITLE.

The word "Civic" is used to show the intention to make it a Theatre with a wide appeal, and not only for the cultured few; also the hope that some day its efforts to provide Drama for the masses will justify direct municipal support; whilst the term "Theatre" is deliberately discarded in favour of "Playhouse" because that is a more accurate description of the promoters' aspirations to make it a place of entertainment and amusement and a common playground for all those who love the art of the Theatre. As a channel for self-expression it will provide opportunities not only for acting, but dress and scenic designing and making, carpentering, lighting and the many needs of theatrical production.

## PERFORMANCES.

During the season 1925-1926, five productions will be given at varying intervals, in the Albert Hall. Each will open on a Friday, and run until and including the following Tuesday. On the Saturday, there will be a Matinee, at 2. Evening performances will commence at 7-30.

## A FREE THEATRE.

Admission to the "Civic Playhouse" will be free; thus Leeds will have the distinction of having the only free Theatre in existence; but to meet the necessarily heavy expenses a silver collection will be taken at each performance.

The privilege of booking their seats will also be granted to those who wish to support the movement by becoming subscribers, and they will also have the first option of attending any supplementary performances that may be arranged.

The subscription is the democratic figure of 6/- (including Entertainment Tax) for the whole series of five productions. The Playhouse having no funds to spend in advertisement urges all readers to become subscribers and to make a point of urging their friends to do so. An assured number of subscribers will enable the Playhouse to make its plans more confidently.

## DIRECTION.

The direction will be in the hands of Mr. Chas. F. Smith, who was an original founder of the Leeds Art Theatre, and is a present Director of the York Everyman Theatre. He was responsible directly for the introduction of the Mystery Play, "The Great World Theatre," to Leeds. He will be assisted by Mrs. Gladys Swannack, as Secretary, and a Dramatic Council of proved experience, including Mrs. M. Hague and Mr. T. Wray-Milnes, both experienced amateur players.

The active support of Mr. and Mrs. Percival Leigh, as Chairman and Vice-Chairman respectively, has been secured. The civic and social character of the Playhouse will receive their special interest. They have already secured influential patronage and help for the movement and are forming a supporting Council.

## PRODUCTION.

The Yorkshire Playwright, Mr. James R. Gregson, Author of "T'Marsdens" and "Young Imeson," will act as producer. The experience gained as a Director of the Leeds Industrial Theatre, and as "lead" in his own plays during their London season, will be invaluable.

LEEDS
REFERENCE
LIBRARY.

# "OVERTURE,"

*A fantastic Comedy by* SUTTON VANE, *author of "Outward Bound."*

## PROGRAMME.

The Characters of the Play are :—

| | |
|---|---|
| **Lady Jasmine** | RUBY WIGODER |
| **Mr. Smith** | FRANK R. QUARMBY |
| **Justice Plush** | T. WRAY MILNES |
| **Mrs. Bagleigh** | MURIEL ESSEX |
| **Youth** | DORIS TATE |
| **Miss Prudence** | DOROTHY HALL |
| **Sebastian Sinclair** | J. WRIGHT |
| **Bill** | T. DESMOND KELLY |
| **Elsie Bagleigh** | MARION GREAVES |
| **James Bagleigh** | GILBERT WATSON |
| **Rosie** | LILIAN ROWE |
| **Major Clayton** | C. D. BUTLER |
| **Rev. Walter Land** | ALFRED SHARP |
| **Mrs. Smith** | PHYLLIS QUARMBY |
| **George** | J. W. GLEW |
| **Sir William Frayne** | W. D. NOBLE |
| **Holman** | WILLIAM FORBES |
| **Willing** | J. W. GLEW |
| **Jilkes** | E. JACKSON |
| **Mr. Greyfield** | HUBERT PADGETT |
| **Liz** | DORIS TATE |
| **Charon Junior** | A. GRAHAM FRENCH |

| | | |
|---|---|---|
| Act 1. | Scene. | The Ante-room. |
| Act 2. | Scene 1. | 33a, Grosvenor Street. |
| | Scene 2. | In the Country. |
| Act 3. | Scene 1. | In Chelsea. |
| | Scene 2. | The Judge's House in Yorkshire. |
| Act 4. | Scene 1. | The Fireplace. |
| | Scene 2. | The Ante-room again. |

The Play produced by JAMES R. GREGSON.

*Stage Managers :* HUBERT PADGETT and WILLIAM FORBES.

Lighting by Messrs. ARDEN and POGSON.

SILVER COLLECTION.—*Expenses of production on a temporary stage are heavy and it is hoped that all will contribute generously in relation to their means.*

## Note the Dates of our Future Productions.

EVENINGS: Friday, Saturday, Monday and Tuesday, at 7-30 p.m.

MATINEE: Saturday, at 2·0 p.m.

| Nov. 20th to 24th | "Oedipus Rex" (*Sophocles*) | .. | *Gilbert Murray* |
| | "The Widow of Ephesus" | .. | *T. Wray Milnes* |
| | First production. | | |
| Dec. 11th to 15th | "The Shining Steps" .. | .. | *James R. Gregson* |
| | First production. | | |
| Feb. 5th to 9th | "The Sphinx" .. .. | .. | *R. R. Whittaker* |
| | First production. | | |
| March 19th to 23rd | "The Mask and the Face" | .. .. | *Fernald* |

For the production of "Oedipus Rex," in November, a mixed crowd of 150 is required. Will ladies and gentlemen willing to take part kindly hand in their names and addresses to the attendants, or write to the Hon. Secretary.

A Theatre that exists by voluntary collections has no excess funds for unnecessary postage or advertising. Will each member of the audience constitute himself (or herself) our representative and make known these and future performances to their friends.

W. S. Maney, Printer, Russell Street, Leeds.

## SOME OF THE PLAYS.

"**THE MASK AND THE FACE.**"
A brilliant and sparkling comedy *a la mode* arranged from the Italian by C. B. Fernald.

"**OEDIPUS REX.**"
The great Greek tragedy of Sophocles, the production of which has taxed the ingenuity of most great dramatic artistes down the ages. In attempting it, Mr. Smith and Mr. Gregson show once again that courage that enabled the "Great World Theatre" and "The Cenci" to be done so splendidly by amateurs in Leeds.

"**THE LITTLE PLAYS OF ST. FRANCIS.**"
The delightful, delicate and whimsical mystical comedies by Mr. Laurence Houman.

"**THE WITCH.**"
A Norwegian Play. A very powerful and dramatic study of mediæval superstition, full of tense situations, a pathetic love interest and all the poetry of John Masefield's translation.

"**THE ADDING MACHINE.**"
A recent success of the London Stage Society. A dramatic and arresting work by an American, who under another name, has a series of successes to his credit. This play is regarded as exemplifying the new methods of technique covered by the description "Expressionism" and as a break-away from the current or "Representational" traditions.

"**EVERYMAN.**"
The beautiful 15th Century morality play that was so successfully performed in the old Guild Hall by the York "Everyman Theatre."

"**THE WIDOW OF EPHESUS.**"
A tale from the famous "Satyricon," of Petronius, made into a poetic comedy by T. Wray-Milnes. One Act.

"**THE SHINING STEPS.**"
A dramatic comedy of Yorkshire life, specially written by James R. Gregson.

"**CÆSAR AND CLEOPATRA.**"
Bernard Shaw at his best. A witty and spectacular comedy.

"**LILIOM.**"
A Hungarian play of great dramatic power, which attracted much attention when produced under another title by Miss Edith Craig, at the Kingsway Theatre.

"**OVERTURE.**"⋯⋯
A three act play by Sutton Vane, the author of "Outward Bound." At the first play dealt with the adventure of death, this deals with the terrible adventure of birth. It is a play written round a big idea, with all. Mr. Sutton Vane's enviable art of being witty about serious matters.

"**THE MACHINE WRECKERS.**"
By Ernst Toller, translated by Ashby Dukes. Toller is the most hopeful portent that has emerged in the German theatre since the war. A grateful country thrust him into prison, and this play concerning the introduction of machinery into industrial England was written there.

K3315 10/35

# Appendix Six

## Melody on Moorside

### The Yorkshire Weekly Post 1931

Famous in the literary from his well-nigh unique position as Yorkshire's native dramatist, born and bred, Mr. J R Gregson has written his first novel. It will be published exclusively in *The Yorkshire Weekly Post*, in instalment form, beginning in the next issue. Mr. Gregson's recent series of pen-pictures of Yorkshire Life, with their vivid drama and sardonic humour, earned tributes from many hundreds of our readers; and there is no doubt that this new triumph of *The Weekly Post* will be even more warmly welcomed.

*Melody on Moorside*, as the Gregson first novel is entitled is as thrilling a piece of dramatic narrative as could be desired. It is a story of a Yorkshire girl whose life was lived among the moor tops. Not altogether a happy story, filled with pathos that rises at times to the level of epic tragedy, *Melody on Moorside* is nevertheless filled with moments of merry humour, and the tang is softened, with a simplicity and sweetness that takes the sting out of the irony

As a picture of a West Riding family – from Anne, or Miss Simplicity as her first lover calls her, to her stern and patriarchal parent, her weakling brothers – *Melody on Moorside* will live forever in the reader's memory. It is unforgettable. Dick Shillitoe, Anne's pathetic husband, the village parson who is her third and last lover, and a host of minor characters, make up a panorama of Yorkshire life, a generation back.

It is a grand yarn, and a supreme achievement as a first novel. *Melody on Moorside* will rank with some of the greatest things that Gregson has done.

On no account should it be missed. There will be a big demand for *The Yorkshire Weekly Post* on Friday next. Make sure of your copy (and subsequent copies) by placing an order for regular delivery with your newsagent.

---

A grand yarn though is probably was, the readership was somewhat divided. Gregson was not averse to writing controversially. Equally, those magazine patrons who disliked it were not averse to objecting in strong terms to it either. To give some indication of the feelings aroused, I have included a selection of the letters received by the magazine, split roughly equally for and against.

### Letters to the Editor

I do not like Gregson, and never did. He makes life seem more dull and commonplace than it is. The ugly side is obvious enough without having to read about it. Give us romance to brighten things up.

> Yours truly
> Edmund Fanway
> Ripon

As one who has persevered with *Melody on Moorside*, I should like to say that in my

opinion it was not fair to Mr. Gregson to publish such an immature and experimental work as his first novel. Most first novels should be burned – as I understand Sir James Barrie did with his first three attempts.
Yours etc.
C Henry Walton
Hull

Why all the fuss about Gregson's first novel? It was not a great book, but a highly commendable effort. In places it was most interesting, although not the lightest of reading. It was however, somewhat above the level of ordinary serial stories, even if it fell short of what the author attempted to do.
Yours truly
Arnold Watlins
Hounslow, London

Gregson will never be a sugar-and-spice best-seller, he sees life too clearly and truthfully. I like him for his candid outspokenness – real Yorkshire and not namby-pamby.
Yours faithfully
Ernest E Elliston
Barnsley

Gregson? – ugh!
Yours candidly
Miss Caroline Beardshaw
Middlesborough

It's all a question of one's attitude to life. Job suffered, but I question whether his attitude to life was ever half so depressing and appalling as Mr. Gregson's. I am deeply sorry for the author of *Melody on Moorside*. What a miserable little man he must be.
Yours truly
Eighty but happy
Kirby Moorside

Mr. Gregson reflects the modern generation very well. What he has to say needs to be said. Speaking for myself I read every word he writes with avidity. Please give us some more of his Yorkshire sketches. He excels in these.
Yours etc.
A C Colne
Headingley, Leeds

Why cannot we have something from the pen of Mr. Gregson every week? I miss him now that *Melody on Moorside* is finished. I know that the grim tragedy of Yorkshire life depicted in the serial may have alarmed people who are excessively sensitive, but it was a chapter from real life and I enjoyed every word.
Yours etc.
D A Bailey
Nether Edge, Sheffield

I am glad to note that Mr. J R Gregson's very unedifying first novel comes to an end in the *Weekly Post* to-day. It is a relief to bid farewell to such unpleasant characters as he portrays. If such people really do exist, is it necessary to bring them to the notice of the public in the form of a novel. Personally I shall carefully refrain in future from reading anything to which his name is attached.

Yours etc.

Winifred Barnett

14, Highfield Crescent, Bingley Road, Heaton, Bradford

I first met James R Gregson when he brought the Yorkshire plays to Scarborough Opera House. Recalling his vivacity then, his happy laugh and his cheerful outlook on life, I am amused (so will he be) to read your vigorous octogenarian correspondent's assumption. What a miserable little man he must be!

Yours etc.

R A H Goodyear

Cloughton, Scarborough

J R Gregson's immature novel, *Melody on Moorside* is causing such controversy that one would imagine it was a literary landmark like *Ulysses*. For my part, I found it very mediocre. It was a good readable yarn, but I should no more think of waxing indignant or enthusiastic over it than I should over *Love on the Cliff Top*, *From Maid to Marchioness*, or any other commercial novel of these days. It won't live; why attempt to assess its ultimate value?

Yours etc.

H G Turner

Keighley

I read with pleasure Miss Winifred Barnet's remarks in reference to your serial which ended a week ago, and would fully endorse her views. Coarse, crude and unconvincing, this story is a gross libel on the inhabitants of the Yorkshire moorland villages, and if this is the best the author can give us some of your readers would feel no regret if his writings disappeared altogether from your otherwise excellent paper.

Yours etc.

C Pentry

Birstall

I thought *Melody on Moorside* utterly loathsome.

Yours truly

John Blunt

Harrogate

Isn't there enough Russian horror in the world today (in all literalness, alas!) without making us read such threadbare imitation – Tchekov rubbish as Gregson's novel? Give me for one such a story as *Red Emeralds* which *The Weekly Post* is now serialising – good, lively, dramatic stories that are clean.

Yours faithfully

Old Reader

Chapel Allerton, Leeds

Gregson's story certainly was rather grim, but isn't it true to life? That's Victorianism, that was! What's the use of shutting our eyes to facts? Yorkshire life still has its more ghastly facets that need to be shown up by a powerful pen. What about the Leeds slums? Why not a tale about life on the dole today in Holbeck? There's a theme for Gregson!

Yours etc.

J G Betts

Moortown, Leeds

I liked *Melody on Moorside*. Strong meat for the timid perhaps, but a change from the usual run of serial stories.

Yours faithfully

Horace Chivers

York

I have been exceedingly amused to read so many acrimonious criticisms of Gregson's novel *Melody on Moorside*, which certainly had qualities which gripped the imagination and made one wonder how the theme would work out. I should like to hear from any person who read the first two instalments and failed to finish the story! Only those who read the tale to the bitter end (and it was a bitter end) are entitled to criticise it, and if they did read it to the end, that in itself is a sufficient proof of Gregson's work. It sometimes leaves a nasty taste, but life is like that.

M W M E

Hyde Park, Leeds

I have been quietly amused by some of the criticisms your readers have to offer J R Gregson's very fine first novel which was published in your columns. Let me say here and now that I, like scores of others I know, enjoyed every moment of it.

We were not of course told the date of which the story began, but to anyone who can remember Yorkshire in the days before the end of the century could easily tell that that was the period to which our Yorkshire writer was referring. One reader, I believe, complained that such characters as Anne and her father could not exist.

May I suggest that this reader should glance through some copies of (shall we say) the *Yorkshire Post* and *Leeds Intelligencer* of between 1880 and 1900? She will see that week after week there were told in the police courts stories of appalling cruelty of apparently respected and religious fathers towards their children. The cruel and hypocritical period in which Anne lived was faithfully depicted by Mr. Gregson. I am waiting for a more mature novel from his pen, but I cannot ask for a more absorbing one.

Yours etc.

J R Byles

Chapel Allerton, Leeds

# Appendix Seven

## Gregson's Popularity in the 1920s

To give some indication of his popularity in the Yorkshire region in the 1920s, the following articles serves as a useful reminder:

The Yorkshire Barrie

> No longer can there be doubt that James R Gregson is a dramatist of quality, for he has been discovered, and discovered in Leeds, where best spirits have dispersed quite finally, of all doubts by giving Mr. Gregson the title of The Yorkshire Barrie. It is true that several of us in Huddersfield for some time held a very high opinion of the dramatic work of Mr. Gregson, but it is difficult for a local lad to become a prophet in his own village.
>
> *Huddersfield Daily Examiner* : January 26th 1922

The article goes on to compare him favourably to Lancashire's Stanley Houghton and Harold Brighouse and the Potteries Arnold Bennett.

The height of his popularity, in Brighouse at least, came in 1928 with the hanging of his portrait in the Rydings Art Gallery.

> *MR. GREGSON'S PORTRAIT*
> Presented to Art Gallery
> Yesterday evening, there was a most interesting ceremony, at the Albert Theatre, when after a performance of *Young Imeson* by the Huddersfield Thespians, before a crowded audience, an oil painting of Mr. J R Gregson was presented to Coun. W E Holland for placing in the Art Gallery at the Rydings. The portrait, which has been painted by Mr. John R Gauld, art master at the Huddersfield Technical School, has been purchased by a number of friends and admirers of Mr. Gregson.
> *Brighouse Echo*: September 27th 1928

The mayor, Alderman A M Denham JP, goes on to say:

> Who could say that in a hundred years from now Mr. Gregson's name would not be as famous as that of Shakespeare, and that Brighouse would not be as famous as Stratford-on-Avon?......Brighouse people would watch Mr. Gregson's career with interest, and the honour they were paying to him would also be a honour to the town.

Perhaps a touch optimistic. However, there's still seventeen years to go, and who knows, one day, Brighouse-on-Calder!

The twenties was undoubtedly the best decade of his career; as playwright, producer and actor he achieved wide regional publicity. Two of his plays, *T'Marsdens* and *Young Imeson* were staged in London, at the Everyman Theatre in Hampstead, in 1923 and 1924 respectively (*T'Marsdens* ran from 30th April to 26th May, which appears to be the maximum run, whilst *Young Imeson* ran from the 17th March to 29th March). *T'Marsdens*, in particular, was tipped to transfer to the West End. Unfortunately, this did not materialize, the problem apparently being that the West End managers were frightened of what London audiences would make of the Yorkshire dialect.

I have not seen either play on stage. I have, however, obtained copies of both plays, and found on reading *T'Marsdens*, the dialect is not as strong or as dominant as I feared. *Young Imeson* has more characters speaking dialect, although strangely, the hero, Ken Imeson, speaks standard English, with no dialect whatsoever, which I feel comes over a little oddly. Perhaps Gregson had deliberately toned down the dialect in order that audiences outside Yorkshire would be able to understand his plays. I have to say that I prefer *T'Marsdens* to *Young Imeson*, although the latter is supposed to be the better constructed play. The hero, to me, does not come across as a particularly likeable character.

*The Brighouse Echo*, reporting on the *Young Imeson* production of November 21st and 22nd, 1921, disagrees with my interpretation :

> There is plenty of West Riding dialect introduced though there is no obsession, whilst the pungent wit and sarcastic retort makes the visitor forget that there is anything of the vernacular in the presentation of the play.

Two things; firstly, the reporter saw the play acted, and I haven't. Secondly, dialect in the 20's was probably stronger and more widely spoken than it is now.

Incidentally, somewhat bizarrely, *T'Marsdens* was once banned. The authorities of a Batley Sunday School refused permission for the play to be performed on their premises. I can only imagine that the main theme of the play, whether or not to allow a nude model to pose for the Municipal Art School, must have brought them out in a cold sweat! The fictional town of Endbridge, where the action takes place, is actually meant to be Brighouse. I have come across Endbridge more than once in his writings. Reverse it and you have Bridge End, a well known part of Brighouse.

# Appendix 8

## An Actor's View of James Gregson as a Producer

### The Fire Breathing Dragon or Rehearsing under Gregson

This a story of pathos, mingled with cruelty.

Once upon a time, dear, gentle readers, a man named Gregson wrote a comedy and christened it *T'Marsdens*. In due course he got together a band of aspiring Thespians, gave them names which they, poor people, cannot break away from even to-day, and declared from now on we will be one happy family. That family, myself being one of them was very happy until – yes, until one Sunday early in October, nineteen twenty two. On that fateful day a band of innocent but optimistic amateurs alighted at the Brighouse station for the dress rehearsal. *T'Marsdens* had come to town with high hopes of creating a furore. Our show was billed for three nights, to be followed later in the week by a screen drama called *The Thunderclap*. It may sound like a paradox, but The Thunderclap revealed itself before *T'Marsdens*.

Entering the Albert Theatre via the stage door, we were confronted by a gloomy dragon disguised as a producer, (Not having tasted human morsels for some time, he appeared gloomier than Hamlet at his gloomiest.)

We will run through act three! thundered the dragon.

Aye, aye sir! responded the company (one had been a sailor).

Under the glare of footlights, and rude remarks interjected by the dragon, we bungled timidly through. When we had finished, the dragon, still gloomy, grudgingly suggested tea.

It is now the plot thickens.

After tea the company, with the exception of the dragon, who had thrust himself into a part, donned on their glad rags and war paint. A storm was gathering. We knew it by the dragon's caustic remarks on our make up.

Half way through the first act, I, poor fool, in the role of John Marsden, miscued.

STOP! STOP!! By the beard of my pre-historic grandfather, STOP!!!

Everybody on the stage commenced knocking at the knees. Instead of the first act of a comedy the scene had a resemblance of a spiritualist meeting. A stage hand weathered the storm with mop and bucket to erase the numerous pools of tears and perspiration from the boards.

Bravely we struggled on for four agonising hours with hearts in our mouths and the fear of the dragon in our little souls. At times he would rave about the stage, at other times bend the pillars in the dress circle with one arm and paw the air with the other. When tired of breathing fire, he would hurl oaths at his perspiring company in crimson English, scarlet Arabic and vermillion Chinese. The pimple on his nose became luminous.  Surely it must have outshone the one Cromwell possessed for brilliance. After the ordeal a parched American would not have touched the companies' spirits. That night I dreamt the dragon had written a Grand Guignol thriller.  I played the hero, he played himself.  The title was *St. George and the Dragon*. One performance sufficed.

*T'Marsdens* went off with a bang, but the only word of praise from the dragon we received was, You'll do!

The same dragon was at the dress rehearsal of the London production, but not as producer.  All he could do was to sit and snort to himself in the stalls.  The spectacle he witnessed was as ghastly as our own, but he writhed in silence – the most profane silence ever heard.

You will have a chance of seeing this dragon in his one-act play, *Liddy*, the last week of Mr. Wareing's vaudeville season.  You will think him modest and kind hearted.  Take it from me.  There are two Gregsons, one a shy and modest playwright, the other a fire-breathing dragon disguised as a producer.

GEORGE BEAUMONT, *Huddersfield Theatre Royal programme : 1923*

# Appendix Nine

## James Gregson and the British Drama League

Mr. J R Gregson's *Melchisedek* produced by the Leeds Civic Playhouse, won the final competition for the Yorkshire area in the British Drama League Festival of Community Drama. Mr. Darlington (the dramatic critic of *The Daily Telegraph*), the adjudicator, commented after the performance, Mr. Gregson is certainly the best of the playwrights I have met who are writing for the competition. In most districts competing I have seen original plays but either of Mr. Gregson's plays (the other was *The Way of an Angel*) would have beaten them. They were written in two very different moods and each play is very good of its kind.

*Leeds Mercury* : December 20th 1926

In the final of the competition, held at the Temperance Hall in London, Gregson put another of his plays in, *Liddy*, which came fourth. A play performed by the Huddersfield Thespians won (*St. Simeon Stylites*). The prize was a trip to New York to take part in the Belasco Cup Competition. The only snag was that they were expected to pay for the trip themselves! They were the first British amateurs to act on a New York stage, in this case, the Bayes Theatre, 44th Street West. They came second, behind a team from Dallas. On the way home, they performed the play at the Arts and Letters Club, Toronto.

Gregson, though a founding member of the Huddersfield Thespians did not go on the trip to New York.

On the whole Gregson was not impressed with the British Drama League Competition. He is quoted as follows :

> Mr. James R Gregson addressed the audience at the close. He expressed his dissatisfaction with the plays he had seen, condemned the lack of enterprise shown in their selection, and suggested that the National Festival of Community Drama was proving of little benefit to amateur societies. Competitors played for safety, said Mr. Gregson, instead of making experiments. Amateur acting of the sort he had seen that evening did nobody any good. The amateur society could only justify its existence by a spirit of enterprise, and the Drama League competitions seemed to be crushing out that spirit instead of fostering it. He feared on that account the festival might have to be written down as a failure.

Unattributed press cutting, circa 1928.

# Appendix Ten

MY FAVOURITE
YORKSHIRE STORY

## Yorkshire Speyks

*by James R. Gregson*

*AFTER five years in the cotton mill, two in a steel foundry and ten in the office of a railway civil engineer, James Gregson turned professionally to the theatre, specialising in such experimental ventures as The Leeds Industrial Theatre and the Leeds Civic Playhouse. Since his first broadcast in 1924 he has been responsible for hundreds of stories, plays and features as writer, actor and producer.*

*Mr. Gregson recalls when Joe and his wife, after an even hotter row than usual, sat sulking, he on one side of the fire, she on the other, with the cat on the rug between them.*

*When it seemed that the sullen silence would never be broken, Joe slowly uncrossed, then recrossed, his legs, sighed and said: "Ee, Ah wish one o' us three were deead. An' Ah doan't meean misen."*

*Just then the cat looked and mewed. "Ah doan't meean thee, nawther!" said Joe.*

---

*As fair an' as false as a new gravestooan!*

IF Shakespeare had heard that, he would have licked his lips and promptly "set it down in his tablets," just as I did when I heard it—except that I put it into my notebook as soon as I got home from the cotton mill.

It was the comment—epitaph, if you'll forgive such an oblique pun—uttered by a disgruntled spinner, retailing an abortive love-affair with a wench who was very much alive and, in the words of another minder, "a bit of a powse."

Whenever I recall that gem of our Yorkshire folk-speech—so typical in its pith, point and poetry—I can smell the warm, oily floor on which we were squatting over our breakfasts.

It was not the first—and by no means the last—of such jewels that I've snapped up, gloated over, hoarded and finally used in my plays.

Here are a few of them—all taken at random from one play:

*Ah can read him better nor big print!*

*If Ah sed 'Trayvle!' shoo'd say 'Lick!'*

*As fluttered as a hen that wants to sit.*

*He'll simmer quietly now he's letten t' lid off!*

*Talk o' t' Devil an' yer'll hear his clogs clattering!*

*He's as much life in him as a bit o' burnt leather.*

*As uneasy as a dog wi' too mony fleas.*

---

*He's a neck like a plucked hen.*

*If tha wants to play hell, it's no use having a referee!*

I CANNOT remember where I heard those, but here is a couple which came in one lively sermon from a vigorous local preacher: "As narrer as a hen between t' eyes," and "Like t' man wi' t' muckrake, shortsighted wi' lookin' after rubbish."

As I type them I can see the robust lay-evangelist darting out of the vestry, bounding up the steps to the pulpit and announcing the first hymn before he got there. Oddly enough, I gave these two gems to my *Ezra Marsden*, who describes himself as a "scientific agnostic"!

One of the earliest entries in my notebook is a comment by my father on an Aunt's pastry: "Tha could shoe hosses wi' it!" And at about the same pre-factory period there is an entry which earns its place, not because it is witty or profound or particularly amusing, but because, phonetically and idiomatically, it is so Yorkshire.

I heard it while following the coal carts from the railway sidings, picking up the bits that fell from the jolting vehicles. A burly carter was at his horse's head, bawling enquiries about the condition of an ailing acquaintance and finally asking: "Has he gotten agate o' gettin' aht o' bed yet?" There is a lovely gaggle of G's.

---

I REMEMBER picking up one little masterpiece of natural descriptive genius while on the staff of the *Leeds Mercury* between the wars. I was sent to interview an ancient matriarch at Scapegoat Hill, not far from where the B.B.C. was to build the towering masts of Moorside Edge.

The story I was after doesn't matter, for I never got it. The old dame was too full of the local gossip, particularly of a "set-to" she'd just had with a "Lady Jane Tape" who was "jumped-up an' too nice to skin onions." The old dame ended her description of this "mimsy-finicky" creature with: "Ay, shoo's one o' that soort that gooas lookin' for lice i' bald heads!"

A similar assignment, this time with a male centenarian in York, threatened at first to be just as frustrating, for I found him obsessed with the case of an old friend and I'd to let him "get it out of his system." This old friend had had a very hard life, dogged by ill-health and ill-luck and was now not expected to leave his bed again.

He had no sooner been struck down, with no prospect of ever being able to enjoy his good fortune, than he'd inherited some thousands of pounds from a distant relative.

---

My centenarian summed up this sadly novel situation with this bit of doleful philosophy: "Ay, Mester Gregson, that's life, that is. God takes away yer teeth an' then he gives yer nuts!" You may question that pessimistic conclusion, but you have to admire its picture-evoking phraseology.

THIS vivid imagery is characteristic of Yorkshire folkspeech, and a fine example which I've heard once or twice is "Ah've licked a cleean thible (wooden porridge-spoon) monny a tahme!" As a picture of hunger and near-starvation it can hardly be bettered. I first heard it on the lips of a cheerful old inmate of a workhouse at a Christmas Party. Her lined face was made more gaunt by the gaudy paper cap she sported.

Nearly all these native "speyks" have a touch of humour about them, from the light and glancing to the mordant and the macabre. And in the ones I think of as typically Yorkshire there's an element of self-mockery, a touch of over-simplemindedness.

An instance of this deliberate over-simplicity I can't resist. It is perhaps the first example I remember meeting. I was walking round Brighouse one evening with my father and, at what we called "t' George Corner," an elderly news-seller pushed a *Yorkshire Evening Post* under our noses with: "Paper, Charlie?" My father bought one and we went on our way. We returned along Commercial Street soon afterwards and the news-seller again, pushed an *Evening Post* under our noses. "Paper, Charlie?" "Nay, tha knows Ah've just bowt one off thee!" "Ay, but (very wheedlingly) 'have another. Tha'll soon read that!"

But I'm getting away from my theme and my space is running out. So, from the scores of entries in my notebook, let me finish with what I consider my favourite—a real plum. It has everything, I think—wit, the brevity that's the soul of wit, humour and commonsense, couched in homely imagery. It's from yon another old dame, who I heard giving this bit of advice to a young "over-fond" bride: "Never put thi husband on a pedestal. He'll nobbut want dusting!"

950

951

# Appendix Eleven

## EVERYMANIA

### 1922
The International Season—contd.

| | | |
|---|---|---|
| 2.1–11.1 (matinées) | The Shadow of the Glen | J. M. Synge |
| (evenings) | The Building Fund | William Boyle |
| | Prunella (cast change 9.1) | Granville Barker and Laurence Housman |
| 23.1–4.2 | Mixed Marriage | St. John Ervine |
| 6.2–4.3 | Fanny's First Play | Bernard Shaw |
| 6.3–25.3 | Arms and the Man | Bernard Shaw |
| 27.3–17.4 | Getting Married | Bernard Shaw |
| 17.4–22.4 (matinées) | Defeat | John Galsworthy |
| | Ile | Eugene O'Neill |
| | The Bargain | Walter Meade |
| | Daily Bread | Jules Renard, trans. Vaughan Thomas |
| 18.4–10.5 | Misalliance | Bernard Shaw |
| 11.5–15.5 | The Pigeon | John Galsworthy |
| 16.5–20.5 | You Never Can Tell | Bernard Shaw |
| 22.5–3.6 | Hedda Gabler | Ibsen |
| 5.6–17.6 | You Never Can Tell | Bernard Shaw |
| | Marlowe Dramatic Society in | |
| 19.6–24.6 | Troilus and Cressida | Shakespeare |
| | Daily Bread | Jules Renard, trans. Vaughan Thomas |
| 17.7–22.7 | In the Zone | Eugene O'Neill |
| | Suppressed Desires | Geo. Cram Cook and Susan Glaspell |
| 24.7–5.8 | Candida | Bernard Shaw |
| 7.8–19.8 | The New Sin | B. Macdonald Hastings |
| | The Constant Lover | St. John Irvine |
| 21.8–2.9 | A Doll's House | Ibsen |
| 4.9–23.9 | Widowers' Houses | Bernard Shaw |
| 25.9–9.12 | Mary Stuart | John Drinkwater |
| 20.12–30.12 (matinées) | Brer Rabbit | Mabel Dearmer and Martin Shaw |
| 22.12–30.12 | Twelfth Night | Shakespeare |

### 1923

| | | |
|---|---|---|
| 1.1–6.1 (matinées) | Brer Rabbit | Dearmer–Shaw |
| (evenings) | Twelfth Night | Shakespeare |
| 10.1–20.1 | Medium | Leopold Thoma |
| | The Perfect Day | Emile Mazaud |
| 29.1–17.2 | The Philanderer | Bernard Shaw |
| 19.2–10.3 | At Mrs. Beam's | C. K. Munro |
| 12.3–24.3 | The Alternative* | Lucy Wilson and Adrian Alington |

126

### 1923—contd.

| | | |
|---|---|---|
| 2.4–28.4 | The Doctor's Dilemma | Bernard Shaw |
| 30.4–26.5 | T'Marsdens | James Gregson |
| 28.5–16.6 | Major Barbara | Bernard Shaw |
| | Private Performance: | |
| 17.6 | Beyond Human Power | Bjornsterne Bjornsen |
| 18.6–7.7 | Candida | Bernard Shaw |
| 9.7–28.7 | Fanny's First Play | Bernard Shaw |
| 30.7–18.8 | Mary Stuart (revival) | John Drinkwater |
| 20.8–15.9 | Magic | G. K. Chesterton |
| 17.9–29.9 | Outward Bound | Sutton Vane |
| 1.10–17.10 (matinées) | Ancient Lights* | Edward Percy |
| 19.10–3.11 | What the Public Wants* | Arnold Bennett |
| 8.11–17.11 | The Second Round | Halcott Glover |
| 29.11–12.12 | The Moral of Vanda* | May Hazel Marshall |
| 18.12 | The Mask and the Face | C. B. Fernald |
| | (Copyright Performance) | |
| 21.12–31.12 | Love in a Village* | Isaac Bickerstaffe, Dr. Arne, arr. Julian Herbage |

### 1924

| | | |
|---|---|---|
| 1.1–5.1 | Love in a Village* | Bickerstaffe–Arne, arr. Julian Herbage |
| 12.1–19.1 | The Painted Lady* | Vera Beringer |
| 5.2–15.3 | The Mask and the Face | C. B. Fernald |
| 17.3–29.3 | Young Imeson* | J. R. Gregson |
| 4.4–7.4 | Monica* | Ernest Cecil |
| 16.4–17.5 | In and Out* | Brandon Fleming |
| 23.5–4.6 | The Tropic Line* | Noel Shannon |
| 11.6–21.6 | The Man of Destiny and Augustus does his bit | Bernard Shaw |
| 24.6–5.7 | Her Daughter* | John Peterson |
| 8.7 | Arms and the Man (Charity Performance) | Bernard Shaw |
| 9.7–9.8 | Getting Married | Bernard Shaw |
| 12.8–16.8 | Low Tide | Ernest George |
| 27.8–30.8 | The Man of Destiny and How he lied to her Husband | Bernard Shaw |
| 11.9–20.9 | False Value* | Lechmere Worral |
| 24.9–18.10 | The Devil's Disciple | Bernard Shaw |
| 27.10–8.11 | Misalliance | Bernard Shaw |
| 10.11–22.11 | Clogs to Clogs* | John Walton |
| 25.11–13.12 | The Vortex | Noel Coward |
| 16.12–22.12 | The Tyranny of Home* | W. Lemon Hall |
| 26.12–31.12 | The Philanderer | Bernard Shaw |

127

# Appendix Twelve

## MISCELLANY

### 1930s FILMS

On the film side, Gregson tells of early involvement in the Gracie Field's film *Sing as we Go* (1934). A video recording of the film was obtained, which features James Gregson as the hen-pecked husband of a Blackpool boarding-house landlady, whilst his wife, Florence, plays Gracie Field's auntie. James Gregson is very good in his comic role, although it is only a small part. His wife actually appeared in more films than he did, appearing with Gracie Fields again in *Look up and Laugh* (1935), with George Formby in *No Limit* (1935), with Ralph Richardson and Ann Todd in *South Riding* (1938) and in J B Priestley's *Good Companions*. In all her films she played a particular type, the grim, no-nonsense Northern housewife. In addition, when Anna Neagle starred in a film about the life of the Yorkshire aviator Amy Johnson, she was hired at £30 a week (a considerable sum in the 1930s) to advise on dialect.

### Radio

He barely touches on his BBC radio work. However, the *Radio Times*, in its programme guide for February 29th 1932, shows a play by James R Gregson, *Sar Alice*, to be broadcast at 8.20pm. In the cast are both James and Florence Gregson. Also broadcast on the same day was Reginald Dixon from the Tower Ballroom, Blackpool, which will bring back memories to a lot of people.

He also gave a series of comic talks on the radio, under the title of *Beckside Chronicles*. It was advertised as being given by Zachariah Briggus (a name which wouldn't have kept his identity secret for long!) and described as a series of humorous incidents in the life of a Northern village, told by one who lives in it. The first episode was entitled 'Mrs Slowwit'.

### Leeds College of Music

Another aspect of Gregson's career not mentioned in his *Autobiography*, was his appointment on to the staff of Professors at the Leeds College of Music (c1929). The advertisement introduces him as The well-known Yorkshire Playwright, Producer and Actor. It goes on to give his specialties as Acting, Gesture, Make-up, Stage Techniques, Special Coaching, Play Production, PlayWriting etc. etc. When they started an 'off-shoot' in Bradford, he was again promoted in an advert. This time fees were mentioned – they would vary according to the type or length of his tuition – although no specific amounts were mentioned.

Nothing has come to light with regard to this professorship or how active he was at the College, or whether it just 'died a death' due to lack of students.

FOUNDED 1894.

## Leeds College of Music,

### Elocution and Drama.

UNDER ROYAL PATRONAGE.

# MR. JAMES R. GREGSON,

*The Well-known Yorkshire Playwright, Producer and Actor,*

RECENTLY ADDED TO THE STAFF OF PROFESSORS.

---

*Acting, Gesture, Make-up, Stage Technique,*

*Special Coaching, Play Production, Play*

*Writing, etc., etc.*

"Leeds does not realise what a fine and true artist it possesses in Mr. Gregson."—Miss Edith Craig.

"In Mr. Gregson you have an undoubted native genius. If you are wise you will treasure him."—Mr. Lennox Robinson, the Irish Playwright.

**Mr. Gregson** has a wide and comprehensive knowledge of all forms of Dramatic and Theatrical Technique with a thorough experience of stage requirements and practice in every department.

As the author of such well-known plays as *T'Marsdens, Young Imeson, Sar' Alice, The Devil a Saint, The Way of an Angel, Liddy, Melchisedek,* etc., etc., he has won golden opinions from the critics for his skilful plot construction and his brilliant character drawing.

His first theatrical productions in Leeds, *The Merchant of Venice, Peer Gynt, The Cenci,* and *Romeo and Juliet,* attracted considerable attention. His work for the Leeds Civic Playhouse and the Huddersfield Thespians is even better known. For the former organisation he directed such successes as *Oedipus Rex, The Adding Machine,* and *The Mask and the Face,* to name only three plays of very different type and

quality. For the Huddersfield Thespians he produced *Androcles and the Lion* and *R.U.R*, amongst other plays. In addition to his work amongst amateur organisations, he has had experience of work in professional theatres, both London and Provincial. He is thus able to approach the problems of stage technique from the point of view of the practical Producer.

As an actor, **Mr. Gregson** is noted for his versatility. His interpretations of his own Yorkshire characters are deservedly popular, but the wide range of his work is better realised when it is known that he has played such parts as "Shylock," "Peer Gynt," "Androcles," "Zero," "Oedipus," "Everyman," "Lob" in *Dear Brutus,* "St. Francis," "Latimer" in *The Dover Road,* "The Nameless Man" in *Granite,* etc. He has played both as an amateur and professional over Yorkshire and Lancashire, has starred in London and toured in Germany. From the actor's point of view, his tuition should be both authoritative and valuable.

**Mr. Gregson's Subjects** will include every branch and detail of stage craft from the art of clear speech to the theory of stage production and play-writing, but he will specialise on these subjects from the point of view of the practical theatre, and will devote special attention to such factors as :—

Interpretation,     Characterisation,
Co-ordination of Detail and Technique,
Individual Tuition in Special Parts
which the Student may select or desire.

**Mr. Gregson** is also prepared to teach his own theory of production, and to arrange for some kind of practical experience for the student.

**Mr. Gregson** is also prepared to read and criticise manuscript plays in a constructive and informative manner.

---

For details of Vacant Times, Fees, etc , for Private Lessons, Coaching Amateur Dramatic Societies, the Production of Plays, etc , application must, in all cases, be made to :—

THE SECRETARY,

COLLEGE OF MUSIC, ELOCUTION & DRAMA,

COOKRIDGE STREET, LEEDS.

TELEPHONE 24641

## J R Gregson's Yorkshire Dramas – Karl Heinrich Thomas

This treatise, presumably some thesis for a degree, is interesting because of the author. He would appear to be German (perhaps of German-British parentage), his address is given as Halle, Dez. And the 1933 puts him at the beginning of Hitler's Chancellorship. His bibliography contains several German books, which he quotes from in his treatise. It is not known who Karl Heinrich Thomas was, or what became of him. Researching the archives in Huddersfield a letter sent by Gregson to an old friend of his, Fred Pennington, dated Christmas 1933 was discovered. In it he comments on receiving a copy of Karl Heinrich Thomas's treatise but is somewhat bemused as to why he was chosen. I don't think they ever met, Gregson writing just two letters, answering various queries. He never mentions Karl Heinrich Thomas in his *Autobiography*, yet he kept his copy of the treatise.

# Index

*n denotes footnote number*

# Illustration Index